THE NEW
CALCULUS OF
ESCALATION

Other Titles of Interest from Georgetown University Press

Arms Control for the Third Nuclear Age: Between Disarmament and Armageddon
David A. Cooper

China's Strategic Arsenal: Worldview, Doctrine, and Systems
James M. Smith and Paul J. Bolt, eds.

Nuclear Command, Control, and Communications: A Primer on US Systems and Future Challenges
James J. Wirtz and Jeffrey A. Larsen, eds.

THE NEW CALCULUS OF ESCALATION

Avoiding Armageddon in Great Power Conflict

MARTIN C. LIBICKI

GEORGETOWN UNIVERSITY PRESS / WASHINGTON, DC

© 2025 Georgetown University Press. All rights reserved. No part of this book may be reproduced or utilized in any form or by any means, electronic or mechanical, including photocopying and recording, or by any information storage and retrieval system, without permission in writing from the publisher.

The publisher is not responsible for third-party websites or their content. URL links were active at time of publication.

Library of Congress Cataloging-in-Publication Data

Names: Libicki, Martin C., author.
Title: The new calculus of escalation : avoiding armageddon in great power conflict / Martin C. Libicki.
Description: Washington, DC : Georgetown University Press, [2025] | Includes bibliographical references and index.
Identifiers: LCCN 2024022174 (print) | LCCN 2024022175 (ebook) | ISBN 9781647125752 (hardcover) | ISBN 9781647125769 (paperback) | ISBN 9781647125776 (ebook)
Subjects: LCSH: Escalation (Military science) | Conflict management. | War. | Nuclear threshold (Strategy)
Classification: LCC U21.2 .L475 2025 (print) | LCC U21.2 (ebook) | DDC 355.02—dc23/eng/20241015

LC record available at https://lccn.loc.gov/2024022174
LC ebook record available at https://lccn.loc.gov/2024022175

♾ This paper meets the requirements of ANSI/NISO Z39.48-1992 (Permanence of Paper).

26 25   9 8 7 6 5 4 3 2   First printing

Printed in the United States of America

Cover design by Jason Alejandro
Interior design by Westchester Publishing Services

CONTENTS

List of Figures   vii

Acknowledgments   ix

Introduction   1

1   Escalation and its Motivations   11
2   Is Cyberwar War?   35
3   The Space between Nonlethal and Lethal War   63
4   Is There a Feasible Local–Global Threshold?   83
5   Conventional Operations against Nuclear Systems   105
6   The Putative Tactical–Strategic Nuclear Threshold   138
7   Will Thresholds Emerge on Their Own?   152

Conclusions   183

Appendix A   Deterrence, Thresholds, and Norms   186

Appendix B   With Nuclear Threats, Might Makes Won't   191

Bibliography   193

Index   229

About the Author   237

FIGURES

Figure I.1 Escalation with and without Thresholds 4

Figure I.2 How Lattices Complicate Escalation Management 6

Figure 7.1 How Inadvertent Escalation Arises from Different Thresholds 153

Figure 7.2 An Escalation Spiral 154

ACKNOWLEDGMENTS

Although many people helped move this work from notion to publication, several people deserve special mention.

The Late David Gompert—a RAND vice president and acting Director of National Intelligence—got me where am I today. He introduced me to the RAND Corporation where I worked for nearly two decades, and then introduced me to the Naval Academy where I now work. He contributed, directly or indirectly, to several of the ideas of this work, including the escalation potential of naval warfare, and the difficulty of ascertaining escalation in a naval standoff-to-cyberwar transition. After having read an early version of this manuscript, his continual question to me was: where and when are you going to publish this? He was a constant and wise sounding board for my ideas, good and less-than-good. We joyfully collaborated for many years designing crisis exercises through which we put midshipmen to test their ability to make difficult policy choices under pressure.

Paul Tortora—former naval intelligence officer and head of the USNA's Center for Cybersecurity Studies—encouraged me to plug away at my research even when it seemed to be moving in circles, and giving me the time to do it. This work has benefited enormously from our constant round of early-morning discussions, notably but not exclusively on the way information technology shaped the war between Ukraine and Russia, and the impact of that use on the threat of nuclear war. I cannot think of anyone I would rather work for.

Mary Ellen and Richard Keyser have generously endowed my chair, one that I have been proud to hold (they also funded some important parts of Hopper Hall, where I teach). Their patronage played a powerful role in giving me the freedom and opportunity to write this. I hope this work has, at least in part, repaid their contribution and patience.

Special thanks are also due to my anonymous reviewers, my editor Donald Jacobs of Georgetown University Press, and an early reader, Michael Guillot of Air University. Their suggestions for expunging unneeded material, adding explanation as needed, and clarifying the rest resulted in a better document with a more consistent line. To this, I must add the many midshipmen who have taken courses of mine in the political science and cyber science departments and whose questions and ripostes forced me to re-examine my thinking on the topic of escalation thresholds and help guide me towards further clarity.

Last, to my wife of nearly forty years, who endured my constant exposition of ideas, helping me toss out those that made little sense.

Introduction

The return of superpower competition has renewed concerns about managing escalation lest what starts as contention culminates in nuclear war. In the Cold War both sides recognized the challenges of escalation management. Each threatened to use nuclear weapons to deter conventional aggression. Although war did not occur, the more that each side threatened to use nuclear weapons to finish off a conventional war, the harder it would have been for them to work out how to confine warfare to conventional weapons if war did break out. After the Cold War ended security problems other than escalation management gained attention. The many escalation dilemmas were never resolved. Thankfully they never had to be.

Today's world is different. There are three superpowers: the United States, China, and Russia (which despite its mediocre military performance in 2022 is still large and well-armed).[1] All have nuclear weapons; all have space programs. All are increasingly dependent on information technology. Their conventional capabilities are comparable if not necessarily equivalent. Most importantly, despite serious asymmetries among them, all can match the other side's crossing any number of thresholds. Granted, tensions among superpowers, in contrast to Cold War struggles, are less about which ideology would be left standing and more like competing nationalisms. Russia is trying to recover its influence in eastern Europe, and China is pushing on its Asian neighbors, notably over Taiwan and in the South China Sea. These may look like local issues, but local issues can become global if both sides read existential fears into the conflict. In a sense today's environment feels more like Europe prior to World War I. But as that war proved, one did not need competing ideologies in order to slaughter others in large numbers. Furthermore, memories of the Cold War are fading, much as World War II is now outside nearly everyone's memory. There's little sense of what great power war means. So escalation dilemmas are back as if new.

Take the fighting in Ukraine. Beginning in 2014, Russia, fearing that open warfare would bring an unwelcome Western reaction, fought Ukraine as a gray zone conflict short of war. Likewise, President Obama held back fearing that arming Ukraine against Russia would lead to a test of wills, which Russia would win for being closer to the conflict and hence more committed. By 2022 Putin concluded that gray zone conflict alone would not achieve his goals and crossed a threshold to war. The United States and its North Atlantic Treaty Organization (NATO) allies responded by sending Ukraine tens of billions of dollars' worth of arms. Yet they hesitated to provide long-range weapons, such as missiles for fear that Ukrainian operations inside Russia would provoke the Russians to escalate to nuclear weapons use or to attack NATO countries.[2] Both sides managed and manipulated fears of escalation at the same time.

In the Cold War the urgent task of preserving the West while avoiding nuclear war compelled many brilliant minds to tackle the problem. Today's strategists are in their debt. But with nuclear weapons came a now-stereotyped set of concerns such as a focus on stability as the ultimate goal, deterrence as the primary means, arms races versus arms negotiations, second-strike capabilities, early warning, the integrity of command and control, the always–never dilemma, the triad (as a hedge against unknown adversary capabilities), the predelegation of authority, the SIOP (Single Integrated Operational Plan, a global target-servicing concept of nuclear operations), declaratory postures, escalation dominance, and more. Escalation questions still reach back to a nuclear-war perspective, not least because nuclear war itself is the ultimate escalation—and nuclear weapons still exist.

Any reintroduction of these frameworks, however, should recognize another influence on escalation dynamics: the emergence of networked information technologies—that is, cyberspace. Precision targeting based on precision information has enhanced the efficacy of weapons and accelerated the shift to knowledge over firepower as the arbiter of battle. Other manifestations of cyberspace range from substantial and continued improvements in systems for C^{4}ISR (command, control, communications, computers, intelligence, surveillance, and reconnaissance) to cyber and electronic operations against such systems.

Granted, early cyberwar thinking was initially laden with many nuclear-era concepts that, while fun to play with, could be misleading if not critically examined. But it is increasingly acknowledged that cyberwar dances its own steps, ones that echo into modern conventional conflict with its hunting and hiding. Its tenets include outcomes that depend on prewar information collection (such as the signatures of targets, detailed terrain data, and the architectures and vulnerabilities of opposing systems); the role of secrecy and surprise in developing unexpected techniques of hunting or hiding; the importance of vulnerabilities and the short half-life of exploits; the rapid struggle between measures and countermeasures (and thence counter-countermeasures, etc.); deception and decoys; the role played by generating and spreading knowledge farther than the other side does; the risk of an entire class of systems put suddenly in peril; red-teaming and experimentation in operational test and evaluation; the pervasive ambiguity associated with assessing—much less predicting—the results of engagements; and the struggle to maintain or, conversely, usurp command and control. A cyber sensibility focuses on what each side knows—and with what confidence. This orientation colors how one assesses escalation decisions.

A cyber, rather than just nuclear, orientation to understanding escalation might not change the answers to the questions that escalation poses. But it could alter the questions. After all, it is easy to believe that we have solved the nuclear escalation problem for having faced it for seventy-plus years without grave penalty. But the role of cyberspace in escalation is new. We have not earned equal confidence in our ability to manage it.

TWO THEMES

Herein, we pursue two themes. The major theme is that thresholds could play a role in managing escalation, notably among the superpowers. An accompanying theme is that the escalation ladder can be more like a lattice, which creates side options that complicate the use of thresholds but also can enhance escalation management.

To explain how thresholds may help modulate escalation, consider the highly simplified Figure I.1. The intensity of conflict reflects two factors: the willingness of each side to fight and each side's fear of what more intense fighting may bring. If the winds of war are heavy and the gravity of consequences is light, the puck of war will slide up the hill—the solid line. If the winds abate and consequences gain weight, the puck will stop sliding. Seriousness and intensity correlate, unsurprisingly. The solid line is escalation by degree (as, for instance, North Vietnam and the United States did from 1964 to 1967).

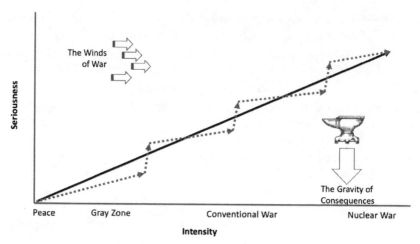

Figure I.1. Escalation with and without Thresholds

Figure I.1 also shows a modified escalation path. Here, the steeper segments in the dotted line represent thresholds. They bend the escalation curve in ways that interrupt movement forward—much as driving up a step is harder than driving up a ramp. Crossing a threshold may not indicate a great increase in intensity. Yet by changing the nature of the conflict, it connotes a hike in seriousness.

Crossing thresholds represents escalation by type. Thresholds themselves can characterize and anchor what both sides are doing. They help make states aware when changes in quantity become changes in quality that make for a different war. Crossing a threshold, however, is clearer than gauging the intensification of combat. Prior restraints are voided. If the other side had also been observing similar restraints, it knows it must choose whether and how to respond. (Salami-slicing, where one side escalates a little and challenges the other side to respond disproportionately, requires the first side to escalate by degree while the other side can only escalate by type.)

Historically the major threshold of conflict was between peace and war.[3] But once the destructive nature of nuclear weapons was appreciated, a second threshold emerged: that between conventional and nuclear war.[4] Both thresholds are being challenged by cyberspace. At the peace–war boundary, cyberwar may become unevenly normalized by states otherwise at peace. At the conventional–nuclear boundary, the growing ability to take out nuclear assets with precision guided weapons and perhaps cyberattacks raises the question of what exactly is the operating threshold before nuclear war.

If older thresholds cannot be relied on, new ones may be needed. Shifts in thresholds are not themselves inherently good or bad. Much will depend on how leaders react to them. The normalization of cyberattacks as peacetime practice may limit what sort of escalation that countries hoping to quash cyberwar might credibly threaten. But some cyberattacks could unexpectedly cross the other side's red lines and lead to violent war. Similarly, a prospect that conventional war can more easily grow into nuclear war would make conventional war more dangerous. Leaders might then avoid conventional war *because* it is more dangerous. This may then lower the risk of nuclear war—or raise it if the lower odds of conventional war are overwhelmed by the higher odds of its turning nuclear.

Thresholds could be likened to rungs to the extent that escalation means one-dimensional movement up or down. Given two levels of conflict, one would be higher than the other. Moving from one level to a higher level would make levels beyond that (including Armageddon) easier to reach, hence more likely.

Escalation scholars, though, have long distrusted the simple ladder metaphor. Alongside vertical escalation (a change in intensity), they have recognized horizontal escalation (when others join the conflict, or when conflict moves into other theaters or media) alongside. Horizontal escalation would have occurred if the Soviet Union had tried to "quarantine" West Berlin during the Cuban missile crisis. As Richard Smoke wrote, "In most real conflicts the potential escalation sequence is more like a ladder that has been bent and twisted out of shape, with all sorts of extras and odd protuberances added on, which vitally affect how the conflict does or does not climb it."[5] To Forrest Morgan,

> the escalation ladder metaphor can be seriously misleading if taken too seriously ... it offers a linear model of a phenomenon that is actually far more complex and ambiguous. There are a host of directions in which a conflict or confrontation can escalate, and, unlike the rungs on a ladder, it is not always clear whether the opponent or a third-party audience will consider one step to be more or less extreme than another, especially when the steps involve dissimilar measures.[6]

Whenever there are multiple escalation routes to the same path (e.g., strategic nuclear war arising from the other side's tactical nuclear use *or* in reaction to the other side's conventional weapons attacks on strategic nuclear assets), intermediate points on separate paths may be hard to compare.

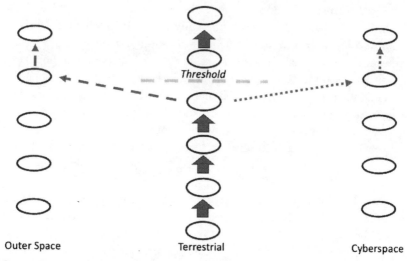

Figure I.2. How Lattices Complicate Escalation Management

Whether movements between intermediate points are escalation could depend on one's perspective.[7] If one side uses tactical nuclear weapons, has the other side escalated if it attacks *strategic* weapons using *conventional* arms? In a standoff over US freedom-of-navigation assertion (FONA) operations near "islands" in the South China Sea,[8] would, say, a Chinese retreat coupled by "unrestricted warfare"[9] in cyberspace that takes down the electric power grid constitute escalation?[10] Chinese forces would have descended from the threatened use of violence and force to methods that are nonviolent and where there is no forced entry. But they would have ascended from targeting military personnel on the field of battle to targeting civilians.

Figure I.2 illustrates this dilemma in general. Start with a local conflict. Each side wants to avoid a global conflict. Both have a rough idea of what that means, which, in turn, denotes the relevant threshold. But each side wishes to win. Both take lateral moves to that end. One side, hoping the other side will settle, carries out cyberattacks of increasing seriousness on the other's infrastructure. The other goes after satellites. Neither side has crossed the threshold because cyberattacks are nonviolent, and space attacks are nonlethal. But if both go far enough (setting aside the art of the possible) the intensity of the conflict can exceed the level that thresholds were meant to prevent.

Those strictures and structures—thresholds and lattices—underlie the prospects and challenges of escalation management. The details now follow.

WHAT WE COVER

The first chapter is largely definitional, covering escalation, motives and inhibitions associated with initiating and responding to it, the role played by the prospect of nuclear Armageddon, and the use of thresholds to modulate or at least shape escalation. Our progression then follows in rough order of intensity from cyberwar to nonlethal operations, conventional combat, operations against nuclear weapons, and operations using nuclear weapons. Each chapter addresses the same question: what are the potentials for thresholds in that region of the conflict spectrum? Correspondingly Chapter 2 asks on what side of the peace–war line cyberwar sits and how it compares to other forms of conflict, notably economic. Chapter 3 examines the prospect of a threshold separating destructive attacks on things—using war in space as an exemplar—from casualty-producing attacks. Chapter 4 looks at escalation in conventional warfare, focusing on the distinction between local and global conflict and the viability of a homeland sanctuary. Chapter 5 examines conventional and cyber operations against nuclear weapons systems and how such operations might lead to the other side's nuclear use. It asks: does the nuclear war threshold mean war *with* or also war *on* nuclear weapons? Chapter 6 considers escalation thresholds that may remain even after the nuclear threshold is pierced. Chapter 7 leverages its predecessors to argue that for many reasons—competing strategic goals, asymmetry even among superpowers, and mismatched understandings of what distinguishes levels of war—thresholds are unlikely to arise on their own. Their emergence requires advocacy followed by give and take. The Conclusions recapitulate the main findings.

Throughout this work we assume rational actors: those that can understand and evaluate their situation, the options available, the effect of pursuing these options (including what the other side might do in response), and the range of possible results—and then make decisions based on what will make them better off by some plausible criteria. Strict rationality, in fairness, is elusive. There is fog and friction. Misperception is common. Leaders often make the worst-case interpretation of the other side's motives. Some leaders put their own welfare before that of their country (the agent problem). Some look backward (e.g., to redeem sunk costs[11] or to exact revenge) rather than forward. They can be overwhelmed by emotions or paralyzed by panic. In a crisis they may think fast rather than slow. Rational leaders may be pressured by political forces of the irrational street. And even if irrational leaders are rare, if they are correspondingly more prone to, say, go nuclear, an unexpectedly large percentage of nuclear crises will require dealing with them. Unfortunately, if rationality is assumed away, any stimulus (e.g., the other side's stepped-up surveillance) can lead to any escalation.

WHAT WE DO NOT COVER

One, this is not an encyclopedia of conflict escalation. We have picked and chosen topics on escalation with a focus on potential thresholds and a tilt toward the effects of cyberspace. We have not looked at, say, other forms of gray zone conflict (e.g., Russia's 2014 use of "little green men" in Crimea) that can erode the distinction between peace and war. We also do not cover other hostile actions short of conflict, such as trade manipulation, traditional espionage and surveillance, the imprisonment of foreign nationals, state-sponsored crime or militia/insurgency activity, the movement of military forces, and quarantines. (Even if thresholds can be applied below the level of conflict, treaties and international law do much of what thresholds do, but in different ways and with different dynamics.)

Two, our discussion of escalation covers changes in action—doing things previously considered off-limits—but not changes in capabilities. In fairness, the distinction between actions and capabilities can be fuzzy. The insertion of Soviet intermediate-range nuclear missiles into Cuba—which would have tripled the Soviet *capability* to hit the United States with missiles—was deemed escalation even though such weapons were never used.[12] It was clearly *escalatory*, in that the United States responded with a blockade—the use of force.

Three, although this book refers to the laws of armed combat (LOAC)—such as the definition of armed attack, the requirements of neutrality, and proportionality—LOAC is not a necessary determinant of whether something is or is not an escalation. It is the other side's reaction that indicates what, in retrospect, was escalatory. LOAC considerations can affect the reaction but are unlikely to dictate them. As Appendix A argues, thresholds are usually poor candidates for formal norms.

Four, we claim no *ipso facto* rules of escalation. Everything is context-dependent. The aim here is not to sketch outcomes or to recommend specific strategies to manage escalation but to lay out a framework for discussing challenges and issues.

INTRODUCTION   9

NOTES

1. Can Russia still be counted as a superpower? Russia's GDP, trade presence, financial power, and conventional military forces do not approach their US counterparts—while China's do. But Russia's cyberspace capabilities, nuclear arsenal, and energy resources are peers to their US counterparts—and China's are not. Russia also exports more military technology to China than it imports. In the long run, Russia's proclivity to use force, its huge size and hence resource base, its population and their educational levels, plus the tendency of losers to fix what made them losers all suggest not counting Russia out as a superpower just yet.
2. See, for instance, Eric Schmitt, Zolan Kanno-Youngs, and Julian E. Barnes, "Zelensky's weapons wish list goes mostly unfulfilled on trip to Washington," *New York Times*, December 22, 2022, https://www.nytimes.com/2022/12/22/us/politics/ukraine-zelensky-biden-weapons.html.
3. Blurred lines are not altogether new. French General Andre Beaufre (*Deterrence and Strategy*, New York, NY: Praeger, 1965, 29–30) wrote over a half century ago, "peace is far more stable than before the advent of the nuclear weapon. But peace has no longer the absolute character it had in the last century: today it is possible to hurl insults at a nation, burn down its embassy, arrest its ships, send hired assassins into its country or give almost open support to political parties without war breaking out."
4. For an early argument that no alternative threshold can substitute for the nuclear/nonnuclear threshold, see Thornton Read, "Limited Strategic War and Tactical Nuclear War," in Klaus Knorr and Thornton Read, *Limited Strategic War* (New York, NY: Praeger, 1972), 67–116.
5. Richard Smoke, *War: Controlling Escalation* (Cambridge MA: Harvard, 1977), 252.
6. Forrest E. Morgan, Karl P. Mueller, Evan S. Medeiros, Kevin L. Pollpeter, and Roger Cliff, *Dangerous Thresholds: Managing Escalation in the 21st Century* (Santa Monica, CA: RAND, 2008), 17.
7. Michael Fitzsimmons ("The False Assure of Escalation Dominance," November 16, 2017, *War on the Rocks*, https://warontherocks.com/2017/11/false-allure-escalation-dominance/) has observed, "contingency planning for escalation is harder than ever. Where in the hierarchy of escalation does a disabling but reversible Chinese attack on U.S. military satellites belong? Is a Russian cyberattack on the U.S. electrical grid more or less escalatory than missile strikes on European bases? This kind of complexity also compounds the challenges of misperception."
8. Thanks to David Gompert, former acting Director of National Intelligence (DNI), for suggesting this logic.
9. Taken after Qiao Liang and Wang Xiangsui, *Unrestricted Warfare*, 1999, https://www.c4i.org/unrestricted.pdf (which, in fairness, has never been official People's Liberation Army [PLA] doctrine).
10. Note the Atlantic Council's Emma Ashford's observations on cyber operations, "the White House clearly views that as far more escalatory than some of the other steps we've taken—the arms, the sanctions, et cetera. Because the calls to use cyber techniques to strike directly at Russian infrastructure, stop Russian trains, make it hard for Russia to fight the war in Ukraine, those seem to be viewed pretty clearly as making the U.S. an actual party to this conflict." ("Transcript: Ezra Klein Interviews Emma

Ashford," *New York Times*, March 18, 2022, https://www.nytimes.com/2022/03/18/podcasts/transcript-ezra-klein-interviews-emma-ashford.html.) Kevin Mandia has stated "there was a decision made somewhere in Russia to not escalate outside of the immediate theater of Ukraine with cyber. And because of that, nobody knows what will trigger an escalation, or what the escalation will be." From Suzanne Smalley, "Nakasone says cyber command did nine 'hunt forward' ops last year, including in Ukraine," *Cyberscroop*, May 4, 2022, https://www.cyberscoop.com/nakasone-persistent-engagement-hunt-forward-nine-teams-ukraine/. Conversely, General Nakasone stated that offensive cyber operations in support of Ukraine are taking place (Alexander Martin, "US military hackers conducting offensive operations in support of Ukraine, says head of cyber command," *Sky News*, June 1, 2022, https://news.sky.com/story/us-military-hackers-conducting-offensive-operations-in-support-of-ukraine-says-head-of-cyber-command-12625139). But without further details, it is difficult to evaluate whether it crossed previously stated Administration barriers. Also note Tyler Bowen, "The logic of escalation and the benefits of conventional power preponderance in the nuclear age," August 19, 2021, https://elischolar.library.yale.edu/gsas_dissertations/, 17: "if North Korea responded to US air strikes on its missile testing sites with a cyberattack against the American energy grid, this would constitute a step up the escalation ladder."

11. Martin Shubik ("The dollar auction game: A paradox in cooperative behavior and escalation," *The Journal of Conflict Resolution*, 15, no. 1 [March 1971], 109–111) administered a game in which two individuals bid for a dollar—but with the proviso that money, once bid, is thereby forfeited. The bidding starts at a nickel, making it seem like a great deal for the winner, but once one player's bid is matched by the other player, both are often motivated to raise the stakes a little (and thus place more money at risk). Even as the bidding exceeds a dollar, thereby guaranteeing that both will have lost more than they gain in the whole transaction, some are still tempted to bid just a nickel more to redeem the original wager.

12. Russia and China have decried, as destabilizing, US actions such as withdrawing from the Anti-Ballistic Missile (ABM) treaty and developing a conventional prompt global strike (CPGS) because both eroded mutual assured destruction (MAD), the premise that all superpowers accepted each other's deterrent as both a fact of life and as a guarantee of stability. Analogously, some Russians believe a similar tacit bargain covers the vulnerability of each other's electric grid to cyberattack; thus, anything the United States does to harden the grid would be seen as similarly destabilizing. But as Brendan Rittenhouse Green (*The Revolution that Failed: Nuclear Competition, Arms Control, and the Cold War* [Cambridge UK: Cambridge University Press, 2020]) argued, the United States never accepted a nuclear stasis during the Cold War, and such refusal never led to destabilization.

1

Escalation and Its Motivations

Escalation—"an increase in the intensity or scope of conflict that crosses threshold(s) considered significant by one or more of the participants"[1]— would seem self-defeating. Two countries squabble. Matters slide from hostility to war. War deepens as each reacts to the other in a tit-for-tat fashion, with no side gaining much edge. Neither planned for this, but neither stops trying to top the other. Both sides grow progressively worse off. Nuclear weapons may be used. If both sides do so, Armageddon could result.

In part because that would be a bad end, it would be good to find ways to modulate escalation. There are many ways to avoid such a fate. A general disposition toward peace and self-restraint certainly helps. So would a resolution of whatever disagreements nations fight over.

But another way to modulate escalation would be through the establishment or recognition of thresholds. These would be barriers to escalation that, at a minimum, would force each side to consider whether crossing them would be worthwhile, and, at a maximum, constitute agreement between two sides that each side's forbearance will be matched by the other's. Thresholds provide stopping points on the path to Armageddon.

To explore the role of escalation thresholds, this chapter first delves into escalation: why countries would initiate it, whether their foes would match it, and the special role of nuclear Armageddon in inhibiting it. In discussing thresholds, we first define them, then discuss their purpose, notably as they may influence inadvertent escalation.

INITIATING ESCALATION

Escalation is not entirely irrational; it has several reasonable motives (in the sense of what countries might gain from escalation as distinct from why they escalate).

One is improving warfighting outcomes. A familiar Cold War scenario starts with conventional Soviet forces invading Europe, which then prompts NATO to contemplate using nuclear weapons lest it be overrun (or, these days, the Russian state decides that not using such weapons jeopardizes its existence). Or countries that start wars face unforeseen events that persuade them to recalibrate how far they must go in order to win.[2] States may also consciously risk inadvertent escalation[3] (e.g., arising from striking nuclear assets) if imposing the controls necessary to ensure against it would hurt military effectiveness. How the war goes may make a difference: the same increase in whatever metric is used to judge the benefits of escalating may be viewed differently if it converts, say, a likely defeat into a possible victory rather than a likely victory to a highly likely one. Similar calculations may spur preemptive escalation.[4] One side tells itself that the other will soon escalate to escape a jam. If holding back leaves it much worse off, it goes first (even if going first converts a possible escalation into a certain one). Preemption was a real worry in the early Cold War years. It may yet return in cases where precision munitions can suddenly take out a large share of another side's assets in a surprise attack (see Chapter 4). But preemption makes sense only if there is high confidence that escalation is coming, the results of waiting and therefore going second are awful, and the reputational consequences of escalating first are tolerable. The need to meet all these conditions should make preemption, especially nuclear preemption, rare: among 67 major external wars between 1816 and 1980, only three, by one account, could be categorized as preemptive: Germany's 1914 attack on Russia, China's 1950 entry into the Korean conflict, and Israel's 1967 attack on Egypt.[5]

A variant on preemption is reacting to the threat that the other side will go first by launching probes, intensifying intelligence collection, redeploying forces, and raising alert levels. The other side sees these actions as prefatory to aggression, which not only validates its own preparations but may cause it to do likewise—thereby validating the first side's own moves.

Two is making the other side drop out first by imposing unaffordable costs or risks on them—a Schelling-esque contest of pain-making and pain-taking.[6] In World War I, with battle lines on the western front hard to move, each side endeavored to wreak so many enemy casualties that the other side would quit in exhaustion and despair. Analysts see Russia's military doctrine as escalating punishment, rather than mounting a stiff defense, to ward off threats to the homeland.[7] As for China, one scholar has written, "China's preferred means of escalating a conventional conflict to coerce an adversary to the negotiating table is to threaten conventional missile attacks, counter-space attacks, and strategic cyberattacks on an adversary's homeland critical infrastructure networks."[8] Escalating to force the other side to quit may be dominant in fights for relative dominance, in contrast to those undertaken achieving specific goals.

States may also escalate an ongoing conflict (especially to the nuclear level) hoping to de-escalate it. The other side would be shocked into realizing that the costs and risks of continuing to fight are much more severe than it realized; it then settles. Here, "de-escalate" is likely a misnomer if the intent is not to modulate conflict but terminate it.

Small escalations may be used to portend a large one and thus serve as a forcing function. "[In] Operation Rolling Thunder, the 1965–1967 bombing campaign ... U.S. planners hoped that gradually increasing the importance of the targets being attacked, striking targets progressively closer to the enemy capital, and increasing the number of sorties flown and the amount of munitions being dropped would make clear to Hanoi that the conflict would eventually escalate to a prohibitively costly level."[9] Incidentally, Hanoi did not flinch. Arguably, "escalation results when one side tries to demonstrate resolve by increasing directed efforts in the diplomatic, military, information, or economic domains."[10]

One side could also escalate as a way of punishing the other side's escalation. An equivalent tit for tat is, by definition, not the initiation of escalation. But if one side concludes that it must meet more than measure for measure,[11] it may escalate the conflict even further. Or, a state could escalate along one path (e.g., a homeland cyberattack) in response to the other side's escalating on another path (e.g., a naval strike on a disputed atoll).

Three is backing up a threat of escalation. Escalation threats (e.g., to use nuclear weapons) can, for instance, be used to protect certain assets (e.g., early-warning satellites). If Russia makes nuclear threats to force a settlement with NATO[12] but NATO does not deem Russian threats credible and keeps fighting, might Russia then use nuclear weapons to show that its threats *are* credible? If the Russians indicate that sufficiently severe sanctions might set off a strategic response,[13] will it react accordingly if sanctions ensue? In fairness, threat mechanics do not always favor escalation. Sometimes one side may deliberately refrain from some escalation in order to retain it as a threat, one to be activated if the other side escalated. Appendix B explains why, particularly with nuclear threats, possible use equates to highly unlikely use.

How much should one side want the other side to know it has escalated? If the goal is military advantage, subtlety is preferred to reduce the likelihood that the other side matches the escalation. If the goals are to signal resolve or give credibility to threats, obviousness is preferred.

Like everything in war, escalation however, can be driven by emotion: for example, to vex the enemy or to give them a taste of their own medicine, to restore one's honor or salve one's pride, to show one cannot be hurt with impunity ("how dare they!"), to deliver justice, or to express entitlement. Leaders may feel that something they have suffered is tantamount to an act of war—which then requires a response.[14] Vladimir Putin's propensity to escalate may stem from his being "an apostle of payback" who believes the West "took advantage of Russia's moment of historical weakness in the 1990s."[15] A country suffering from air strikes but lacking air power may consider sabotage or terrorism to be like-for-like—while the other side may see restraints discarded, hence escalation. A country whose soldiers face attacks by, say, robots and knowing that robots do not suffer may deem the contest unfair and look for people to strike, hoping to make the other side suffer as they do. All that noted, the existence of emotions does not mean the absence of rational thinking. Rising to leadership requires manipulating emotions rather than being manipulated by them. Sounding emotional is one thing, acting from emotion quite another.

Escalation can also arise from accident (errors in operations) or inadvertence (errors in judgment). Navigational error probably explains Germany's first bombing of London's residential neighborhoods, an act that put both sides' cities in play for further air attack.[16] Escalation might result from a lapse in command and control, for example, actions carried out by a subordinate ally, a rogue unit, or a third party. If two sides have very different views of what actions are comparable, one side may think it is responding to an escalation vigorously while the other thinks it is initiating it anew. Examples include China's demonstrating a blockade of Taiwan after the visit of House Speaker Nancy Pelosi, or Russia's attacks on Ukraine's infrastructure after the latter's attack on the Kerch bridge connecting Crimea to the Russian mainland (a rationale that now looks like an excuse).

In a way, every escalation must be a response to some change. If a state thought itself best off fighting at one level, something must have changed to convince it to fight at a higher level. That something could be a change in circumstances, shifting perceptions (e.g., of the other side's aims), or a growing gap between expectations and reality (e.g., the other side is unyielding). If that change should have been anticipated, escalation may then be evidence of miscalculation (even if it is the other side that escalates in response to an attack). Miscalculations may also result from a failure to anticipate the other side's innovations. If, say, drone swarms prove to be as militarily effective as some think[17] *and* the other side cannot field something similar *and* various countermeasures (e.g., counter-UAV guns, electronic warfare, cyberattack) avail naught *and* drone swarms, themselves, are not considered escalation by type, then a sharp shift in military outcomes may lead the other side into initiating its own escalation.

In principle, the stakes at hand should dictate the level of military commitment (at least by those who start or join wars). Small issues ought not lead to large wars; if they do, something went wrong. Accordingly, for example, the United States and China should never fight a big war over "islands" in the South China Sea (as distinct from China's enforcing claims over the whole South China Sea). Unfortunately, the logic may be stood on its head if the stakes at hand reflect the means used. As the Vietnam War escalated, fears about the reputational costs of failure grew.[18] US policymakers became more anxious to have their policy succeed. The US interest in how Afghanistan was governed rose substantially once the United States committed forces there in response to the September 11 attacks. If the Chinese, say, took down the US electric grid with cyberattacks in the hope of dissuading a US intervention over Taiwan, that act alone could raise the US stake in showing it could not be pushed around—and, thus, its stake in preserving Taiwan's freedom. Similarly, increasing hostility from one side can raise the urgency felt by the other side to quash its foe.

As a rule, the prospect of escalation—particularly by the losing side—tends to reduce the interest and thus investment in the prospect of winning at one level, when the other side, if losing, can escalate to a higher level. If NATO were to convince Russia that victory against Ukraine would lead to NATO's intervention, would Russia bear the same costs and take the same risks it is now taking to achieve such a victory—or would it hold back its resources to take on NATO? Both the French and the United States may have hesitated to go for a knock-out blow in Vietnam lest doing so would invite Chinese intervention.[19] Eisenhower's strategy of brinksmanship in the 1950s led to less investment in conventional war-winning capability; if NATO could not win the conventional war, there were other options. The inferior party at the lower level would likely want to husband its effort because it has the choice to escalate; the superior party, unless convinced the other side will escalate anyway, must maintain the effort in case the inferior side does not escalate. The goal of the superior party, therefore, should be to win just enough to convince the other side to settle, but not too much to warrant escalation.

MATCHING ESCALATION

Because an escalation tit-for-tat spiral requires two players, the choice to match escalation matters as much as the choice to initiate it. In principle, if one side escalates, the military benefits to the other side from then escalating should not be that much different than if the other side escalated *de novo*. Yet, if the other side were holding back from something that would be militarily advantageous in hopes that its opponent was similarly self-restrained, then the one side's initial escalation voids the rationale for the other side's forbearance. Or, one side's escalation may force the other side into an agonizing reappraisal; it then sees its foe as more hostile or more heedless than earlier thought. In a contest of wills, the side that fails to match escalation may look as if it is dropping out.

Matching the other side's escalation also helps reestablish the idea that escalation carries consequences—perhaps to where the other side reimposes its former self-restraint, or at least does not escalate further. Indeed, countries may want to overmatch escalation as a way of ensuring against further escalation from the other side. But the urge to match may also be cynical (I've always wanted to do this; now I can), angry (I've restrained myself, but they haven't, so let it rip), or revanchist (now they know what it feels like).

Escalation may also go unanswered. Leaders may refuse to respond to signal their virtue. Or they lack a good military rationale: operating across the threshold is impossible or at least not cost-effective. In some cases, it may require delegating too much authority to the field. Even if something the other side did *could have been* regarded as crossing a threshold, acting otherwise may show it regards the threshold as intact and should still govern both sides' behavior. Continued self-restraint allows the other side to go back to its earlier rules. Holding off still leaves room to escalate when better prepared—especially if the next violation is more damaging or more obvious. A lack of reaction may also arise from one side's determination to lay out its own path. Secretary of Defense Harold Brown's 1979 observation, "Soviet spending has shown no response to U.S. restraint—when we build, they build; when we cut, they build,"[20] reflected not only Soviet determination but also its indifference to the prospect of influencing what the United States did.

Many of the factors that might prevent a response to escalation—such as resource shortages, inappropriate technology, political constraints, and strategic philosophies—are the same as those that limit escalation in the first place. The one side could reason: your failure to escalate because you are weak just allows us to escalate with impunity.

Nevertheless, not every act of escalation is escalatory—in the sense of inducing the other side to escalate. And some actions—such as Ukraine retaking the Kharkiv oblast in September 2022—cannot be considered escalation but are escalatory because it induced the other side to escalate. Escalation by one side matters most when it is escalatory: that is, when it persuades the other side to itself escalate, thereby setting up further cycles of escalation and response. In that light, consider the following statements on the Ukraine war: "We need to make our own judgments about what counts as escalation . . . and not defer to Putin on these questions,"[21] or UK Foreign Minister David Cameron saying that only "where a NATO soldier is killing a Russian soldier" would there be escalation.[22] It is precisely the other side's reaction that would give escalation added significance.

The logic of an escalation spiral necessarily assumes that the odds of escalation in response exceed the odds of escalation *ab initio*. Otherwise, each side's decision is largely independent of the other side's. In practice and retrospect, the fact that the other side escalated may be only one of many reasons why military outcomes are disappointing and demand upping intensity levels. The all-too-human tendency to assume that what you did accounts for what they do may exaggerate your influence on their decision making. A spiral must also assume that someone *over*-matches the other side; if one side is careful to no more than match its adversary and both see this correctly, then there is no spiral.

FEARS OF ARMAGEDDON SHOULD ALSO INHIBIT ESCALATION

Among superpowers, fears of Armageddon resulting from successive escalation can inhibit such escalation even if the next step is well below the nuclear level.[23] In the wake of the 2019 terrorist attack in Kashmir, an *Economist* article was headlined, "Skirmishing between India and Pakistan could escalate: Two nuclear-armed states shoot down each other's planes."[24] In 2020 John W. Nicholson, former commander of US Forces Afghanistan, wrote, "If true, this [Russia's paying bounties to Taliban for killing US forces in Afghanistan] would constitute both a reckless miscalculation and a major mistake by the Russians and the Taliban. History shows that such mistakes and miscalculations often lead to war. And, of course, the consequences of a conflict between Russia and the United States, both nuclear superpowers, could be catastrophic for the planet."[25]

As Thomas Schelling argued "Small wars embody the threat of a larger war; they are not just military engagements but 'crisis diplomacy.'"[26]

Responsible leaders, in a superpower confrontation, should therefore be expected to assess the odds that this or that move would result in mutual destruction—even if such odds are never written down.[27] The greater the odds of such disaster, the greater should be the inhibition to push matters.[28]

It would be irrational for states to light off a nuclear attack and thereby suffer great harm[29] unless utterly convinced that no other choice exists.[30] But getting there through escalation is disturbingly plausible. Knowing that the other side also fears Armageddon does not mean it cannot happen. The path there could reflect interactions whose outcome is uncertain because neither side knows how its foe will react to this or that circumstance. There are accidents and incidents, the outcomes of battle, third countries, bureaucratic maneuvering, and national politics in the mix. Leaders may believe a very limited nuclear strike, particularly if carried out just as a signal, could scare others into suing for peace. A leader, having backed a red line with a nuclear weapon—that is then crossed—may prefer starting a nuclear war (hoping, perhaps, to see only a few weapons used) to losing the credibility necessary to maintain nuclear deterrence or at least its nuclear-backed red lines.

In the Cuban missile crisis, President Kennedy estimated that the *a priori* risk of all-out nuclear war was between a third and a half.[31] These days the odds of Armageddon from a similar standoff should be lower (smaller nuclear inventories and the shift toward counterforce targeting suggest that the level of global destruction from an all-out nuclear war would also be less). Secure second strike has sharply cut the need for (and value of) preemption. There are more nuclear options than the SIOP. There is less automaticity; US missiles stopped having predesignated target assignments after the Cold War ended. There are more counterforce options, including those that do not use nuclear weapons. Unfortunately, when everyone thinks the odds of Armageddon are low, they may be apt to take greater risks, thereby raising those very odds.

Fears of starting a great (if nonnuclear) war have also inhibited escalation. Outside powers in the Spanish Civil War calculated that some otherwise attractive military options could precipitate a catastrophic pan-European war, which no one wanted. This includes Hitler, because he was not yet ready for one[32]—until 1939, when he was. Even after Hiroshima both the United States and China, while fighting each other in Korea, refrained from attacks outside the Korean peninsula for fear of general war.[33] Avoiding the risk of an unrestricted war with China over Vietnam was important enough to overshadow fears of escalating into a nuclear war. But these days the primary ultimate restraint has nuclear roots.

The tenet that the fear of Armageddon should further dampen the urge to escalate admits of two exceptions.

One is a strategy of deliberately passing the onus for nuclear escalation to the other side who would then settle rather than continue, much less escalate. Per Schelling, deterrence "often depends on getting into a position where the initiative is up to the enemy and it is he who has to make the awful decision to proceed to a clash."[34] Per Robert Powell, "During a crisis, each state exerts coercive pressure on its adversary by acting in ways that vary the risk of disaster. Eventually, one of the states finds the risk too high and withdraws."[35] Where that point lies may depend less on escalation dominance and more on which side has the better escalation path at a particular point. In the Cuban missile crisis, the first move was the Soviets putting missiles in Cuba at a time when they had far fewer intercontinental missiles than the United States did. Presumably the Soviets considered that the resulting odds of Armageddon were low compared to the strategic advantages from evening up the nuclear balance (in an era when nuclear war seemed sufficiently likely to justify taking such risks). The second move was the United States quarantining Cuba. US leaders must have believed that the harm in facing a sharp hike in the number of Soviet missiles that could reach the United States plus the loss to US credibility (by doing nothing after having publicly warned the Soviet Union not to put missiles in Cuba) exceeded the heightened risk of nuclear war. That put the onus back on the Soviet Union—which had few good options. Its naval inferiority around Cuba obviated its breaking the quarantine. Making a new ruckus about West Berlin would have only extended the crisis without resolving it. The United States, meanwhile, had cards left to play—notably an air attack on Cuba or a ground invasion. Every day the crisis continued was a day when something—such as a U-2 incident, of which there were two that week—could push both countries to war. The Soviet Union found its least bad strategy was to seek terms (winning two concessions: a public pledge not to invade Cuba and a private pledge to remove missiles from Turkey). Passing the onus may work even for subnuclear threats.[36]

The other exception is the stability–instability paradox—the belief that having a nuclear stalemate (stability) encourages countries to escalate at lower levels of conflict (fostering instability).[37] Nuclear weapons, accordingly, have freed Pakistan to wage the 1998 Kargil war, the 2001 terrorist attack on India's Parliament, and the 2019 terrorist attack in Kashmir. The escalation route from terrorism to nuclear war would have had three steps: one by Pakistan (e.g., a terrorist act), the second by India (to conventional war), and the third by Pakistan (to a nuclear strike). Pakistan's leaders felt freed from the fear of losing a war to India's superior conventional military,[38] since India's doing so would raise the risk of nuclear war beyond India's tolerance. Although India did carry out a conventional attack against a Pakistani military facility that supported the 2019 terrorist attack in Kashmir, the air raid sparked no further escalation (it helped that Pakistan was satisfied to have shot down an Indian pilot, later repatriated). But the entire incident may have resulted in both countries living "in a world where more forms of escalation short of major conventional war may be possible."[39] The Russian war on Ukraine also indicates the three-step feature of the paradox. Russia invaded Ukraine with only modest fears of nuclear war precisely because NATO would *not* automatically be involved. The onus would be on NATO to escalate the war by intervening. But NATO countries feared that if they did intervene, Russia might use nuclear weapons, thereby raising the risks of Armageddon to uncomfortable levels. NATO's expected discomfort correspondingly lowered the probability that Russia's invading Ukraine would raise the odds of Armageddon too high for its comfort. Thus, the fear of nuclear war (the highest level) increased the prospects of a Russian invasion of Ukraine (the third-highest level) because it inhibited NATO from entering the war (the second-highest level). Conversely, nuclear weapons likely inhibited conventional combat in Cold War Europe because both sides believed that escalation to the next level (nuclear war) was far too likely.[40] There were few if any third-level options (e.g., terrorism, proxy wars) made more attractive just because escalation to general war was less attractive. Overall, though, because the paradox needs three potential levels of conflict, the fillip it gives to escalation must take place two levels down from Armageddon.[41] (Even if nuclear-armed countries might be encouraged to start wars because their own sovereignty is protected by their nuclear deterrence, their existence is newly threatened if the other side has nuclear weapons as well.)

THE DEFINITION AND PURPOSE OF THRESHOLDS

Thresholds, as noted, can help manage escalation, first by denoting when a party is moving to a new stage of conflict, and second by creating a basis for both sides to agree not to go further. They may be defined in terms of either ends or means.

A change in ends might be a threshold between cyberattacks on military targets to those on civilian targets and, within these targets, from information systems to physical systems. These shifts may be regarded as escalation even if the same means are used. Using surface-to-air missiles against manned aircraft could be regarded as escalation if previously used only against drones (see Chapter 3). Going after the other side's nuclear weapons that were previously off limits (see Chapter 5) may be deemed escalation. Shifting from counterforce to counter-value nuclear targeting could be considered escalation (see Chapter 6) even if the choice of weapons did not change. Defining a threshold in terms of effects, however, could create problems of inadvertent escalation whenever effects vary from intentions or are difficult to measure to both side's satisfaction.

An example of a change in means might be a shift from cyberattacks to kinetic attacks—even if the targets stay the same.[42] Crossing thresholds may carry serious consequences even when intensity has not immediately increased—because the *potential* costs and casualties using one means may be far higher than with other means. Going from cyberwar to kinetic war takes one from an arena in which no one has died directly to one in which tens of millions have (e.g., the 60 million of World War II). Escalating to nuclear war could jeopardize billions, not just millions.

Thresholds can help modulate conflict even if they are only unilateral. A well-defined threshold can be how leaders know they are crossing over from one type of war to another. It may mark when conflict or confrontation has passed a point of no return, short of a full conflict resolution. Walking back across the threshold would signal failure or resignation that would be more obvious than, say, drawing down forces (who, one can say, did their job and can now leave). Designating boundaries can inhibit mission creep of the sort that brought US forces in South Vietnam from tens of thousands to a half a million over three years without very much to mark any transition. The marking of thresholds can also be used as part of a nation's narrative that it has seized the high moral ground (e.g., by recognizing the "sanctuary of space"). They can signal intentions—we won't unless you do.

Thresholds, though, are more useful when bilateral.[43] Each side, mindful of this or that threshold, would limit its own military efforts in the belief that the other side also will. Correspondingly a threshold is not only a threat but a promise, albeit perhaps tacit. Therein lies a relationship between deterrence and escalation management. The core concept of deterrence is: if you do this, I will do that. But behind that threat is a corresponding and converse promise: if you don't do this, I won't do that. When statesmen and scholars talk about the credibility of deterrence, they usually refer to one side's belief in the other side's doing "that." The converse promise of restraint gets less attention. By contrast, a promise by one side that it will respect a threshold if the other side does so shifts the emphasis to the credibility of the promise. Is the other side trustworthy? Will it stick to the deal, however implicit?

Will it try to cheat? When assessing the other side's character, the question of whether its threats are credible is different from the question of what its promises are worth.

For escalation of both degree and type, the more likely it is that the other side will respond, the weaker the case for initiating escalation. Thresholds fit nicely into this calculus. Crossing an understood threshold would raise the odds of a retaliatory escalation because it would be noticeable; its nature would be less debatable. As Edward Guest has argued of escalation, "Indeed, adversaries have incentives to act as though they interpret U.S. retaliation as disproportionate even if they do not perceive it as such."[44] Establishing thresholds reduces their ability to do so justifiably. Furthermore, a country that would burst through tacit constraints at the lower level necessarily weakens its ability to credibly promise self-restraint at higher levels.

Thresholds convert analog risk into digital risk. Without thresholds, a state that engaged in hostilities at say, level A, may contemplate raising the intensity to level B. Further intensity gets the state to level C; much greater, to level D. Moving from level A to level B, from level B to level C, or from level C to level D all carry some risk of escalation from the other side. With a threshold that, say, separates level B from level C, moving from level A to level B poses less risk of escalation from the other side; ditto, in moving from level C to level D. But moving from level B to level C makes a corresponding response from the other side more likely—and thus must be carefully considered.[45] Similarly, if two parties are testing one another, mutually recognized thresholds convert the question, "where will they go," into the question, "will they go there?" This helps explain why credibility at lower levels of intensity matters to credibility at higher levels. It also turns escalation strategy into a more tractable information problem.[46]

A threshold's universality, symmetry, clarity, and robustness should all improve the likelihood that both sides can work with it.

Universality refers to which thresholds apply in which conflicts. One universal threshold is the nuclear taboo[47]—first visible in President Truman's decision not to use nuclear weapons in the Korean War. Offering thresholds too specific to one conflict may appear self-serving. Yet, some reasonable thresholds are context-dependent; for example, they apply to land conflict but not naval conflict. Distinctions must also make logical sense. Russia's use of hypersonic cruise missiles (having previously used only subsonic cruise missiles) could only be deemed an escalation[48] only if speed is a relevant criterion.

Symmetry also helps. In principle, thresholds can be asymmetric—tantamount to two red lines, one from each side. After all, the foregoing definition referred to thresholds "considered significant by *one or more* of the participants." One side could believe that tactical nuclear weapons are those with warheads under 100 kilotons but understand that the other side believes that tactical nuclear weapons feature warheads of 200 kilotons or less. The other side's using 150-kiloton weapons does not constitute crossing the tactical–strategic line as the other side defined it—so the threshold is still intact. Bilateral asymmetry is possible: so, touching the US homeland with war (Chapter 4) may more surely lead to further escalation than if it were done to Russia or China, but the latter may be more sensitive to threats to their regime's stability. In practice, it is hard to see one side allowing the other side to do what it cannot and still stay within the same threshold. The better articulated and the more widely broadcast the thresholds, the more they must be the same for both sides for them to be deemed unfair and illegitimate. The 2022 claim by Russia's spokesman, Dmitry Peskov, that an attack on a fuel depot in Belgorod Russia was escalation[49] abuses the term—unless one can argue that Russian strikes on Ukraine sat at a lower level of escalation than Ukrainian strikes back. Internal debates on whether thresholds should be observed are facilitated by observing that the other side observes the same constraints; they shape the rules of that conflict. Conversely, to return to whether Russian use of hypersonic cruise missiles breaks a threshold, the fact that Ukraine had nothing similar in its kit bag suggests such a threshold would have limited meaning in that conflict.

Clarity has two aspects. Can one side determine whether something it might do *would* cross a threshold? Can the other side determine whether such an action *did* cross a threshold? That is a matter of correct characterization and attribution. It is difficult to make a threshold out of an act that cannot be confidently characterized or attributed: for example, implanting cyberattacks for later use, surreptitious attacks on satellites that look like internal failure, forms of electronic warfare that look like random static, hidden mines yet to be activated, or the sabotage of equipment to fail mysteriously. A threshold that one side believes it can cross obscurely will not maintain much respect. A move that cannot be confidently attributed to the other side may also tempt cheating. Uncertain attribution, admittedly, is more of a peacetime than wartime problem. Once war starts, a move that is costly to make or requires unique capabilities would generally be attributed to the enemy because third parties lack the willingness or the means for carrying it out.

Robustness reflects the prospect that one threshold defined by type can resist pressures that arise when subthreshold activities are so intense that crossing the threshold does not appear to be escalation in comparison. Posit a threshold, for instance, separating cyberattack from kinetic attack. Then a cyberattack kills thousands (e.g., by shutting down the electric power grid). The pressure for kinetic retaliation may be hard to resist; a threshold so crossed ceases to be a serious one. Another element in robustness is that actions within the threshold do not, in practice, call for the other side to cross the threshold as a military response. For instance, a threshold that allows trespass (e.g., by air) but does not allow responses to a threshold (e.g., by air defense) would appear unstable.

It is unclear what thresholds were during the Cold War. Herman Kahn's classic work[50] posited 44 levels of conflict from "Ostensible Crisis" to "Spasm or Insensate War." These levels were separated by six thresholds: (1) Don't Rock the Boat, (2) Nuclear war Is Unthinkable, (3) No Nuclear Use, (4) Central Sanctuary, (5) Central War, and (6) City Targeting. But no one knows if such thresholds inhibited escalation, because neither the United States nor the Soviet Union had reached "Barely Nuclear War" (the 15th level). There was also very little indication that each side of the Cold War saw the same thresholds: the United States was tight-lipped about its nuclear strategy and Soviet Union even more so: it was Truman, not Stalin, who announced in 1949 that the Soviet Union became a nuclear power. Herman Kahn helpfully noted that countries did not have to operate at each of the 44 levels on the way up. They could and likely would jump a few steps at a time—simplifying but not solving the problem of determining which thresholds had been mutually recognized and would therefore guide behavior.

Sometimes, escalation involves behavior that few thought to forbid for having deemed it impossible or strategically pointless. Even before invading Ukraine, Russia had become adept at discovering imaginative annoyances. They include the 2016 hack of the Democratic National Committee, GPS jamming, using mini-submarines to embarrass Swedish defenses, buzzing NATO ships, approaching the border of NATO countries with jets, cordoning off a large part of the Black Sea for "exercises," killing their domestic enemies within other countries, and sponsoring mercenaries. China built artificial islands in the South China Sea and used massed fishing boats to harass the neighbors' commercial maritime activities. The problem with novelty is that what one side thinks is clearly on its side of the line for not having been called out may not strike the other side the same way.

Thresholds, like information technology standards,[51] must be recognized by the relevant parties as influencing behavior to be effective. One can infer thresholds from patterns of state behavior (e.g., the nuclear taboo). One can theorize thresholds, as Herman Kahn did. States can unilaterally declare them or judge the behavior of other states against them. But even though the opinion of third parties (e.g., polities, thinkers, and allies) can influence escalation decisions, thresholds matter strategically only if both sides believe they matter intrinsically or believe the other side takes them seriously as restraints.

As a rule the effective judge of whether an action crossed a threshold would be the other side, who must choose whether to react by also crossing the threshold. If both sides were on the same ladder, then the other side's options would be obvious: do nothing, meet the escalation, or, if bold, beat it. But if conflict choices are arrayed on a lattice, the other side may well respond with a lateral move. Reactions need not match the action for thresholds to reinforce mutual restraint. Thus, the most useful metric of whether a point on one path is escalation vis-à-vis a point on the other path may be which is more escalatory—that is, which provokes the other side to itself escalate. Such a metric entails positive considerations (how will the other side take this) rather than normative ones (what is a fair equivalence). Tractable thresholds in the two-dimensional option space of a lattice must themselves be two-dimensional. The question of what lies within the boundary of play replaces the question of what lies below some rung. Thomas Schelling points out that a threat is more credible to an adversary if it is perceived as "in the same currency, to respond in the same language, to make the punishment fit the character of the crime."[52] But if carrying out such threats is unavailable or unattractive, then thresholds will have to encompass more choices, many being lateral moves.

The case for thresholds admits of one serious dilemma. Countries, to bolster deterrence, may want others to think that there is no limit to what may ensue if they misbehave. Yet if deterrence fails and fighting ensues, the benefits of stopping before approaching Armageddon suddenly become quite appealing. This dilemma has been well-recognized by US researchers: "Applying disincentives to the outbreak of war almost always conflicts with maintaining disincentives to escalation after the war has begun. The United States scares the other side into remaining at peace by the prospects of uncontrolled escalation; but US planners then must work hard, after peace has ended, to make sure the predictions of escalation are not confirmed."[53] And foreign researchers: "Everything that increases the likelihood of escalation in advance contributes to deterrence but also makes it, by definition, more difficult to limit war if it breaks out after all."[54] And policy officials such as Henry Kissinger: "On the one hand we want the Soviets to think that the situation might get out of hand, while on the other hand we want to persuade them not to let it get out of hand."[55] When President Biden said, "I don't think there's any such thing as an ability to easily lose a tactical nuclear weapon and not end up with Armageddon,"[56] he was essentially talking up deterrence (do not use tactical nuclear weapons) at the expense of later escalation control (once the nuclear taboo is broken, the prospects dim for any higher nuclear-use threshold). Combatants may regret not having thoroughly discussed their expectations for conflict management with the other side—were it not for the very fact that such discussions could make it harder to credibly threaten unlimited consequences.

THRESHOLDS AND INADVERTENT ESCALATION

Thresholds should also make inadvertent escalation less likely by making both sides aware of what level they are fighting at—aka "agreed competition."[57] If something unexpected that might prompt escalation occurs, both sides would at least know the risk that they might be fighting at levels neither wants, and avoid going there. These days fears of inadvertent escalation abound.[58] In the summer of 2022 with the Russo-Ukraine war on boil and China's reaction to Speaker Pelosi's visit to Taiwan on simmer, the prospect of inadvertent escalation was leveraged to argue that the United States should back off confronting Russia and China. In late July Bonnie Glaser and Zack Cooper maintained "Chinese leaders would want to avoid war with the United States, but might be willing to risk an escalation such as challenging Ms. Pelosi's plane or flying military aircraft directly over Taiwan for the first time. Inadvertent escalation would be a real risk."[59] Samuel Charap and Jeremy Shapiro argued, "Western leaders should understand that the risk of escalation stems from the complete incompatibility of their goals with the Kremlin's."[60] Liana Fix and Michael Kimmage wrote, "The war's invisible rules may be fully apparent to Putin but less so to his commanding officers, many of whom are dealing with the frustration of battlefield setbacks, equipment problems, inadequate manpower, and a Ukrainian military that has fought with skill and resolve. Their adventurism could encourage an air or missile strike outside of Ukraine—for example, to halt the passage of weapons into Ukraine."[61] Elsewhere they noted, "Accidental escalation may, in fact, be even more frightening than deliberate escalation, since the latter holds within it the possibility of deliberate de-escalation."

Thresholds should remove some ambiguity about what actions constitute escalation, but false understandings, altered understandings, and forces beyond leadership control, may nevertheless, lead to inadvertent escalation, even with thresholds.

One type of false understanding arises when one side uses the other side's actions as an excuse. In early 1965 the United States started a sustained bombing campaign against North Vietnam, justified by a Viet Cong attack in Pleiku (South Vietnam) that killed several US servicemen. When asked about whether the two were related, McGeorge Bundy, President Johnson's national security advisor, commented that "Pleikus are like streetcars."[62] Sooner or later, one would come along.

Misunderstanding may come from each side's thinking it observed the relevant thresholds but the other side thinking otherwise. The Chinese Coast Guard has been carrying out aggressive operations[63] in the apparent belief that they are short of war. What might happen if other countries felt differently and then damaged such vessels? Forces beyond leadership control could include anything that induces a demand for escalation ("Remember the *Maine!*") that leaders find hard to resist.

Otherwise, those with a serious interest in preventing conflict from getting out of hand have options when thresholds exist. Beforehand, each side could issue standing orders that anticipate the fog of war but nevertheless prevent crossing such thresholds. Afterward, the side that inadvertently escalated could signal (e.g., by conspicuous reprimand) that overreaction is not tolerated. The other side could stay its hand while investigating whether the one side's operations had permanently changed. Actions during the Cuban missile crisis, where both sides had a strong interest in mutual restraint, show restraint can be communicated.

Paradoxically, reducing the odds of inadvertent escalation may not lower the odds of Armageddon. Schelling's discussion of a "threat that left something to chance" posited that escalatory actions short of all-out nuclear war would be inhibited precisely because of the odds that, despite neither side wanting to go there, matters would culminate in nuclear war.[64] Even today, "When fears of inadvertent escalation are lower, conflict is more likely. Low fears of inadvertent escalation are particularly likely when only one side in a dispute has nuclear weapons, making it important to be cautious when applying evidence from those situations to mutual vulnerability."[65] This paradox applies to thresholds in general. If a threshold short of nuclear war could be relied on, then the inhibition to escalate from the fear of nuclear war would correspondingly decline. But if such assurance is overestimated, conflict could rise to the threshold level and then, unexpectedly, beyond, thereby raising the risk of Armageddon beyond where it would have been in the absence of thresholds.

NOTES

1. Morgan et al., *Dangerous Thresholds*, 8. Some borderline cases merit mention. Germany's invasion of Poland was not an escalation of its stand-off over Danzig; the latter was just a pretext. Conversely a permanent reaction to some action clearly meant to be temporary might be considered escalation.
2. Brendan Rittenhouse Green, Caitlin Talmadge ("Then what? Assessing the military implications of Chinese control of Taiwan," *International Security*, 47, No. 1 [Summer 2022], 7–45) argues, in several places, that the prospect of losing Taiwan in a war with China would mean that the United States would have to escalate to antisatellite operations and attacking Chinese over-the-horizon radar in any major conflict.
3. The classic word on that subject being Barry Posen, *Inadvertent Escalation: Conventional War and Nuclear Risks* (Ithaca NY: Cornell University Press, 1991).
4. From Stephen Flanagan et al, *A Framework of Deterrence in Space Operations* (Santa Monica, CA: RAND, 2023), 24: "The Chinese military . . . contend that, in advance of any military engagement, the United States (referred to as the 'strong enemy') will first conduct high-intensity space information reconnaissance operations that are decidedly different from such operations in peacetime. The nature of these operations constitutes a preemptive 'first shot' in space combat operations, thus warranting a Chinese response."
5. See Dan Reiter, "Exploding the powder keg myth: Preemptive wars almost never happen," *International Security*, 20, No. 2 (Fall 1995), 5–34. The 67 were taken from the Correlates of War database.
6. Robert Pape (*Bombing to Win* [Ithaca, NY: Cornell University Press, 1996]) argues that if nuclear weapons are not involved, it is nearly impossible to get countries to quit fighting by attacking their civilians, much less threatening to do so.
7. From Michael Kofman, Anya Fink, and Jeffrey Edmonds, "Russian strategy for escalation management: Evolution of key concepts," *Center for Naval Analyses*, April 13, 2020, https://www.cna.org/CNA_files/PDF/DIM-2020-U-026101-Final.pdf, 3: "While a number of the concepts discussed across the Russian military-analytical community, such as 'strategic deterrence,' appear developed and refereed at the level of national political leadership, military strategy or planning is not the same as political strategy writ large . . . we do not claim to know what the Russian political leadership will choose to do in a particular contingency." But they later (p. 74) add, "Although we cannot predict what choices Russia's political leadership might make, it is less likely to be self-deterred if its military establishment has developed several plausible options for escalation management and war termination from crisis to large-scale war."
8. Fiona S. Cunningham, "The maritime rung on the escalation ladder: Naval blockades in a US-China conflict," *Security Studies*, 29, No. 4 (2020), 730–768.
9. From Morgan et al., *Dangerous Thresholds*, 31–32.
10. Brendon Valeriano, "Managing escalation under layered cyber deterrence," *Lawfare*, April 1, 2020, https://www.lawfareblog.com/managing-escalation-under-layered-cyber-deterrence.
11. As Winston Churchill said (July 14, 1941): "if to-night the people of London were asked to cast their vote whether a convention should be entered into to stop the bombing of all cities, the overwhelming majority would cry, 'No, we will mete out to the

Germans the measure, and more than the measure, that they have meted out to us.'" From *National Churchill Museum*, "Do Your Worst; We'll Do Our Best," https://www.nationalchurchillmuseum.org/do-your-worst-well-do-our-best.html.

12. Or the wider notion of "escalation control." Jay Ross ("Time to terminate escalate-to-de-escalate—It's escalation control," *War on the Rocks*, April 24, 2018, https://warontherocks.com/2018/04/time-to-terminate-escalate-to-de-escalateits-escalation-control/) observes that an escalate-to-de-escalate strategy was used by US Secretary of Defense Robert McNamara in the early 1960s. Dave Johnson ("Russia's conventional precision strike capabilities, regional crises, and nuclear thresholds," *Livermore Papers on Global Security*, No. 3, February 2018, 67) argues that "Moscow will not limit itself to 'escalating out of failed conventional aggression,' but is prepared to escalate in defense of gains made through successful conventional aggression in line with the 'aggressive sanctuarization' concept." Kristin Ven Bruusgaard ("Russian nuclear strategy and conventional inferiority," *Journal of Strategic Studies*, 44, No. 1 [2021], 3–35) maintains that when Russia had a weak military, "threats to national security" was the official trigger (*circa* 2010), but when its military strengthened, its posture became more restrictive ("the very existence of the state").

13. In 2014 then-prime minister Dmitry Medvedev declared that cutting off Russia from SWIFT (an international banking network) would be tantamount to "a declaration of war." From Marina Shagina, "How disastrous would disconnection from SWIFT be for Russia?" *Carnegie Moscow*, May 28, 2021, https://carnegiemoscow.org/commentary/84634.

14. E.g., "may feel compelled to respond militarily either because it perceives the violation of its territory as an act of war itself...." From Rebecca Hersman *et al.*, "Under the nuclear shadow: Situational awareness technology and crisis decisionmaking," *Center for Strategic and International Studies*, March 2020, https://www.csis.org/analysis/under-nuclear-shadow-situational-awareness-technology-and-crisis-decisionmaking.

15. Quoting William J. Burns, former US ambassador to Russia, from David Sanger, "Russia's missile test fuels U.S. fears of an isolated Putin," *New York Times*, April 20, 2022, https://www.nytimes.com/2022/04/20/us/politics/russia-putin-missile-test.html.

16. "On August 24, a small force of German bombers accidentally attacked London. In response, the Royal Air Force launched its first raid against Berlin on the following night, which, in turn, contributed to the German decision to begin the Blitz." From Morgan, *Dangerous Thresholds*, 26. Intelligence errors can have a similar effect: China's embassy in Belgrade was bombed accurately in 1999, but in the erroneous belief that it was a Serbian supply ministry.

17. Benjamin Jensen, "Bringing the Swarm to Life: Roles, Missions, and Campaigns for the Replicator Initiative," *War on the Rocks*, February 13, 2024, https://warontherocks.com/2024/02/bringing-the-swarm-to-life-roles-missions-and-campaigns-for-the-replicator-initiative. But see Stacie Pettyjohn, "Evolution not revolution: Drone warfare in Russia's 2022 invasion of Ukraine," *Center for New American Studies*, February 2024, https://s3.us-east-1.amazonaws.com/files.cnas.org/documents/CNAS-Report-Defense-Ukraine-Drones-Final.pdf.

18. Smoke, "War: Controlling escalation," 286.

19. For France (1953), "Letourneau [France's high commissioner for Indochina], in turn, restated his position that it was 'not the policy of his government' to seek a military victory in Indochina, that indeed victory probably was unattainable because of the

likelihood that the Chinese would intervene in Indochina to prevent such an outcome." (George W. Allen, *None So Blind: A Personal Account of the Intelligence Failure in Vietnam* [Chicago: Ivan R. Dee, 2001, p. 46] cited in Fredick Logevall, *Embers of War* [New York: Random House, 2012, p. 443.]) For the United States (1965), Robert McNamara felt that with perhaps even 600,000 US troops on the ground, the Americans could prevent the North Vietnamese from "sustaining the conflict at a significant level" but at that point the Chinese could be expected to intervene (Lieutenant General Harold G. Moore (Ret.) and Joseph L. Galloway, *We were Soldiers once... and Young*, [New York: HarperCollins, 1992] p. 400 cited in Kai Bird, *The Color of Truth* [New York: Simon and Schuster, 2000, p.48]).

20. Statement before a joint meeting of the House and Senate Budget Committees on January 31, 1979, regarding the fiscal 1980 budget.

21. Evelyn N. Farkas (deputy assistant secretary of defense for Russia/Ukraine/Eurasia from 2012 to 2015), "We can do more to help Ukraine without provoking World War III: In aiding Ukraine, why are missiles fine but fighter jets unthinkable?" *Washington Post*, March 11, 2022, https://www.washingtonpost.com/outlook/2022/03/11/ukraine-no-fly-escalation-humanitarian/.

22. Andrew McDonald and Hans von der Burchard, "UK to Germany: Sending Taurus missiles won't escalate Ukraine war," *Politico*, March 7, 2024, https://www.politico.eu/article/sending-taurus-missiles-to-ukraine-wont-escalate-war-uk-tells-germany-cameron/.

23. Glenn H. Snyder and Paul Diesing, *Conflict among Nations: Bargaining, Decision Making and System Structure in International Crises* (Princeton, NJ: Princeton University Press, 1977) maintains that leaders worry a great deal about escalation spirals, even when their odds are low.

24. *Economist*, "Skirmishing between India and Pakistan could escalate," February 28, 2019, https://www.economist.com/briefing/2019/02/28/skirmishing-between-india-and-pakistan-could-escalate.

25. John W. Nicholson, "Opinion: The US must respond forcefully to Russia and the Taliban. Here's how," *Washington Post*, July 13, 2020, https://www.washingtonpost.com/opinions/the-us-must-respond-forcefully-to-russia-and-the-taliban-heres-how/2020/07/13/df13ed6c-c529-11ea-b037-f9711f89ee46_story.html.

26. Thomas Schelling, *Arms and Influence* (New Haven CT: Yale University Press, 1966), 33.

27. US policymakers, entering a large-scale guerilla war (Vietnam) for which the United States had little relevant experience, rarely inquired into the odds of its ending in quagmire, much less an outright defeat. In Leslie Gelb and Richard Betts, *The Irony of Vietnam: The System Worked* (Washington, DC: Brookings, 1979), 127, there was only one mention of any probability for a particular outcome. Conversely, McGeorge Bundy was, himself, more apt to talk in terms of probabilities (Kai Bird, 2017). When contemplating the consequences of pressing the West on Berlin in the late 1950s, "Khrushchev's rule of thumb was that the probability of a general war... was about 5 per cent. To look at this from the other end of the stick: that meant 95 per cent estimated success—excellent odds for a gambler." From Campbell Craig and Sergey Radchenko, "MAD, not Marx: Khrushchev and the nuclear revolution," *Journal of Strategic Studies*, 41, No. 1–2 (2018), 219.

28. Lawrence Freedman ("General deterrence and the balance of power," *Review of International Studies*, 15, No. 2 [April 1989], 199–210) has observed, "Nuclear war, even if

the worst excesses of city busting and 'nuclear winter' can be avoided, will be so horrific that only the most extreme political pressure would make it worth tolerating the slightest risk of this coming to pass. So long as there is a measurable risk that a confrontation could end up with nuclear detonations there is every incentive to avoid the confrontation."

29. As Robert Jervis ("Why nuclear superiority doesn't matter," *Political Science Quarterly*, 94, No. 4 [Winter 1979/80], 628–29) and others observed, the existence of nuclear weapons placed certain traditional military goals—such as seizing serious territory or forcibly removing a government—off the table. This conclusion, he more controversially argued, was robust against large variations in the size of a country's stockpiles or its nuclear strategy.

30. A standard caveat applies: even rational albeit short-sighted leaders may escalate to get themselves out of a short-term jam and overlook long-term consequences, such as raising the odds of disaster. See, for instance, Christopher Clark, *The Sleepwalkers: How Europe Went to War in 1914* (New York, NY: Harper, 2013). Herman Kahn's thesis (see his *On Escalation: Scenarios and Metaphors* [New York, NY: Praeger, 1965]) of a step-by-step march to Armageddon seemed to require a great deal of sleepwalking so that leaders could ignore how such a story ends.

31. Theodore Sorenson, *Kennedy* (New York NY: Harper & Row, 1965), 705.

32. Smoke, "War: Controlling escalation," 49–79.

33. See John Speed Meyers, "Mainland Strikes and U.S. Military Strategy Towards China: Historical Cases, Interviews, and a Scenario-Based Survey of American National Security Elites," Dissertation, Pardee RAND Graduate School, August 2019, 66 and 73–74.

34. Schelling, *Arms and Influence*, 44.

35. Robert Powell, *Nuclear Deterrence Theory* (Cambridge MA: Harvard, 1990), 33.

36. "Zelensky may have crossed the line and fired a drone into Russia, at least in part, to force Putin into this position—either of having to accept Russia's military vulnerability (which could trigger Putin's own political vulnerability) or having to escalate the war (which could bring the US and NATO to engage in it more directly.)" From Fred Kaplan, "What Ukraine's drone strike deep in Russian territory means," *Slate*, December 6, 2022, https://slate.com/news-and-politics/2022/12/ukraine-drone-strike-putin-russia.html.

37. Robert Rauchhaus ("Evaluating the nuclear peace hypothesis: A quantitative approach," *Journal of Conflict Resolution*, 53, No. 2 (April 2009), 258–277) uses statistical analysis to argue that nuclear weapons do shift conflict to the lower end of the scale.

38. See for instance Simit Ganguly and Devin Hagerty, *Fearful Symmetry: India-Pakistan Crises in the Shadow of Nuclear Weapons* (Seattle: University of Washington Press, 2015) and Paul Kapur, *Dangerous Deterrent* (Palo Alto, CA: Stanford, 2007).

39. Rohan Mukherjee, "Climbing the escalation ladder: India and the Balakot crisis," *War on the Rocks*, October 2, 2019, https://warontherocks.com/2019/10/climbing-the-escalation-ladder-india-and-the-balakot-crisis/. See also Paul Kapur, "India and Pakistan's unstable peace: Why nuclear South Asia is not like Cold War Europe, *International Security*, 30, No. 2 (Fall 2005), 127–52.

40. In the early 1950s, General Bernard Montgomery, Deputy SACEUR, said, "I want to make it absolutely clear that we at SHAPE are basing all our planning on using atomic and thermonuclear weapons in our defence. With us, it is no longer: 'they may possibly be used.' It is very definitely, 'they will be used if we are attacked'" (from "A look through

a window at WWIII," *Journal of the Royal United Services Institute*, 99, No. 596 [November 1954], 508).

41. So, for instance, the argument (see Prashant Hosur Suhas and Christopher K. Colley, "It's still the Indian Ocean: Parsing Sino-Indian naval competition where it counts," May 7, 2024; https://warontherocks.com/2024/05/its-still-the-indian-ocean-parsing-sino-indian-naval-competition-where-it-counts): "A fully equipped Chinese navy could easily overwhelm the Indian navy, but it would also leave the Chinese mainland wide open to attack from China's primary rival, the United States," can be challenged by the prospect that an opportunistic naval conflict between China and the United States would be inhibited by the risk that matters would escalate to the nuclear level. Thus, the odds that a US-China naval war would go nuclear inhibits the US from starting one (whether or not as India's ally is secondary), which enables China's strike on India.

42. Could using autonomous systems (see, e.g., Paul Scharre, *Army of None: Autonomous Weapons and the Future of War* [New York, NY: W.W. Norton, 2018]) cross a threshold? If so, how could the other side know that a system that could be manned is, in fact, autonomous—much less how autonomous such systems really are (i.e., what kind of command and control is being exercised over the system)?

43. Austin Carson (*Secret Wars* [Princeton, NJ: Princeton University Press, 2018]) observes that states often keep their interventions secret where exposure might spark the other side to escalate. Secrecy can be understood as a threshold: those who place evident value on being covert have good reason to restrain themselves since some forms of war cannot be plausibly hidden. Often, he adds, the other side will not be fooled but knows that making such intervention public would backfire. The one side may no longer be inhibited from escalating into carrying out operations that cannot be hidden. A dependence on second-party discretion and third-party ignorance to stay below a threshold, however, makes it easy for a threshold to be crossed by surprise.

44. Edward Guest, "Qualities precede quantities: Deciding how much is enough for U.S. nuclear forces," *RAND*, September 2023, https://www.rand.org/pubs/perspectives/PEA2555-2.html.

45. This echoes the distinction between "crunchy" and "soggy" systems as described by Nico Colchester ("Crunchiness," *Financial Times*, October 24, 2006): "Crunchy systems are those in which small changes have big effects leaving those affected by them in no doubt whether they are up or down, rich or broke, winning or losing, dead or alive."

46. "Step-by-step escalation could serve to measure the other side's responses while maintaining the option to recalibrate and avert an unmanageable crisis." From Hamidreza Azizi, "How Iran and its allies hope to save Hamas," *War on the Rocks*, November 16, 2023, https://warontherocks.com/2023/11/how-iran-and-its-allies-hope-to-save-hamas/.

47. See Rebecca Davis Gibbons and Keir Lieber, "How durable is the nuclear weapons taboo?" *Journal of Strategic Studies*, 42, No. 1 (2019), 29–54, which ponders whether the taboo is rooted in strategic logic (my nonuse will be rewarded by their nonuse) or moral logic (analogous to what applies to incest or cannibalism). Nina Tannenwald (*The Nuclear Taboo* [Cambridge, UK: Cambridge University Press, 2007]) argues the latter.

48. "Russia claims it destroyed a Ukrainian ammunitions depot with hypersonic missiles.... If confirmed, it would mark a dramatic escalation of Russia's brutal campaign to crush the pro-Western government in Kyiv" from Courtney Kube, Dan De Luce,

and Corky Siemaszko, "Moscow's claim about firing hypersonic missiles could be more hype, experts say," *NBC News*, March 21, 2022, https://www.nbcnews.com/news/world/moscows-claim-firing-hypersonic-missiles-hype-experts-say-rcna20925. See also former Secretary of Defense Leon Panetta on March 15, 2022: "by using hypersonic missiles like this he is escalating the war in Ukraine.... I think this is a dangerous escalation" (https://www.youtube.com/watch?v=-rECMnJ50WA: 2:00 to 2:07 and 2:38 to 2:42).

49. Robyn Dixon, Miriam Berger, and David L. Stern, "Russia accuses Ukraine of helicopter strike on Belgorod fuel depot," *Washington Post*, April 1, 2022, https://www.washingtonpost.com/world/2022/04/01/russia-belgorod-fire-helicopter-ukraine/.

50. Herman Kahn, *On Escalation*. For a similar look at escalation levels and thresholds, see Loch K. Johnson, "On drawing a bright line for covert operations," *American Journal of International Law*, 86, No. 2 (April 1992), 284–309. Its treatment is almost purely descriptive: an illustrative superstructure exists solely to distinguish what is below and what is above some "bright line." And because the discussion is only about one player (operating in the context of international law), there is nothing about any need for consensus to make a threshold more than arbitrary.

51. See, for instance, Martin Libicki, *Quest for the Common Byte* (Boston, MA: Digital Press, 1994 and 2016).

52. Schelling, *Arms and Influence*, 145.

53. George H. Quester, "War termination and nuclear targeting strategy," from Desmond Ball and Jeffrey Richeson, eds., *Strategic Nuclear Targeting* (Ithaca, NY: Cornell University Press, 1986), 291.

54. Raymond Aron, English translation in Stanley Hoffman, *Janus and Minerva: Essays in the Theory and Practice of International Politics* (London: Westview Press, 1987), 60 (originally *Penser la Guerre*, Clausewitz, Vol. 2 [Paris: L'âge Planétaire, 1976], 162–63).

55. Minutes of Verification Panel Meeting, Washington, August 9, 1973, 3:40–4:31 P.M.; from Todd Bennett, ed., *Foreign Relations of the United States, 1969–1976, Volume XXXV, National Security Policy, 1973–1976* (Washington, DC: GPO, 2014), 105.

56. https://www.whitehouse.gov/briefing-room/speeches-remarks/2022/10/06/remarks-by-president-biden-at-democratic-senatorial-campaign-committee-reception/.

57. From Kahn, *On Escalation*. See also Michael P. Fischerkeller and Richard J. Harknett, "Persistent engagement, agreed competition, cyberspace interaction dynamics, and escalation (IDA NS D-9076)," *Institute for Defense Analysis*, May 2018, https://www.ida.org/-/media/feature/publications/p/pe/persistent-engagement-agreed-competition-cyberspace-interaction-dynamics-and-escalation/d-9076.ashx.

58. For instance, Rebecca Hersman et al. ("Under the nuclear shadow: Situation awareness technology and crisis decisionmaking," CSIS, March 2020; https://www.csis.org/analysis/under-nuclear-shadow-situational-awareness-technology-and-crisis-decision making) argues that using many types of surveillance technologies may affect escalation dynamics. This argument is broadened in Rebecca Hersman, "Wormhole escalation in the new nuclear age," *Texas National Security Review*, 3, No. 3 (2020), 90–109, https://tnsr.org/2020/07/wormhole-escalation-in-the-new-nuclear-age/. But these treatments do not broach the question of what the other side would gain by escalating to war or whether normalization of intrusive surveillance might squelch escalation.

59. Bonnie S. Glaser and Zack Cooper, "Nancy Pelosi's trip to Taiwan is too dangerous," *New York Times,* July 28, 2022, https://www.nytimes.com/2022/07/28/opinion/china-us-taiwan-pelosi.html.
60. Samuel Charap and Jeremy Shapiro, "The U.S. and Russia need to start talking before it's too late," *New York Times,* July 27, 2022, www.nytimes.com/2022/07/27/opinion/ukraine-russia-us-diplomacy.html.
61. Liana Fix and Michael Kimmage, "What if the war in Ukraine spins out of control? How to prepare for unintended escalation," *Foreign Affairs,* July 19, 2022, https://www.foreignaffairs.com/articles/ukraine/2022-07-18/what-if-war-in-ukraine-spins-out-control.
62. David Halberstam, *The Best and the Brightest* (NY: Random House, 1972), 533.
63. See, for instance, Damien Cave, "China creates a coast guard like no other, seeking supremacy in Asian seas," *New York Times,* June 12, 2023, https://www.nytimes.com/2023/06/12/world/asia/china-coast-guard.html: "'The idea,' he [John Bradford, a retired US Navy commander and senior fellow in the Maritime Security Program at the S. Rajaratnam School of International Studies in Singapore] added, 'is that it's more effective because you're less likely to push up the escalation ladder because they're lightly armed. But when a coast guard vessel gets missiles on it, how is it different from a navy vessel except for the color of the paint on the hull?'"
64. Thomas Schelling, "The threat that leaves something to chance," *RAND,* 1959, https://www.rand.org/pubs/historical_documents/HDA1631-1.html.
65. Paul C. Avey, "Just like yesterday? New critiques of the nuclear revolution," *TSNR,* 6, No. 2 (Spring 2023), https://tnsr.org/2023/04/just-like-yesterday-new-critiques-of-the-nuclear-revolution/.

2

Is Cyberwar War?

I think it's more than likely we're going to end up, if we end up in a war—a real shooting war with a major power—it's going to be as a consequence of a cyber breach of great consequence.[1]

President Biden, July 2021

Could cyberwar—the systematic use of hostile cyberspace operations to manipulate digital systems for political or military ends—be a step between peace and war that could grease an unwanted transition between the two?[2] Those inclined to dismiss the importance of cyberwar to escalation dynamics can point to a general lack of strategic consequence from cyberattacks to date (the Stuxnet worm, which stymied Iran's nuclear progress, excepted[3]). But as digitization and artificial intelligence—hence dependence and vulnerability—continue to advance, cyberwar could become far more consequential.

The importance of cyberwar to the escalation question is reflected in a question that arises after major cyberattacks: is this an act of war?[4] Increasingly, the answer has been no—in that no country has responded to any cyberattack by using force. In that way, cyberwar is becoming normalized in the current environment just as cyberespionage has been. But will it remain so if the effects of cyberwar exceed mere annoyance to become hazardous or more debilitating? And if cyberattacks become a stepping stone to war, what kind of war would it be? Cyberattacks alone hardly challenge territorial integrity or political independence.[5] Escalation to the use of force that also does not challenge these ends (e.g., the tit for tat between Israel and Iran over Syria) is more likely than escalation to the use of force that *does* challenge them. And the former type of war may have very different escalation dynamics than the latter.

Accordingly, we take up two questions. First, is cyberwar tantamount to war, or has it been normalized in the same way espionage has been? Second, how does cyberwar compare on the escalation lattice to other unfriendly actions such as economic sanctions or the provision of intelligence to combatants?

THE PERILS OF AMBIGUITY OVER CYBERWAR

Agreement among rivals that cyberwar is a peacetime activity *or* agreement that it is a wartime activity are both less escalatory than disagreement on whether cyberwar belongs in war or peace. Here is why, expressed in terms of three alternative perspectives.

Assume, first, that cyberattacks that disable (or, worse, destroy) important systems are universally deemed tantamount to war. Potential aggressors believe that engaging in cyberwar will cause others to see it as war, thereby justifying escalation to the use of force. So thinking, aggressors would hold off unless either they (1) are prepared to go to war anyway, (2) believe their targets are disinclined to wage war even though they believe that the aggressor has, or (3) hope the other side will not characterize or attribute the attack with enough confidence to react. So the bar to cyberwar is high. Critical information systems suffer no state-fostered interference. But crises may erupt from accidents, the mis-characterization of cyberespionage as preparations for cyberwar, misattribution, or claims that some cybercrimes (e.g., ransomware attacks on critical infrastructure such as Colonial Pipeline's) are state cyberattacks by proxy.

Assume, second, cyberattacks are not deemed a use of force or an act of war. Others may respond in kind to hostile cyberspace operations but not violently. Such kinetic peace, though, is won at the cost of putting up with the depredations of cyberwar. Stability holds, but information and other digital systems remain at risk.

Last, assume opinion is split. Some leaders think cyberattacks do not make for war; others do. If aggressors believe the former and their targets believe the latter—and can do something about it—a confrontation between the two can lead to unexpected kinetic conflict. For instance, the aggressor wages cyberwar because the step up from everyday hostility is small; to them, cyberwar does not justify a response that uses force. The target reacts to cyberwar by using force because they do not see a transition from cyberwar to physical war as a huge step. Neither side has, in its view, crossed a threshold: the aggressor does not believe that its actions constitute war, but the target concludes that war has already started and the primary question is how best to conduct it. For stability, this is the worst outcome.

It matters whether thresholds are defined in terms of means—which would differentiate cyberwar and kinetic war—or effects. In the latter case, a cyberattack that broke things and hurt people would cross a threshold. But something like the 2017 NotPetya cyberattack, which cost their victims collectively $5 to $10 billion but did not physically injure anyone, would not. Since most cyberattacks—particularly distributed denial of service (DDOS) attacks—are mere nuisances, a threshold might be understood as some minimum level of physical damage. But actual effects may be difficult to measure unambiguously. They may look nothing like intended effects because the cyberattack failed (quite common) or conversely, the malware used ran amok or induced unexpected cascading damage.

IS CYBERESPIONAGE A STEPPING STONE TO WORSE?

Collecting information is not considered a legitimate *casus bello* under the *jus ad bellum* norms of the law of armed conflict (LOAC) and has rarely led to war in the past. So, cyberespionage—which comprises most hostile state activity in cyberspace—should never lead to worse. But several features suggest cyberespionage *might* be escalatory.

One, changes in quantity may imply changes in quality. Traditional espionage stole information about or from one or a handful of people. Cyberespionage, though, can steal information about tens of millions—as China's 2015 theft of US Office of Personnel Management (OPM) records files did. South Korea spent almost a billion dollars to redo its national identity system after it was compromised by North Korea.[6] Botnets could steal information from millions of machines. Conceivably, a populace enraged over its privacy being violated could force policymakers to "do something" about the other side's spymasters, and that "something" could immediately or after several back-and-forth steps cross over into conflict. That noted, the OPM hack had no such effect. Neither, of course, would undiscovered intrusions.

Two, even after decades of effort in distinguishing cyberespionage and cyberattack, the media and politicians conflate the two. The narrative path that starts with one, proceeds through the other, and culminates in kinetic attack remains wide open.

Three, the early stages of both cyberattack and cyberespionage—penetration of the target system and lateral movement within it—are largely the same. Indeed, cyberattacks often must be preceded by reconnaissance in the form of cyberespionage. Thus, detecting an intrusion into critical systems may alarm defenders who infer that a cyberattack is being prepared. Such discoveries *could* induce preemptive escalation. But that would depend on extant tensions between the attacker and defenders. Preemption without other indications and warnings of physical war makes little sense.

Four, active defenses against cyberespionage, notably "persistent engagement," can easily include cyberattacks, undertaken to affect the ability of the other side's hackers to use their own systems (albeit to harm others). The target of these active defenses may easily shrug this off as spy-versus-spy games that imply nothing higher. But leaders inclined to strike back can use these games to argue that they did not go first. And, if one side is unlucky, the target of some active defense may be deemed a sensitive system.

Five, while the risk to human spies constrains spying, there are few similar risks to hackers that would act as a corresponding constraint (as is also true with unmanned espionage platforms such as UAVs). By contrast, the need to trade a spy to get back the pilot of the U-2 plane shot down in 1960 (coupled with the diplomatic crisis caused by the incident) ended U-2 flights.

So, if cyberespionage is deemed tantamount to cyberattacks, and cyberwar is like war, what prevents invasive acts of cyberespionage from setting off a chain reaction unwanted by both sides?

FORMAL NORMS-MAKING HAS NOT ANSWERED THAT QUESTION

Despite some consensus that there *should* be norms of international behavior to tame the Wild West of cyberspace, if norms mean that countries refrain from operations otherwise in their interest, then there are none today nor any likely tomorrow.

Proposed norms for cyberspace have come from three sources: an extension into cyberspace of LOAC norms, multilateral negotiations; and bilateral agreements, such as the Xi–Obama agreement of September 2015.

The proposition that LOAC applies in the virtual world as it does in the physical world would seem self-evident, and it does remain official US policy. Strictures on violations of sovereignty, the use of disproportionate force, gratuitous attacks, perfidy, and the violation of neutrality reflect basic national and human rights; they are medium-agnostic. But LOAC was written to modulate death, injury, and destruction from war, and cyberattacks have yet to do much of any of that. The toll from cyberspace operations is measured in time and money—both of which fall outside the scope of LOAC. Even though the published Tallinn Manual[7] discusses countermeasures (what one state can do to make another state stop behaviors that levy time and money costs), such a right to self-defense is a norm that permits rather than forbids behavior. As for cyberespionage, the Manual is silent (except to moot it as a violation of national sovereignty).

Multilateral attempts to create norms specific to cyberspace have not fared much better. The most official such endeavor is the UN Group of Governmental Experts (GGE), whose high-water mark was a 2013 agreement among superpowers (and others) that LOAC did cover cyberspace.[8] But no longer had Russia's and China's diplomats come home and unpacked than their governments concluded that even such a simple agreement was not really what they had meant. Subsequent GGE sessions fared worse. Expectations should be tempered about the revival of the process begun in 2019.[9]

The Convention on Cybercrime of the Council of Europe (aka the Budapest Convention) binds members to help each other solve cybercrimes and arrest cybercriminals. Although signatories do comply, the Convention cannot be considered a global norm because Russia (which shields many cybercriminals from prosecution[10]) and China are prominent nonsignatories. The Convention also imposes no restrictions on what *states* can do in cyberspace. Other initiatives to establish norms include those by Microsoft[11] and the Paris[12] declaration. Russia's 2021 reaffirmation that states should not hack each other's critical infrastructure in peacetime was also not expected to curb its behavior.[13]

The closest the superpowers have come to an observed norm in cyberspace was a 2015 agreement between presidents Xi of China and Obama of the United States to cease cyberespionage against commercial firms undertaken to gain an edge in commercial competition. A subsequent G20 agreement extended that agreement globally.[14] For the first time, a major country had agreed to stop doing something that had (debatably) benefited it. Alas, while the agreement significantly reduced Chinese cyberespionage at first, Chinese cyberespionage levels began, in early 2017, to return to form albeit more discreetly and discretely.[15]

Two problems bedevil norms-making in cyberspace—and correspondingly, threshold formation.

One is attribution. Granted, rarely does a major cyberattack take place without one or more cybersecurity companies (e.g., FireEye, Symantec,

Crowdstrike, Sophos, Kaspersky, or Checkpoint) and now governments assigning blame. But how cyberattacks are attributed is generally opaque and lacks details. Private companies protect their proprietary methods. Governments shy from explaining their judgments when doing so might put sensitive intelligence sources and methods at risk; for instance, information gleaned from having hacked into the hackers' systems cannot be touted without admitting as much.[16] The relevant paragraphs in the US Department of Justice case that North Korea was behind the cyberattack on Sony contained all of 140 words.[17] The case claiming that Russians penetrated the Democratic National Committee cited only a consensus of the US intelligence community.[18] So those inclined to skepticism can easily maintain their doubts. The accused can then blandly assert that such accusations reflect animus against them, not evidence. In fairness, once cases get to court, evidence *is* presented and convictions often result. Since 2014 the United States has energetically indicted[19] state-hired or at least state-supported actors, suggesting it has similar evidence—but none so indicted have been extradited to appear in court.[20]

The other problem is asymmetry. Take the Xi–Obama agreement. China forewent operations that profited it; the United States forewent operations that it had no interest in—while giving itself a pass on those types of cyber-espionage against commercial companies that *did* interest it (e.g., hacking commercial firms to find exploitable flaws in their products or looking for indicators of terrorist activity). There was no comparable behavior from the United States that China both wanted to modulate and had a reasonable prospect of so doing: no US administration, for instance, could credibly promise China to squelch the free speech of dissidents. As a rule, countries agree to asymmetric deals only under the pressure of coercion—which, in the Obama era, was sanctions. The Trump administration, however, called out many Chinese trade practices, not just intellectual property theft via cyberspace.[21] Trade restrictions followed, irrespective of China's conformance with the Xi–Obama deal. So, from China's perspective, why keep the deal's terms? The broader rule applies: norms established in state-to-state negotiations require proponents to give up something as well as receive if such norms are to enjoy mutual buy-in.

From the US (or, broadly, Western) perspective, matters are unlikely to improve. Relations with Russia soured in 2014 after Crimea was taken; relations with China did likewise because of trade disputes. It does little good to plead that Western states have advocated and adopted a set of norms-like practices. They are not going to fight one another. But what matters are norms that forbid unwanted Russian or Chinese behaviors and thereby also reduce the risks of escalation stemming from such behaviors.

CAN NORMALIZATION STAND IN FOR NORMS?

In contrast to norms that say what states should not do, normalization is a process by which some practice persistently carried out by at least one serious country becomes accepted as inevitable.[22] Once certain activities are normalized through consensus, the odds that they will escalate to violent conflict should be substantially reduced—even if such practices are not necessarily condoned.

An example of annoying behavior becoming normalized was the Soviet practice of parking trawlers to eavesdrop on US naval exercises in open waters.[23] The United States initially objected to this practice, but when the Soviets adamantly maintained that their behavior was permitted, the United States grudgingly accepted this as a normalized state of affairs. Similarly, what started in 2017 as a controversial NATO intercept of a Russian transport carrying its defense minister (missile-armed Russian fighters got involved) became, by 2020, a near-daily and uncontroversial event.[24]

One advantage of normalization over norms is that it can emerge without a formal consensus—but it can leave countries at odds over what, in fact, has been normalized. As Max Smeets has observed of the United States,[25] many types of cyberspace operations have raised US government objections, but few if any were deemed acceptable. Because countries are not going to give up cyberspace operations, the failure to draw distinctions between allowed and disallowed behavior will persuade others to ignore objections to the latter.

The process of using state behaviors to determine what has been normalized must deal with two questions: which countries, and what behaviors? One can easily omit North Korea and Iran as they are rogue states. To set North Korea's deeds as the standard normalizes bank robbery.[26] To set Iran's deeds as a standard would normalize computer trashing (notably those of Saudi Aramco and Las Vegas Sands) and attacks on infrastructure (carried out against Israel and Saudi Arabia).

Russia is a superpower. Yet its overall behavior, at least since late 2013, has crossed limits (e.g., taking territory from a neighboring country) that even the postwar Soviet Union adhered to. Russian hackers have interfered in the politics of the United States, the United Kingdom, and several other countries; may have implanted malware in the electrical grid of the United States and Europe;[27] did take down the power grid in Ukraine (in the years before the 2022 invasion); and corrupted software exported by Ukraine as well as software used by tens of thousands of organizations (the Solar Winds hack). Using Russia as the standard would require accepting such activities as normalized; it is certainly not in the US interest to do so. Note that the denial of such activities by Russia[28] presents normalization difficulties if Western countries did likewise unto Russia—only for Russia to deny having done as much itself.

Accepting Chinese actions as normalized is somewhat easier. China is not fighting the concept of a world order so much as its place in it. It has carried out a great deal of cyberespionage; yet its (known) cyberattack activity (Taiwan aside) has been limited to DDOS attacks on dissidents and dissident-used websites such as Github. But normalizing actions by China then means accepting cyberespionage for commercial purposes (see above) and via border gateway protocol (BGP) hacks.[29]

US power, sophistication, and web of alliances all make it even easier for its practices to define normalized behavior in cyberspace. Having advocated norms of responsible state behavior in cyberspace, whatever it has already done in cyberspace should not lead to an escalated response if someone else did it. So what can be considered normalized behavior because the United States has already done it? *First* would be cyberattacks to impede the production of nuclear weapons and their delivery systems: for example, Stuxnet[30] and (reportedly) one on North Korean medium-range missiles.[31] *Second* would be mass surveillance to select a handful that represent people of interest (China's hack of OPM suggests it sees no problem doing likewise).[32] In a sense, this is how signals intelligence has always worked; see also DARPA's proposed Terrorist Information Awareness program.[33] *Third* is "persistent engagement," intrusions into adversary systems to stop or impede hostile cyberspace activity. Although the one operation claimed in the press—a DDOS attack to stymie Russia's Internet Research Agency[34]—was small potatoes, it may have been but one of many. *Fourth* is *reportedly* inserting malware in infrastructure. In early June 2019 the *New York Times*[35] claimed (without immediate pushback from the Administration) that the US CyberCommand (CYBERCOM) did that within the Russian electric grid—perhaps to deter Russia's activating malware suspected to lurk in the US grid. If press reports of *Nitro Zeus* are correct,[36] the United States had booby-trapped Iran's electric grid *before* reports surfaced that Iran had done the same to the US grid.[37] *Fifth* is to implant attacks into hostile information systems. Specifically, days after a US Global Hawk was shot down by Iranian batteries, the United States purportedly carried out cyberattacks against an intelligence group that built a database to monitor civilian shipping.[38] Using cyberattacks as a tit-for-tat would appear to be, itself, unexceptional—but if it takes weeks and more likely months to prepare a cyberattack, then these implants must have *preceded* the Iranian attack (unless Iran's Islamic Revolutionary Guard Corp networks were so easy to penetrate that it could have been done in the few days).

The creeping normalization of cyberwar or at least its preparations may seem to be escalation in cyberspace vis-à-vis past practice. But this development is also counterescalatory in that, with so much now normalized, it takes a novel or larger incident to push countries into physical combat.

Electronic warfare, notably GPS jamming and spoofing, is undergoing a similar normalization.[39] North Korea routinely jams GPS transmissions into South Korea, interfering with the management of airport traffic.[40] Even before invading Ukraine, Russia spoofed GPS signals in the Black Sea, leading some ships to read their position well inland.[41] It may also have interfered with automated identification system (AIS) readings there.[42] And China carried out GPS jamming near some of its ports.[43]

ESCALATION DYNAMICS WITHIN CYBERSPACE

Action–reaction cycles in cyberspace have, so far, been rare. The clearest ones all involve Iran: Israel's 2020 cyberattack on one of Iran's ports in retaliation to an cyberattack on Israel waterworks facilities,[44] the Iranian DDOS attacks on US banks (in 2012) as possible retaliation for having suffered Stuxnet (revealed in 2010), or arguably cyberattacks on Saudi Aramco (2012) in response to cyberattacks on Iran's refineries.

Long lead times help explain the relative lack of tit-for-tat cycles. It usually takes months to years to lay in a cyberattack (DDOS attacks aside). Stuxnet, itself, was years in the making. Seeking a specific rather than general failure (e.g., to create a cascading electrical failure rather than to knock a single electrical generator offline) can take longer. Accelerating preparations risks mistakes that lead to premature discovery and removal. Adding to the delayed reaction is the time required to characterize a cyberattack (e.g., was it an accident, a design flaw, or a cyberattack?), attribute it (particularly if a skilled attacker takes pains to look like someone else[45]) in the absence of self-identification,[46] and discern intentions from it.

The loose gearing between action and reaction may also inhibit a tit-for-tat cycle in cyberspace. The point of tit-for-tat is to establish in the other side's mind that it will reap what it sows. But errors may lurk within the cycle. What the original attacker thinks it did may differ from what the other side believes it did. The other side's response may be different from the attack (e.g., each side may have very different target sets). The retaliator's intentions may look very different from their effects. The original attacker's perception of the effects may differ from the actual effects. So, what looks as like-for-like to one side may appear unlike-for-like to the other. The more these issues are understood, the less attractive is tit-for-tat as a discipline mechanism. To state the obvious: the less likely is tit-for-tat, the less likely is escalatory tit-for-tat.

The escalation of tactical cyberwarfare carried out to support kinetic warfare is largely meaningless; when lethal attacks are in bounds, how can cyberattacks, regardless of how severe, be out of bounds (even if deemed unchivalrous because they rely so heavily on deception)? What bounds might exist are likely to be cyberattacks beyond the battlefield: against clearly civilian targets, outside the arena of conflict, or against nuclear systems. The other side may react by expanding the theater of operations or bringing nuclear weapons into play. But a lot would depend on how consequential such cyberattacks are.

ESCALATION BEYOND CYBERSPACE

Even if cyberwar, itself, is not kinetic war, might it lead there? George Beebe has argued, "cyber technologies, artificial intelligence, advanced hypersonic weapons delivery systems and anti-satellite weaponry are making the U.S.-Russian shadow war much more complex and dangerous than the old Cold War competition.... in a highly connected world in which financial networks, commercial operations, media platforms, and nuclear command and control systems are all linked together in some way, escalation from the cyber world into the physical domain is a serious danger."[47]

No country has made it clear what it would do in response to a cyberattack; there are only hints. Thus, no failure to respond would necessarily dent its credibility. US officials have stated on background that a cyberattack on the electric grid would draw a forceful response.[48] The 2018 Nuclear Posture Review indicated that a non-nuclear attack on the homeland *could* draw a nuclear response (earlier drafts were more explicit about naming cyberattacks). A 2013 Defense Science Board, as noted, mooted nuclear retaliation against a sufficiently lethal cyberattack.[49] Back in the 1990s, when Russia's conventional military was on its back, leaders deemed a sufficiently large cyberattack a strategic attack that could merit a strategic—which is to say nuclear—response.[50] Some speculated at the time that Russia's spring 2021 build-up of forces near Ukraine was a response to the Biden administration's threat to retaliate in cyberspace for Russia's SolarWinds hack[51] (in retrospect, it was not). Perhaps a country would escalate to kinetic warfare following a devastating cyberattack to demonstrate that it is still strong[52]—even if harming civilian infrastructure should not affect the other side's immediate ability to respond.

Might kinetic force be justified to disarm the other side's hacking capability? In June 2019 Israel bombed a building in Gaza that it said housed Hamas hackers[53]—but that was in the middle of a broader bombing campaign and not in response to any specific cyberattack. If Israel was punishing Hamas as a way of bolstering deterrence (aka "cutting the grass"), its leaders may have asked themselves: why not go after its hackers as well? Of note, Israel has yet to suffer a serious cyberattack for which the use of destructive force would represent comparable pain delivered to the other side.

Two events in early 2021 suggest why the scale of a cyberspace operation may itself be escalatory. In one, Russians inserted malware in a software update (from SolarWinds) and thereby infected 18,000 customers. Even though hackers neutered their malware in every target but the hundred or so of interest to it,[54] a tough US response was mooted based on the 18,000 customers temporarily infected rather than the hundred or so who remained infected.[55] In another instance a Chinese hacking group, Hafnium, exploited vulnerabilities in the Microsoft Exchange server to plant a web script into target networks that would give them reentry privileges. Initially, they targeted just a few dozen organizations. But when a patch loomed, Hafnium, in fear of being denied future access, dropped web scripts into every one of some 30,000 organizations it infected.[56] The United States pondered retaliation against the Chinese as well. Despite differences between cyberespionage and cyberattack, the penetration mechanisms are similar, and at this juncture the retaliation logic may also be similar.[57] The nature of cyberspace creates an unexpected impetus for escalation. Once a *cyberattack* exploit is developed and proliferated, detonating one might lead to every other such exploit being discovered in target systems and swiftly eradicated. This fact favors detonating all at once (this may explain the simultaneous detonation of booby-trapped pagers carried by Hezbollah members[58]), but the resulting shock makes escalated retaliation more likely.

If the distinction between a nonlethal and lethal cyberattack is the one that triggers retaliation, it may take time to figure out how many if any were harmed. Cyberattacks are more likely to hurt people indirectly rather than directly. For instance, taking down 911 service could delay getting urgent medical help; some may die from events that they would otherwise have survived.[59] An electrical power outage may kill from intolerable cold or heat (tens of thousands may have died in Europe's August 2003 heat wave), crippled hospitals, or shortages of medicines or food. Yet it could take careful statistical methods to determine how many people died. Although the immediate death toll in Puerto Rico from Hurricane Maria was 64, it took three months of statistical research to conclude that 3,000 more people died than would otherwise have been expected from demographic trends.[60] The consequences of a broad cyberattack on critical infrastructure—and thus the justification for a violent response—will hardly be any clearer any faster. By then feelings may have cooled down. Perhaps the threat of force might apply sooner if cyberattacks continue, especially in more damaging form. But cyberattacks do not repeat very easily when targets respond by cranking up their own cybersecurity. It is harder to imagine a forceful response to a cyberattack when tempers have abated.

Research also suggests that cyberattacks are less likely to garner a retaliatory—much less an escalated—response than would comparably damaging kinetic attacks. One study "suggests that cyberattacks create a threshold that restrains the escalation of conflict.[61] Americans are less likely to support retaliation with force when the scenario involves a cyberattack even when they perceive the magnitude of attacks across domains to be comparable."[62] To date there have been only two (disputed) incidents where violence was *possibly* employed to retaliate for a cyberattack: the death of Iran's cyber leader[63] in retaliation for a cyberattack on a tunnel in Haifa, Israel, and a strike on an Israel-linked oil tanker in retaliation for a hack on Tehran's rail system.[64]

So maybe what starts in cyberspace would stay in cyberspace. Such a consensus—one not yet formally endorsed by the major powers—may not survive cyberattacks that kill directly or, more generally, become a much worse problem.

ESCALATION INTO CYBERWAR FROM ECONOMIC SANCTIONS

Although Russia's economic responses to being hit by economic sanctions were relatively weak (as befit its weak economy), Russian could have used cyberattacks to press the West for sanctions relief.[65] Would that have been escalation?[66] And would it have lubricated a transition between economic "war" and kinetic conflict among nuclear powers?

As of this writing Russia has not carried out much in the way of consequential cyberattacks on the West—and much of what it did was aimed at hobbling supplies going to Ukraine.[67] Western customers of Russia's February hack of Viasat satellite terminals meant to cut Ukrainian wartime communications were, at most, collateral damage.[68] Maybe because Putin's hackers only had six weeks' notice of the invasion,[69] they had too little time to prepare serious hacks in retaliation for sanctions. Yet by 2024, that rationale lost its explanatory power. Perhaps Russia believes that cyberattacks on US critical infrastructure could free CYBERCOM to target Russian military systems.

Would a Russian cyberattack on Western systems be escalation vis-à-vis sanctions? It may be, if escalation is understood as one side doing something that both sides hitherto refrained from doing. Otherwise the answer may depend on where cyberwar sits on the escalation lattice. Russian officials have called economic sanctions and especially its cut-off from SWIFT as acts of economic war, with the clear implication that they stand at the same level as violent warfare.[70] But sanctions are the converse of trade, a set of arrangements freely entered into. Thus they can be freely exited from as well (subject to contract law and trade agreements). LOAC does not recognize sanctions, even *qua* economic warfare, as the use of force. Correspondingly, being victimized by sanctions cannot justify the use of force. Cyberattacks, conversely, are imposed by attackers on victims; they are nonvoluntary.

From another perspective, economic sanctions can be far more economically damaging than the most expensive cyberattack—NotPetya. Even a 2 percent drop in Russia's GDP from their effects, as happened in 2022, could cost $40 billion a year (measured by exchange rates) to $80 billion a year (measured by purchasing power parity). It would take a wildly successful cyberattack campaign to wreak greater costs. By such criteria cyberwar would likely be less costly, hence not escalation. The West in general may push back on such an equivalence, in part because it enjoys a clear advantage in economic sanctions but has no such obvious advantage in cyberwar. But for just that reason the West's foes may favor the opposite.

Again, different perceptions about cyberwar's place in the escalation lattice may grease the transition from economic sanctions to kinetic warfare. One side imposes sanctions on the other side, which suffers large losses and then retaliates with cyberattacks to cause comparable losses to make the one side stop sanctions. The one side deems cyberwar to be war. It could retaliate with kinetic attacks. A potential firebreak might differentiate cyberattacks that leave casualties (hence like war) from those that do not (hence unlike war). But given the difficulties of predicting the effects of cyberattacks, such a firebreak may be crossed unintentionally.

CYBERATTACKS TO SIGNAL ESCALATION INTO KINETIC ATTACKS

Several analysts, reflecting on the Russo-Ukrainian War, have argued that cyberspace operations on novel targets or at unprecedented levels would be used to signal that further escalation would follow. A July 2022 RAND report examines four escalation paths that Russia might take.[71] Of the four escalation scenarios contemplated, one of them "would likely" begin with a nonkinetic attack, and two more of them "could begin with nonkinetic attacks." Eric Schlosser, author of *Command and Control*, considered a reverse scenario: "The United States could launch a crippling cyberattack on the Russian command-and-control systems tied to the nuclear assault and leave open the possibility of subsequent military attacks."[72]

But would cyberattacks be a reliably read and hence useful signal? There is little evidence that world leaders think that being under cyberattack signals something else, but they could. In 2014 a relatively low-level intrusion into servers maintained by the bank JPMC was interpreted by some White House officials as Russia's reaction to being sanctioned after it took Crimea (in actuality, it was a cybercrime incident out of Israel).[73] The May 2021 Colonial Pipeline ransomware attack, which led to a spate of gasoline lines, might have been colored similarly if it had taken place right after the invasion of Ukraine.

Would it be wise, though, to signal with an operation that cannot work reliably? A country that intends to move forces, sail ships, fly aircraft, or launch spacecraft is likely to succeed at doing so. But a cyberattack on a seriously defended target could fail. It may fail at a stage (e.g., at a firewall) where no one notices that anyone tried. It could fail at a stage where it is detected but its intent and authorship were unclear (if so, would the attacker want to confess to something both malicious and incompetent?). It may fail at a stage where it is noticed and attributed but where failure itself raises the question of how serious the attackers were.

Even if cyberattacks did succeed, would the target read them as a signal for some kind of *kinetic* attack? Maybe not, particularly in an already violent context, such as the Russo-Ukrainian war. Cyberattacks use nonviolent means and rarely break things or hurt people. So how would they connote greater violence to come? Indeed, the opposite might be inferred. Introducing a nonviolent form of conflict may signal a desire to remove the conflict from a violent contest in one domain to a nonviolent contest in another.[74]

THE ESCALATION POTENTIAL OF INFORMATION ASSISTANCE

One country's supplying information to another at war has traditionally not made it a co-belligerent. But as the flow of tactical intelligence increasingly influences who wins wars, this assessment may change.

In the 1980s the United States provided intelligence from space assets to Iraq (fighting Iran) and to the UK (fighting Argentina), allowing the recipients to understand the other side's dispositions and, in some cases, to target more efficiently. The United States (and likely the United Kingdom) has provided real-time intelligence to Ukraine to detect the particulars of a Russian invasion,[75] possibly locate Russian artillery,[76] help kill generals,[77] and sink a ship.[78] Cyber operations, logistics support, remotely hosted training, and simulation are other forms of assistance that superpowers can provide their clients without putting themselves at direct risk or leaving visible fingerprints. The less direct exposure, the fewer the paths to escalatory confrontations—as long as it is covert.

International law may hold that providing intelligence suffices to render one a co-belligerent.[79] "If the U.S. were providing targeting information to a foreign party, and we're closely involved in targeting decisions, we're directing those forces and they're acting as a proxy for us," said Scott R. Anderson, a former State Department official who was the legal adviser for the US Embassy in Baghdad. "That might be seen as getting close to the line of actually attacking Russia, at which point Russia could arguably respond reciprocally."[80]

The more that third-party tactical intelligence matters to a war's outcome, the more the other side gains by objecting to it. This creates two escalation pathways to violence. One arises if the target state demarches outside parties demanding an end to assistance via cyberspace, but the information keeps flowing and the target state feels it must make good on the threat. Here is where the ambiguities of cyberspace matter. Maybe the outside party thinks it can hide its activity—but it cannot, especially if what exposes the information transfer is not forensic analysis but intercepting battlefield information within the other side's systems that can only have come from third parties. The second pathway arises if the target state turns to preemption, or what is almost as bad, raises alert levels as a hedge, which then sparks the third party to do likewise—especially if it does not understand why because it thinks that the instigating cyber operations were still undetected. Then something happens.

Dangers increase when intelligence assets are physically present on or near the battlefield. Third-party sensors outside the war zone could be targeted (a US Reaper UAV was attacked by Russian warplanes). Or third parties may figure that if sensors were being targeted outside the war zone's lines, they may as well operate inside the lines. Even if UAVs are destroyed, the lack of casualties (see the next chapter) may limit pressures on their owner to retaliate. But if the UAV's owner asserts a right to collect information and targets the other side's *manned* surface-to-air missiles in its own self-defense, and casualties result, open conflict may follow. Each response could have crossed a line in the eyes of the other but not its own: the side that targets the UAV elides the distinction between intelligence and the use of force, and the side with the UAV elides the distinction between the lethal and nonlethal use of force. But escalation has clearly occurred. It is unclear whether manned intelligence assets (e.g., radar-carrying aircraft and Aegis-equipped ships) that sit outside the theater would fare better. They are more likely to shoot back in self-defense (but correspondingly less likely to be shot at for that very reason).

Cyberwar in support of an ally is more hostile than providing information. Yet disagreement over whether cyberwar is war, its nonlethality, and the ambiguities of attribution may all limit—but not end—the risks to the outside party if caught. Andrei Krutskikh, Putin's top cyber advisor, has alleged that the United States had, "unleashed cyber aggression against Russia and its allies . . . [using Zelensky and] the IT Army created by him to carry out computer attacks against our country as a battering ram. . . . We do not recommend that the United States provoke Russia into retaliatory measures."[81] Such an argument alludes to some vague threshold yet to be crossed and thus provides no useful way for Russia to use threats to forestall more serious US cyberoperations. Falsely accusing an outside power of already having intervened makes it harder to threaten the outside power when it really does intervene. Cyberspace operations in theater that hobble, disrupt, or destroy superpower assets, however, may create problems.[82]

ALLIANCES MAY COMPLICATE ESCALATION IN CYBERSPACE

Alliances always add complications to escalation decisions, especially those from cyberspace.

A state facing an alliance may well judge its foe's thresholds by looking at the least restrained alliance member. Although it could dismiss that member as unrepresentative, it would more likely conclude that the alliance wants to have it both ways: to be seen as restrained because most members are, but gaining an edge when one member exceeds such restraints (e.g., by attacking the other side's homeland infrastructure). Escalation could follow that one member's crossing thresholds.

If so, an alliance interested in avoiding escalation needs *all* its members to restrain themselves accordingly. The odds that a rogue alliance member will cross a threshold can be tamped down by the prospect that such escalation will be noticed and called out by other alliance members. The assumption that escalation *will* be noticed is plausible for many military operations—except in cyberspace.

Cyberattacks are not unique in being difficult to attribute: covert actions, deniable militia activities, and stealth weaponry also present attribution problems. But attribution is harder when the target itself is not trusted and may have an interest in shifting the blame from a rogue member to the alliance as a whole. The odds that a state will let its foes peek inside its affected systems to do forensics are microscopic (even Japan, a US ally, did not want CYBERCOM officials peering into systems of theirs hacked by the Chinese[83]).

If the alliance does not trust all of its members to restrain themselves *and* the potential for escalation matters, the most straightforward approach is for alliance members to work together so closely that one member's going rogue will be detected in time. Conversely, some members snooping into other members' networks to detect their preparing cyberattacks would erode alliance cohesion. Normally the most militarily aggressive member of NATO, the United States, was also the most militarily capable. As such its actions were a proxy for the entire alliance. But when it comes to assisting Ukraine, several NATO countries that were part of the Soviet Union or the Warsaw Pact appear to be more aggressive vis-à-vis Russia and Belarus. By contrast the United States appears to be more cautious than many, and thus perhaps rightly concerned about what its allies might do in cyberspace.

CONCLUSIONS

The fear that cyberattacks can lead to escalation remains.[84] This is particularly the case if cyberwar epitomizes a broader information war effort that could include electronic warfare (EW), psychological operations, and coercive surveillance: all nondestructive, ambiguous, and persistent to where they can plausibly be used together for purposes where such traits are critical.

Yet it is neither certain nor particularly likely that cyberwar can push countries to war if they are otherwise disinclined to it. Escalation presumes that cyberwar is successful at the technical level and that success makes it difficult *not* to respond, either for political reasons or to regain some military balance. The unexpected escalation to physical war requires an aggressor who does not see cyberwar as tantamount to violence, and a target who determines that yes, it is—and needs a violent response. In principle, the only way cyberattacks should persuade a rationale state to escalate to kinetic conflict is if (1) *future* such cyberattacks would be intolerable, (2) there are no other ways to ward off or mitigate such attacks, and (3) the use of force would end such cyberattacks or at least reduce them to a tolerable level without leading to something worse. Meeting each criterion is nontrivial; meeting all is unlikely.

Increasingly, cyberwar appears to be in the process of being normalized in that it is seen as distinct from war. The Russian invasion of 2022 was clearly a higher state of war than the gray zone takeover of Crimea and the eastern Donbass—but the level of *successful* cyberspace activity by Russia in both cases was comparable. Persistent engagement—if it did entail cyberattacks on other countries' hackers—appears to be an escalation vis-à-vis the cyberespionage activity that it is intended to suppress, but reaction to such escalation has been muted. In what other military domain would an ongoing attempt to degrade the other side's capabilities be normalized?

Could this change? Do cyberattacks occupy a low niche on the escalation spectrum because of their inherent nonviolent and transitory character or because their efficacy, so far, has been unimpressive compared to serious violence? Are cyberwar's consequences so awful that countries are restraining themselves for fear of mutually assured disruption? Or more prosaically, have the results of cyberwar been so restrained as more system operators take cybersecurity seriously that making major consequences becomes hard to achieve?

The place of cyberwar on the escalation lattice remains undecided. In the early months of the Russo-Ukrainian war, commentators saw cyberattacks (on the West) as an act of escalation *up* from death and destruction (against Ukraine). Secretary of Defense Robert Gates placed cyberattacks between heavy conventional warfare and tactical nuclear weapons: "It [the war in Ukraine] could also end in a Russian escalation, perhaps in the form of cyberattacks or even tactical nuclear weapons."[85] The Atlantic Council's Richard Hooker listed "employing cyber tools" as the first of Putin's escalation options, ahead of WMD use.[86] David Sanger also placed cyberattacks first, "if Mr. Putin believes that his conventional military forces are being strangled, he will turn to stepped-up cyberattacks on Western infrastructure, chemical weapons or his arsenal of tactical, 'battlefield' nuclear weapons."[87]

Andrea Kendall-Taylor and Michael Kofman lumped cyberattacks with nuclear weapons as options for a desperate Putin.[88] In the other direction, analysts have mooted cyberattacks as a satisfactory result to Russian nuclear weapons use in Ukraine[89] or even a dissuasive tool beforehand.[90] The same inflation of cyberwar appears in a RAND assessment of a hypothetical war with China[91] as well as the DoD's assessment.[92] So, the probable effects of cyberattacks notwithstanding, a cyberattack may be an escalation—if and only if both sides see it that way.

NOTES

1. "Biden warns cyberattacks could lead to a real shooting war," *Reuters*, July 27, 2021, https://www.reuters.com/world/biden-warns-cyber-attacks-could-lead-a-real-shooting-war-2021-07-27/.
2. See also Erica Lonergan and Shawn Lonergan, *Escalation Dynamics in Cyberspace* (Oxford UK: Oxford University Press, 2023).
3. See Jon Lindsay, "Stuxnet and the limits of cyber warfare," *Security Studies*, 22, No. 3 (2013), 365 to 404.
4. See, for instance, Yevgeny Vindman, "Is the SolarWinds cyberattack an act of war? It is, if the United States says it is," *Lawfare*, January 26, 2021, https://www.lawfareblog.com/solarwinds-cyberattack-act-war-it-if-united-states-says-it.
5. Might there be two types of wars? "It may be argued ... that the use of force which is not accompanied by an attempt to violate territorial integrity or political independence is not contrary to the obligations of Article 2 [of the UN charter]." Ian Browlie, *International Law and the Use of Force by States* (Oxford UK: Clarendon Press, 1963), 265–6. The author goes on to reject these arguments, but the repeated use of "territorial integrity" and "political independence" suggests that countries may view the use of force differently if these bedrock values are not at risk. See also "The legal significance of the state of war in the period since 1920 and the problem of defining war," 384–401, same volume.
6. Alex Hern, "North Korean 'cyberwarfare' said to have cost South Korea £500m," *The Guardian*, October 16, 2013, https://www.theguardian.com/world/2013/oct/16/north-korean-cyber-warfare-south-korea.
7. The Tallinn Manuals are generally considered the most systematic and consensus-based treatment of how LOAC may apply to cyberspace operations. See Michael Schmitt et al., *Tallinn Manual 2.0 on the International Law Applicable to Cyber Operations* (Cambridge UK: Cambridge University Press, 2017).
8. See, for instance, Bart Hogeveen, "The UN norms of responsible state behaviour in cyberspace," UNODA, March 2022, https://documents.unoda.org/wp-content/uploads/2022/03/The-UN-norms-of-responsible-state-behaviour-in-cyberspace.pdf.
9. Alex Grigsby, "The United Nations doubles its workload on cyber norms, and not everyone is pleased," *Council on Foreign Relations*, November 15, 2018, https://www.cfr.org/blog/united-nations-doubles-its-workload-cyber-norms-and-not-everyone-pleased.

10. E.g., see Nicole Perlroth, "Online security experts link more breaches to Russian government," *New York Times*, October 28, 2014, https://www.nytimes.com/2014/10/29/technology/russian-government-linked-to-more-cybersecurity-breaches.html; or Mark Johnson, "Russia issues travel warning about US, citing threat of 'kidnapping,'" *IB Times*, September 3, 2013, http://www.ibtimes.com/russia-issues-travel-warning-about-us-citing-threat-kidnapping-1402265.
11. Scott Charney et al., "From articulation to implementation: Enabling progress on cybersecurity norms," *Microsoft*, June 2016, https://query.prod.cms.rt.microsoft.com/cms/api/am/binary/REVmc8.
12. *The Paris Call for Trust and Security in Cyberspace*, December 11, 2018, https://www.diplomatie.gouv.fr/IMG/pdf/paris_call_text_-_en_cle06f918.pdf.
13. Ellen Nakashima and Joseph Marks, "Russia, U.S. and other countries reach new agreement against cyber hacking, even as attacks continue," *Washington Post*, June 12, 2021, https://www.washingtonpost.com/national-security/russia-us-un-cyber-norms/2021/06/12/9b608cd4-866b-11eb-bfdf-4d36dab83a6d_story.html.
14. For the communique and a discussion on it, see Cody Poplin, "Cyber sections of the latest G20 leaders' communiqué," *Lawfare*, November 17, 2015, https://www.lawfareblog.com/cyber-sections-latest-g20-leaders-communiqué.
15. Adam Segal et al., "Hacking for ca$h: Is China still stealing Western IP?" *Australian Strategic Policy Institute*, September 24, 2018, http://apo.org.au/node/194141.
16. Ben Buchanan, *The Cybersecurity Dilemma: Hacking, Trust and Fear between Nations* (Oxford, UK: Oxford University Press 2017).
17. FBI, "Update on Sony investigation," December 17, 2014, http://www.fbi.gov/news/pressrel/press-releases/update-on-sony-investigation. There are 140 words in those paragraphs that presented the evidence of North Korean involvement.
18. Office of the Director of National Intelligence, "Assessing Russian activities and intentions in recent US elections," January 6, 2017, https://www.dni.gov/files/documents/ICA_2017_01.pdf.
19. Against China see Ellen Nakashima, "Indictment of PLA hackers is part of broad U.S. strategy to curb Chinese cyberspying," *Washington Post*, May 22, 2014, http://www.washingtonpost.com/world/national-security/indictment-of-pla-hackers-is-part-of-broad-us-strategy-to-curb-chinese-cyberspying/2014/05/22/a66cf26a-e1b4-11e3-9743-bb9b59cde7b9_story.html. Against Russia see "United States v. Viktor Borisovich Netyksho et al," Case 1:18-cr-00215-ABJ Document 1 Filed 07/13/18, https://www.justice.gov/file/1080281/download. Against Iran see Ellen Nakashima and Matt Zapotosky, "U.S. charges Iran-linked hackers with targeting banks, N.Y. dam," *Washington Post*, March 24, 2016, https://www.washingtonpost.com/world/national-security/justice-department-to-unseal-indictment-against-hackers-linked-to-iranian-goverment/2016/03/24/9b3797d2-f17b-11e5-a61f-e9c95c06edca_story.html.
20. The arrest and conviction of Karim Baratov is close to an exception; see David Shepardson, "Canadian who helped Yahoo email hackers gets five years in prison," *Reuters*, May 29, 2018, https://www.reuters.com/article/us-yahoo-cyber/canadian-who-helped-yahoo-email-hackers-gets-five-years-in-prison-idUSKCN1IU2OE.
21. See, for instance, US Office of the Special Trade Representative, "Findings of the investigation into China's acts, policies, and practices related to technology transfer, intellectual property, and innovation under Section 301 of the Trade Act of 1974,"

March 22, 2018, https://ustr.gov/sites/default/files/Section%20301%20FINAL.PDF.
22. See Brandon Vigliarolo, "77% of security leaders fear we're in perpetual cyberwar from now on," *The Register*, August 27, 2022, https://www.theregister.com/2022/08/27/in-brief-security/.
23. See David Frank Winkler, *The Cold War at Sea: High-Seas Confrontation between the United States and the Soviet Union* (Annapolis, MD: Naval Institute Press, 2000).
24. See, for instance, Ralph Clem, "Risky encounters with Russia: Time to talk about real deconfliction," *War on the Rocks*, February 18, 2021, https://warontherocks.com/2021/02/risky-encounters-with-russia-time-to-talk-about-real-deconfliction/.
25. Max Smeets, "There are too many red lines in cyberspace," *Lawfare*, March 20, 2019, https://www.lawfareblog.com/there-are-too-many-red-lines-cyberspace.
26. Matt Burgess, "North Korea's elite hackers are funding nukes with crypto raids," *Wired*, April 3, 2019, https://www.wired.co.uk/article/north-korea-hackers-apt38-cryptocurrency.
27. Lily Hay Newman, "Russian hackers haven't stopped probing the US power grid," *Wired*, November 28, 2018, https://www.wired.com/story/russian-hackers-us-power-grid-attacks/.
28. President Putin has compared those who hacked the DNC to "artists." See Andrew Higgins, "Maybe private Russian hackers meddled in election, Putin says," *New York Times*, June 1, 2017, https://www.nytimes.com/2017/06/01/world/europe/vladimir-putin-donald-trump-hacking.html.
29. Chris Demchak and Yuval Shavitt, "China's maxim—Leave no access point unexploited: The hidden story of China Telecom's BGP hijacking," *Military Cyber Affairs*, 3, No. 1 (2018).
30. Something like Stuxnet may have been used against North Korea, albeit without effect. See Joseph Menn, "Exclusive: U.S. tried Stuxnet-style campaign against North Korea but failed—sources," *Reuters*, May 29, 2015, https://www.reuters.com/article/us-usa-northkorea-stuxnet/exclusive-u-s-tried-stuxnet-style-campaign-against-north-korea-but-failed-sources-idUSKBN0OE2DM20150529.
31. David Sanger and William Broad, "Trump inherits a secret cyberwar against North Korean missiles," *New York Times*, March 4, 2017, https://www.nytimes.com/2017/03/04/world/asia/north-korea-missile-program-sabotage.html.
32. For instance, see Ellen Nakashima and Joby Warrick, "For NSA chief, terrorist threat drives passion to 'collect it all'," *Washington Post*, July 14, 2018, https://www.washingtonpost.com/world/national-security/for-nsa-chief-terrorist-threat-drives-passion-to-collect-it-all/2013/07/14/3d26ef80-ea49-11e2-a301-ea5a8116d211_story.html.
33. See, for instance, John Markoff, "Threats and responses: Intelligence; Pentagon plans a computer system that would peek at personal data of Americans," *New York Times*, November 9, 2002, https://www.nytimes.com/2002/11/09/us/threats-responses-intelligence-pentagon-plans-computer-system-that-would-peek.html.
34. Ellen Nakashima, "U.S. Cyber Command operation disrupted Internet access of Russian troll factory on day of 2018 midterms," *Washington Post*, February 27, 2019, https://www.washingtonpost.com/world/national-security/us-cyber-command-operation-disrupted-internet-access-of-russian-troll-factory-on-day-of-2018-midterms/2019/02/26/1827fc9e-36d6-11e9-af5b-b51b7ff322e9_story.html. "Persistent engagement" has

also been associated with botnet take-downs, but such activity largely took place outside hostile countries.
35. David Sanger and Nicole Perlroth, "U.S. escalates online attacks on Russia's power grid," *New York Times*, June 15, 2019, https://www.nytimes.com/2019/06/15/us/politics/trump-cyber-russia-grid.html.
36. David Sanger and Mark Mazzetti, "U.S. had cyberattack plan if Iran nuclear dispute led to conflict," *New York Times*, February 16, 2016, https://www.nytimes.com/2016/02/17/world/middleeast/us-had-cyberattack-planned-if-iran-nuclear-negotiations-failed.html.
37. For instance, see Andy Greenberg, "The highly dangerous 'Triton' hackers have probed the US grid," *Wired*, June 14, 2019, https://www.wired.com/story/triton-hackers-scan-us-power-grid/.
38. AFP, "US launched cyberattacks on Iran after drone shootdown: reports," *AFP*, June 22, 2019, https://news.yahoo.com/us-launched-cyber-attacks-iran-drone-shootdown-reports-232123877.html.
39. "The jamming and spoofing of satellites has become somewhat common, and without strong repercussions these adverse activities could gradually become normalized." Todd Harrison et al., "Space threat assessment 2020," *Center for Strategic and International Studies*, March 2020, https://www.csis.org/analysis/space-threat-assessment-2020. From Nicholas Wright, "China and escalation in the 'gray zone-entangled space age,'" in Nicholas Wright ed., *Outer Space; Earthly Escalation? Chinese Perspectives on Space Operations and Escalation*, August 2018, 9: "In 2014, Russia jammed GPS signals in Ukraine during the Crimean conflict (Sukhankin, 2017; InformNapalm.org, 2016, 2017). This grounded some remotely piloted aircraft, and caused GPS loss for radios and phones. Independent Ukrainian analysts report that from 2014 to 2017 Russia used six different jamming and radio monitoring platforms in Ukraine, including the R-330Zh jammer and the R-381T2 ultra-high frequency radio monitoring system." See also Selam Gebrekidan, "Electronic warfare confounds civilian pilots, far from any battlefield," *New York Times*, November 21, 2023, https://www.nytimes.com/2023/11/21/world/europe/ukraine-israel-gps-jamming-spoofing.html.
40. Choe Sang-Hun, "North Korea tried to jam GPS signals across border, South Korea says," *New York Times*, April 1, 2016, https://www.nytimes.com/2016/04/02/world/asia/north-korea-jams-gps-signals.html.
41. Matt Burgess, "To protect Putin, Russia is spoofing GPS signals on a massive scale," *Wired*, March 27, 2019, https://www.wired.co.uk/article/russia-gps-spoofing.
42. H.I. Sutton, "Positions of two NATO ships were falsified near Russian Black Sea naval base," *USNI News*, June 21, 2021, https://news.usni.org/2021/06/21/positions-of-two-nato-ships-were-falsified-near-russian-black-sea-naval-base.
43. See, for instance, Mark Harris, "Ghost ships, crop circles, and soft gold: A GPS mystery in Shanghai," *Technology Review*, November 15, 2019, https://www.technologyreview.com/2019/11/15/131940/ghost-ships-crop-circles-and-soft-gold-a-gps-mystery-in-shanghai/.
44. Joby Warrick and Ellen Nakashima, "Officials: Israel linked to a disruptive cyberattack on Iranian port facility," *Washington Post*, May 18, 2020, https://www.washingtonpost.com/national-security/officials-israel-linked-to-a-disruptive-cyberattack-on-iranian-port-facility/2020/05/18/9d1da866-9942-11ea-89fd-28fb313d1886_story.html; and Ronen Bergman and David M. Halbfinger, "Israel hack of Iran port is latest salvo in

exchange of cyberattacks," *New York Times*, May 20, 2020, https://www.nytimes.com/2020/05/19/world/middleeast/israel-iran-cyberattacks.html.

45. See, for instance, Andy Greenberg, "The untold story of the 2018 Olympics cyberattack, the most deceptive hack in history: How digital detectives unraveled the mystery of Olympic Destroyer—and why the next big attack will be even harder to crack," *Wired*, October 17, 2019, https://www.wired.com/story/untold-story-2018-olympics-destroyer-cyberattack/.

46. The best examples are Israel's coy attempts to credit itself with Stuxnet and a group that, even more coyly, called itself "Fancy Bears" (echoing a designation given by a cybersecurity firm, Crowdstrike, to the Russian-based group "Fancy Bear"), giving itself credit for breaking into a database managed by the Democratic Party of Wisconsin (Paul Srubas, "Russians suspected of hacking Wisconsin Dems," *USA Today*, January 24, 2017, www.usatoday.com/story/news/politics/2017/01/24/russians-suspected-hacking-wisconsin-dems/97023222/).

47. George Beebe, "We're more at risk of nuclear war with Russia than we think," *Politico*, October 7, 2019, https://www.politico.com/magazine/story/2019/10/07/were-more-at-risk-of-nuclear-war-with-russia-than-we-think-229436.

48. An anonymous official in the US government mused, "If you shut down our power grid, maybe we will put a missile down one of your smokestacks," from Siobhan Gorman and Julian E. Barnes, "Cyber combat: Act of war," *Wall Street Journal*, May 31, 2011.

49. Defense Science Board, *Task Force Report: Resilient Military Systems and the Advanced Cyber Threat*, 2013, http://www.acq.osd.mil/dsb/reports/ResilientMilitarySystems.CyberThreat.pdf. See also Scott D. Sagan and Allen S. Weiner, "The U.S. says it can answer cyberattacks with nuclear weapons. That's lunacy." *Washington Post*, July 10, 2021, https://www.washingtonpost.com/outlook/2021/07/09/cyberattack-ransomware-nuclear-war/.

50. Stephen Blank, "Can information warfare be deterred?" *Defense Analysis* 17, No. 2 (2001), 121–38; and Matthew Campbell, "'Logic bomb' arms race panics Russians," *The Sunday Times*, November 29, 1998.

51. Andrew Kramer, "Russian troop movements and talk of intervention cause jitters in Ukraine," *New York Times*, April 9, 2021, https://www.nytimes.com/2021/04/09/world/europe/russia-ukraine-war-troops-intervention.html: "Before the tanks started rolling, Russia had been telegraphing a possible response to the Biden administration's promise of a tougher line with Moscow. The Biden administration had said it would pursue cyberoperations and sanctions to retaliate for Russian cyberattacks and election meddling. Russia, some analysts say, is now essentially daring the United States to follow through while its tanks are on the Ukrainian border."

52. Hal Brands, "Getting ready for a long war with China," *American Enterprise Institute*, July 2022, https://www.aei.org/research-products/report/getting-ready-for-a-long-war-with-china-dynamics-of-protracted-conflict-in-the-western-pacific/. Should this [round of network warfare that can cause collapse of the adversary's economy] happen, the United States might consider drastic remedies.

53. Erica D. Borghard and Jacquelyn Schneider, "Israel responded to a Hamas cyberattack with an airstrike. That's not such a big deal," *Washington Post*, May 9, 2018, https://www.washingtonpost.com/politics/2019/05/09/israel-responded-hamas-cyberattack-with-an-airstrike-thats-big-deal/.

54. Jon Porter, "White House now says 100 companies hit by SolarWinds hack, but more may be impacted," *The Verge*, February 18, 2021, https://www.theverge.com/2021/2/18/22288961/solarwinds-hack-100-companies-9-federal-agencies. Dmitri Alperovitch and Ian Ward ("How should the U.S. respond to the SolarWinds and Microsoft Exchange hacks?," *Lawfare*, March 12, 2021, https://www.lawfareblog.com/how-should-us-respond-solarwinds-and-microsoft-exchange-hacks) argue that Russian hackers inserted commands to kill their own malware that wound up in the systems they had no interest in.
55. David E. Sanger, Julian E. Barnes, and Nicole Perlroth, "Preparing for retaliation against Russia, U.S. confronts hacking by China," *New York Times*, March 7, 2021, https://www.nytimes.com/2021/03/07/us/politics/microsoft-solarwinds-hack-russia-china.html.
56. Brian Krebs, "At least 30,000 U.S. organizations newly hacked via holes in Microsoft's email software," *Krebs on Security*, March 5, 2021, https://krebsonsecurity.com/2021/03/at-least-30000-u-s-organizations-newly-hacked-via-holes-in-microsofts-email-software/.
57. From David Sanger, "After Russian cyberattack, looking for answers and debating retaliation," *New York Times*, February 23, 2021, https://www.nytimes.com/2021/02/23/us/politics/solarwinds-hack-senate-intelligence-russia.html: "At a White House briefing last week, Anne Neuberger, President Biden's new national security adviser for cyber and emerging threats, said the White House was preparing a comprehensive response because of 'the ability of this to become disruptive.' She was referring to the possibility that the same access that gave the Russians the ability to steal data could, in the next phase of an operation, enable them to alter or destroy it."
58. *Al-Monitor*, "Exclusive: Hezbollah suspicions forced Israel to expedite Lebanon pager attack," September 18, 2024; https://www.al-monitor.com/originals/2024/09/exclusive-hezbollah-suspicions-forced-israel-expedite-lebanon-pager-attack.
59. See Melissa Eddy and Nicole Perlroth, "Cyberattack suspected in German woman's death," *New York Times*, September 18, 2020, https://www.nytimes.com/2020/09/18/world/europe/cyber-attack-germany-ransomeware-death.html.
60. Frances Robles et al., "Official toll in Puerto Rico: 64. Actual deaths may be 1,052," *New York Times*, December 9, 2017; https://www.nytimes.com/interactive/2017/12/08/us/puerto-rico-hurricane-maria-death-toll.html. Later estimates were closer to 3,000; Milken Institute School of Public Health of the George Washington University, "Ascertainment of the estimated excess mortality from Hurricane Maria in Puerto Rico," August 27, 2018, https://publichealth.gwu.edu/sites/g/files/zaxdzs4586/files/2023-06/acertainment-of-the-estimated-excess-mortality-from-hurricane-maria-in-puerto-rico.pdf.
61. Sarah Kreps and Jacquelyn Schneider, "Escalation firebreaks in the cyber, conventional, and nuclear domains: Moving beyond effects-based logics," 2019, https://ssrn.com/abstract=3104014. See also Jacquelyn Schneider, "Cyber and crisis escalation: Insights from wargaming," 2017, https://paxsims.files.wordpress.com/2017/01/paper-cyber-and-crisis-escalation-insights-from-wargaming-schneider.pdf.
62. Nadiya Kostyuk and Yuri M. Zhukov, "Invisible digital front: Can cyberattacks shape battlefield events?" *Journal of Conflict Resolution* 63, No. 2 (2017), 1–31. See also Benjamin Jensen and Brandon Valeriano, "What do we know about cyber escalation? Observations from simulations and surveys," *Atlantic Council*, November 2019, https://www.atlanticcouncil.org/wp-content/uploads/2019/11/What_do_we_know_about_cyber_escalation_.pdf.

63. See "Cyber-terrorism shut down Israel's Carmel Tunnel," *Info Security*, October 28, 2013, http://www.infosecurity-magazine.com/news/cyber-terrorism-shut-down-israels-carmel-tunnel/ for reports of the September 2013 Haifa cyberattack; and Damien McElroy and Ahmad Vahdat, "Iranian cyber warfare commander shot dead in suspected assassination," *Telegraph*, October 2, 2013, http://www.telegraph.co.uk/news/worldnews/middleeast/iran/10350285/Iranian-cyber-warfare-commander-shot-dead-in-suspected-assassination.html. Israel announced the Haifa cyberattack *after* the Iranian's death was reported.
64. *Times of Israel*, "TV: Israel believes Iran struck ship in response to cyberattack on train system," August 1, 2021, https://www.timesofisrael.com/tv-israel-believes-iran-struck-ship-in-response-to-cyberattack-on-train-system/.
65. "Statement by President Biden on our nation's cybersecurity," March 21, 2022 (https://www.whitehouse.gov/briefing-room/statements-releases/2022/03/21/statement-by-president-biden-on-our-nations-cybersecurity/): "I have previously warned about the potential that Russia could conduct malicious cyber activity against the United States, including as a response to the unprecedented economic costs we've imposed on Russia alongside our allies and partners."
66. Dmitri Alperovitch ("The dangers of Putin's paranoia," *Foreign Affairs*, March 18, 2022, https://www.foreignaffairs.com/articles/russia-fsu/2022-03-18/dangers-putins-paranoia) argued, "Before jumping headlong into a potentially dangerous spiral of cyber-escalation, the United States and its allies should first use all of the economic tools at their disposal." This logic implies that all major cyber operations sit higher on the escalation ladder than the most severe economic sanctions. See also "Dmitri Alperovitch on the risks of escalation," *Economist*, February 24, 2022, https://www.economist.com/by-invitation/2022/02/23/dmitri-alperovitch-on-the-risks-of-escalation: "If America and its allies stay the course on economic sanctions, Russia could further escalate the conflict in other ways. Carrying out cyber-attacks against American and European financial institutions and energy infrastructure is one. Having already exhausted the power of economic sanctions, America and its European allies would have few choices other than to respond to these attacks with offensive cyber-strikes of their own. This pattern of tit-for-tat cyber retaliation could place Russia and the West on a worrying path. It could end with the conflict spilling out of cyberspace and into the realm of a hot conflict."
67. Andrzej Kozłowski, "Polish cyber defenses and the Russia-Ukraine war," *Council on Foreign Relations*, January 18, 2023, https://www.cfr.org/blog/polish-cyber-defenses-and-russia-ukraine-war. For a broad assessment of Russia's failure to generate consequential cyberattacks, see Jon Bateman, "Russia's wartime cyber operations in Ukraine: Military impacts, influences, and implications," *Carnegie Endowment*, December 2022, https://carnegieendowment.org/2022/12/16/russia-s-wartime-cyber-operations-in-ukraine-military-impacts-influences-and-implications-pub-88457.
68. See, for instance, Matt Burgess, "A mysterious satellite hack has victims far beyond Ukraine," *Wired*, March 23, 2022, https://www.wired.com/story/viasat-internet-hack-ukraine-russia/.
69. The Microsoft Digital Security Unit ("Special report: Ukraine, An overview of Russia's cyberattack activity in Ukraine," *Microsoft*, April 27, 2022, https://query.prod.cms.rt.microsoft.com/cms/api/am/binary/RE4Vwwd) indicated that Russian cyber operators were mobilized six weeks before the invasion, but it also argues that even then Russian hackers were still avoiding targets in NATO.

70. "Russian Foreign Minister Sergey Lavrov... [says] he believes that the West has declared 'total war' on Russia." From Cameron Jenkins, "Kremlin official says West has declared 'total war' on Russia," *The Hill*, March 25, 2022, https://thehill.com/policy/international/russia/599722-lavrov-says-west-has-declared-total-war-on-russia/.
71. Bryan Fredrick et al., "Pathways to Russian escalation against NATO from the Ukraine war," *RAND*, July 2022, https://www.rand.org/pubs/perspectives/PEA1971-1.html. It is difficult to see what kind of nonkinetic attack, if not a cyberattack, the authors had in mind.
72. Eric Schlosser, *Command and Control* (London UK: Penguin, 2013). This particular suggestion was a paraphrase of a discussion with Rose Gottemoeller, former US negotiator for the New START arms control treaty.
73. Michael Corkery, Jessica Silver-Greenberg, and David Sanger, "Obama had security fears on JPMorgan data breach," *New York Times*, October 8, 2014, http://dealbook.nytimes.com/2014/10/08/cyberattack-on-jpmorgan-raises-alarms-at-white-house-and-on-wall-street/.
74. See, for instance, Brandon G. Valeriano and Benjamin Jensen, "De-escalation pathways and disruptive technology: Cyber operations as off-ramps to war," (November 10, 2020) in Scott Shackelford, Frederick Douzet, and Chris Ankersen (eds.), *Cyber Peace: Charting a Path towards a Sustainable, Stable, and Secure Cyberspace* (Cambridge, UK: Cambridge University Press, 2022).
75. Helene Cooper and Julian E. Barnes, "U.S. considers warning Ukraine of a Russian invasion in real-time," *New York Times*, December 23, 2021; https://www.nytimes.com/2021/12/23/us/politics/russia-ukraine-military-biden.html.
76. *Economist*, "Artillery is playing a vital role in Ukraine," May 2, 2022, https://www.economist.com/europe/2022/05/02/artillery-is-playing-a-vital-role-in-ukraine.
77. Julian E. Barnes, Helene Cooper, and Eric Schmitt, "U.S. intelligence is helping Ukraine kill Russian generals, officials say," *New York Times*, May 5, 2022, https://www.nytimes.com/2022/05/04/us/politics/russia-generals-killed-ukraine.html. But, "The administration has sought to keep much of the battlefield intelligence secret, out of fear it will be seen as an escalation and provoke President Vladimir V. Putin of Russia into a wider war." The White House has, accordingly denied as much; see Jack Shafer, "Opinion | The White House treats the public like morons. Again.," *Politico*, May 5, 2022, https://www.politico.com/news/magazine/2022/05/05/white-house-morons-public-russia-generals-ukraine-00030476.
78. Shane Harris, Paul Sonne, Dan Lamothe, and Michael Birnbaum, "U.S. provided intelligence that helped Ukraine sink Russian warship," *Washington Post*, May 6, 2022, https://www.washingtonpost.com/national-security/2022/05/05/us-intelligence-ukraine-moskva-sinking/.
79. Mark Mazzetti, Helene Cooper, Julian E. Barnes, and David E. Sanger, "For the U.S., a tenuous balance in confronting Russia," *New York Times*, March 19, 2022, https://www.nytimes.com/2022/03/19/us/politics/us-ukraine-russia-escalation.html: "As a matter of international law, the provision of weaponry and intelligence to the Ukrainian Army has made the United States a co-belligerent." But Yann Schmuki ("The law of neutrality and the sharing of cyber-enabled data during international armed conflict," in the *15th International Conference on Cyber Conflict* [Tallinn, Estonia: CCDCOE, 2023]) argues that doing so only violates a state's claim to being neutral.

80. Shane Harris and Dan Lamothe, "Intelligence-sharing with Ukraine designed to prevent wider war," *Washington Post*, May 11, 2022, https://www.washingtonpost.com/national-security/2022/05/11/ukraine-us-intelligence-sharing-war/.
81. David Ignatius, "The U.S.-Russia conflict is heating up—in cyberspace," *Washington Post*, June 7, 2022, https://www.washingtonpost.com/opinions/2022/06/07/us-russia-conflict-is-heating-up-cyberspace/.
82. For a deeper discussion of this issue see Martin Libicki, *Cyberspace in Peace and War* (Annapolis, MD: Naval Institute Press, 2021), 284–5.
83. Ellen Nakashima, "China hacked Japan's sensitive defense networks, officials say," *Washington Post*, August 8, 2023, https://www.washingtonpost.com/national-security/2023/08/07/china-japan-hack-pentagon/.
84. The *Summary DoD Cyber Strategy* (https://media.defense.gov/2023/Sep/12/2003299076/-1/-1/1/2023_DOD_Cyber_Strategy_Summary.PDF, 2) states, "As it campaigns in cyberspace, the Department will remain closely attuned to adversary perceptions and will manage the risk of unintended escalation."
85. From David Ignatius, "As Ukraine braces for a second round, the West has a duty to stand up," *Washington Post*, April 7, 2022, https://www.washingtonpost.com/opinions/2022/04/07/ignatius-russia-ukraine-heavy-weapons/. See also *Economist*, "History will judge Vladimir Putin harshly for his war," February 26, 2022, https://www.economist.com/leaders/2022/02/26/history-will-judge-vladimir-putin-harshly-for-his-war: "should Mr Putin seize a large swathe of Ukraine, . . . bloated by victory, he will subject [the Baltic states] to the cyberattacks and information warfare that fall short of the threshold of conflict."
86. Richard D. Hooker, "Climbing the ladder: How the West can manage escalation in Ukraine and beyond," *Atlantic Council*, April 21, 2022, https://www.atlanticcouncil.org/in-depth-research-reports/report/managing-escalation-in-ukraine/.
87. David E. Sanger, "Behind Austin's call for a 'weakened' Russia, hints of a shift," *New York Times*, April 25, 2022, https://www.nytimes.com/2022/04/25/us/politics/ukraine-russia-us-dynamic.html. See also Anton Troianovski and David E. Sanger, "Russia issues subtle threats more far-reaching than a Ukraine invasion," *New York Times*, January 16, 2022, https://www.nytimes.com/2022/01/16/world/europe/russia-ukraine-invasion.html: "if the conflict escalates further, American officials believe that Mr. Putin could be drawn to cyberattacks—easy to deny, superbly tailored for disruption and amenable to being ramped up or down, depending on the political temperature."
88. Andrea Kendall-Taylor and Michael Kofman, "Russia is down. But it's not out." *New York Times*, June 2, 2022, https://www.nytimes.com/2022/06/02/opinion/russia-ukraine-war-nato.html. See also Peter Clement, "Putin's risk spiral: The logic of escalation in an unraveling war," *Foreign Affairs*, October 26, 2022, https://www.foreignaffairs.com/ukraine/putin-risk-spiral-logic-of-escalation-in-war: "Should Putin's winter strategy fail . . . [he] may well follow up on his oft-cited threats to 'use all available means.' One possible option is large-scale cyberattacks on Western infrastructure." See also Jonathan Guyer, "What US weapons tell us about the Russia-Ukraine war: The debate around which weapons to send to Ukraine, explained," *Vox*, March 29, 2023, https://www.vox.com/world-politics/2023/3/29/23652435/debate-weapons-ukraine-abrams-leopard-tanks-biden-zelenskyy: "But Russia still may escalate, says Miranda Priebe, a political scientist at the Rand Corporation. 'Nuclear escalation isn't the only thing I worry about.

Russia still has a lot of cards to play.' Those may include increased strikes on civilians and Ukrainian infrastructure, or massive cyberattacks."
89. Greg Herken, Avner Cohen, and George M. Moore, "3 scenarios for how Putin could actually use nukes," *Politico*, May, 16, 2022, https://www.politico.com/news/magazine/2022/05/16/scenarios-putin-nukes-00032505: "The U.S. and NATO could also respond [to Russian nuclear use] by use of non-kinetic means like cyber warfare."
90. Kristin Ven Bruusgaard, "How Russia decides to go nuclear: Deciphering the way Moscow handles its ultimate weapon," *Foreign Affairs*, February 6, 2023, https://www.foreignaffairs.com/ukraine/how-russia-decides-go-nuclear: "Western and Ukrainian leaders could then take steps to persuade Russian officials to reverse course [towards nuclear use]. Such steps could . . . include increasing the pressure on Moscow through unconventional coercive measures, such as cyberattacks."
91. Timothy R. Heath, Kristen Gunness, Tristan Finazzo, "The return of great power war," (Santa Monica, CA: RAND, 2022), 116: "A desire to bring [a Sino-U.S.] war to a close and restore economic growth and social stability could lead to the experimental use of even more destructive escalatory options, including tactical nuclear weapons, cyberattacks on civilian infrastructure, and attacks on space infrastructure." See also Steven Wertheim, "Can America really envision World War III?," *New York Times*, December 2, 2022, https://www.nytimes.com/2022/12/02/opinion/america-world-war-iii.html: "Second, each side would be tempted to escalate. This summer, the Center for a New American Security held a war game that ended with China detonating a nuclear weapon near Hawaii. 'Before they knew it,' both Washington and Beijing 'had crossed key red lines, but neither was willing to back down,' the conveners concluded. Especially in a prolonged war, China could mount cyberattacks to disrupt critical American infrastructure. It might shut off the power in a major city, obstruct emergency services or bring down communications systems."
92. Department of Defense, *Military and Security Developments Involving the People's Republic of China 2023*, 140: "In the event of a protracted conflict [over Taiwan], the PLA might choose to escalate cyberspace, space, or nuclear activities in an attempt to end the conflict . . ."

3

The Space between Nonlethal and Lethal War

As thresholds separating peace from war are challenged, could a new threshold—one separating nonlethal from lethal operations—emerge among states that take death more seriously than destruction? The Space Shuttle *Challenger* disaster and the World Trade Center attack, for example, destroyed both life *and* property. Yet far more people knew how many people died in each than how much property was damaged; seven astronauts made much more news than having to replace a $3 billion spacecraft.

When President Trump responded to Iran's June 2019 shoot-down of a US Global Hawk with a cyberattack rather than an air raid, he justified his decision by his unwillingness to hurt people; the Iranian attack, itself, had left no casualties. Even the Pentagon's alternative of sinking a missile-laden Iranian boat was designed to "warn the Iranians to evacuate the vessel, videotape them doing so, then sink the boat with a bomb or missile strike. The end result would be zero casualties, which [Secretary of Defense] Shanahan and [Joint Chiefs of Staff Chairman] General Dunford argued would be a proportional response."[1] When missiles struck Saudi Aramco's oil processing facilities, also with no reported casualties, the United States carried out not a lethal response but a cyberattack that affected Iran's ability to spread "propaganda."[2] In January 2020 an Iranian missile strike against a US base in Iraq (in retaliation for an assassination of Iran's general Soleimani) did not kill people[3]; the president cited this fact to justify not counter responding. Michael Horowitz[4] has argued that, "Some norms already seem to be developing in the use of drones—for example, as the Turkey/Russia encounter in 2016 shows, countries are already treating the shooting down of a drone as less serious than the shooting down of an inhabited aircraft." Russia essentially ignored one and reacted harshly to the other.[5] In mid-March 2023, Russian jets shot down a US UAV over the Black Sea, but there was little US response.[6]

A threshold distinguishing between life and property gives leaders space to place certain options off the table when pressed to respond to a destructive attack. Conversely a reprisal that crosses such a line would more easily be deemed an act of escalation and disproportionate. But such forbearance also protects the aggressor's actions by reducing some of the retaliation risk from its acts.

In examining the potential for a threshold between destructive-but-nonlethal attacks and lethal attacks, we start with space satellites. Apart from the International Space Station, all can be disabled or even destroyed with minimal risk of direct human casualties (the odds of anyone on the ground being hit by satellite debris are miniscule, but loss of weather satellites can cause casualties indirectly). Because satellites are both highly valuable and highly vulnerable and the United States depends on satellites more than its rivals do, confining warfare to space is not guaranteed. Similar logic is then applied to assessing the viability of a broader nonlethal threshold.

NONLETHAL SPACE WAR CAN BE STRATEGICALLY CONSEQUENTIAL

China's People's Liberation Army (PLA) believes that great power war entails seeking to "achieve and maintain information superiority for the operational system while simultaneously seeking to degrade or undermine an adversary's operational system in the information battlefield."[7] It recognizes that "US targets in an AirSea Battle–style campaign were to include Chinese command and control networks, missile sites, intelligence, surveillance, and reconnaissance (ISR) assets, air defense systems, and submarines, with the goal of 'executing a blinding campaign against PLA battle networks,'"[8] But China has the assets to attempt as much itself.

To demonstrate the plausibility of a nonlethal attack with strategic import, imagine a scenario where China's leaders conclude that their best way to counter the Quad (a working relationship between the United States, Australia, India, and Japan) would be to neutralize Japan. Its strategy would be to isolate Japan from US assistance long enough to coerce the country into sundering its relationship with the United States and then impose measures to prevent backsliding.

To that end, the US ability to defend Japan using conventional forces would be sharply compromised. Several communications satellites used by

US forces would be silenced; so would key transponders on commercial communications satellites. Doubts would be raised over whether US surveillance satellites were functional. Electronic interference in frequencies used by militaries would be sharply increased. American UAVs would go missing. Deployed US ships would be forced to slow down their operations; from what cause would not be obvious.

Japan then would be asked to renounce its mutual defense pact with the United States and allow Chinese firms to build out a controlling share of Japan's communications infrastructure (not just 5G mobile services). Doing so would allow China to introduce its Great Firewall into Japanese communications.[9] The effect would be subtle; little would be blocked—except anything that criticized China in general, or China's intervention into Japan, in particular. Rejecting China's demands, though, would bring war.

Japan's leadership understood that the United States would aid Japan to protect the latter's sovereignty. Indeed, if physical destruction had caused the loss of US satellites, the United States would be effectively at war anyhow, albeit in the commons of outer space. But since China had not been deterred by that prospect, matters came down to the military balance. The US ability to fight in the Western Pacific would be severely crippled. True, no ship sank. No one was hurt. And there were enough communications to enable real-time command and control from Hawaii (headquarters of the US Pacific Command) and Washington, DC. However, there were sharp drops in the bandwidth available to support all the various forms of reach-back (e.g., equipment monitoring and maintenance, imagery and other intelligence, and video-teleconferencing as well as simulation and decision-support). The United States would have a hard time fighting as it had trained.

Here a world in which the United States had the immediate strength to deter Chinese threats to Japan suddenly became a world where the United States could not extract painful military damage to China without receiving more than like damage in return. Given months the United States could return to parity and perhaps even gain enough advantage to force a peace. Some satellites could be replaced. Geosynchronous satellites could be repositioned from the Atlantic to the Pacific. UAVs could be moved in from other theaters. Fiber optics could be repaired. But as John Mearsheimer[10] has argued, countries are not deterred by the prospect of long-term loss so much as the diminished prospects of quick victory. The United States could, and most likely would, attack Chinese space, external communications, and surveillance assets as a reprisal-in-kind. Doing so, though, would not change the correlation of forces very much or quickly. The United States needed such assets to fight in the Western Pacific. China had far less need for its counterpart operations—especially if it conceded that it could not, anyway, effectively target US ships beyond the range of its air-breathing reconnaissance assets.

If the Chinese attack on US assets had resulted in fatalities—which it had not–the result would have been a Pearl Harbor moment; no US president could avoid responding. But no casualties resulted from China's attacks on US assets. Japan was not yet attacked. China was not necessarily going to be deterred by the prospect of facing US forces in a conventional fight because it might do well enough in the first year of combat. And while Japan, if it acceded to China's demands, would cease to be a US ally and lose some of its sovereignty, China did not threaten to eliminate Japan's democracy, much less occupy Japan. As far as public messaging was concerned, the United States would respond like-for-like against the Chinese attacks—once these attacks were characterized and attributed. But would going on to wage lethal war be deliberate escalation?

China's actions, in this scenario, would create a narrative of conflict that served to give the other side a way of saving face while standing down. Few NATO countries, for instance, wanted to come to Ukraine's assistance in 2014. A narrative that Crimean "independence" reflected local sentiment or that the fighting in eastern Ukraine was a civil war rather than a proxy invasion made it easier to hold off. As the *Economist* explained,[11] "[The West] connived in Mr. Putin's pretense that he had not invaded eastern Ukraine—even though in a furtive tricksy way he plainly had—because to say otherwise would have required a drastic response." An obvious invasion would have forced NATO governments to do something—which they did in 2022. Likewise, an attack that left no US casualties would make it easier to limit the response to in-kind retaliation and sanctions if the United States would prefer not starting a lethal war.

What of a nuclear response? The US arsenal is still much larger than China's, but not so much so that the United States could preemptively rid China of its capability to wipe out some US cities with its surviving nuclear weapons. It is one thing for the United States to say it retained the option to use nuclear weapons to defend its Asian allies, but another to go first and use nuclear weapons to help Asian allies fend off non-nuclear aggression—much less nonlethal aggression. The Chinese should reflect that getting into lethal combat with the United States would make Armageddon more likely. That prospect would weaken the credibility of any threat they make against US allies in Asia and thereby *could* nullify the prospects of this scenario. But not entirely or always.

Key to this scenario is the central role of satellites in enabling US war in the western Pacific. Circa 2000 US military strength against China's was larger and its dependence on space a bit less than it is today; losing satellites might have weakened the ability to wage war with China but not to where the United States would initially lose. Circa 2035, if China's military continues to improve faster than America's—by no means certain—the US ability to prevail in the western Pacific in the first year may be in doubt even if its satellites go untouched. But in the meantime access to space makes a difference. So would a nonlethal attack on these satellites escalate into lethal war? Correspondingly, could destructive but nonlethal attacks, such as those on satellites, be credibly deterred by the threat of lethal war if the latter is viewed as crossing a threshold?

So let us look more closely at space warfare as the epitome of nonlethal warfare.

ON SPACE WARFARE

The art of the possible in space offense and defense reflects how and where outer space is used.[12] Escalation decisions, correspondingly, will reflect not only whether the sanctuary of space has been violated but the economic and military implications of such violations.

Almost all defense-related satellites sit in one of four types of orbits: low earth orbit (LEO: roughly 200 to 1,500 miles up), medium earth orbit (MEO: almost 13,000 miles up), geosynchronous earth orbit (GEO: 22,400 miles up and over the equator) and highly elliptical orbit (HEO: largely to stare at the upper latitudes of the northern hemisphere). The lower the orbit, the easier it is for earth-based space weapons to reach them; the same rocket that can get a kilogram into GEO can get roughly 5 kilograms into LEO. Also, the lower the orbit, the shorter the flight time to hit a satellite there; by contrast "a typical launch trajectory to geosynchronous orbit takes more than four hours to reach apogee."[13] This gives satellites more time to evade contact and its owners more time to react.

In these orbits fly many types of satellites. *Communications* satellites (commsats) are found in LEO and GEO. GEO contains several hundred large and expensive satellites owned by a wide variety of commercial firms, governments, and international organizations. Satellites in GEO can be found in the same place in the sky, allowing antennas to be permanently pointed to such locations. Such satellites can be moved to a new orbital slot given a few weeks' notice. Because most of the world's GEO commsat bandwidth is in private hands, governments that lose access to their own or their allies' satellites can buy or command commercial bandwidth even if a substitute is neither instant nor entirely adequate (military commsats are better protected against EW and cyberattacks) and not always available if the owner is also being pressured by the other side. Sitting in LEO are multiple commsat constellations,[14] the most ambitious being the privately owned Starlink, with more than 7,000 satellites as the summer of 2024 ended. *Surveillance* satellites sit in LEO (taking high-resolution imagery including electro-optical and cloud-penetrating radar satellites) and GEO (looking for electronic emissions useful for surveilling oceans and infrared signatures useful for detecting missile launches). LEO satellites are not designed for real-time surveillance and battle management (it would have required something like the canceled US SBIRS-Low constellation to do both). Although the destruction of imaging satellites would eliminate updating, the data already collected (e.g., for populating maps) would remain. Precision navigation and timing (PNT) satellites such as GPS orbit in MEO. Although the US military has access to more precise and jamming-resistant location information[15] than other GPS customers do, those others profit greatly from location services. Indeed it is precisely such third-party benefits and the consequent risk of political blowback from ending PNT services that may protect the GPS and like constellations—Europe's Galileo, China's BeiDou, and Russia's Glonass.[16]

Attackers have the choice of temporarily disabling satellites through jamming, dazzling, hacking, or (the most escalatory) destroying satellites.

Electronic jamming can disable communications satellites, the data-communications channels of other satellites (e.g., GPS), and satellites that collect RF signals for surveillance and targeting. Although jammers can be located and disabled, they are far cheaper to buy in quantity than satellites are. An intermittent jammer on a mobile platform can also be very hard to track long enough to hit it. Satellite jamming comes in two forms: downlink jamming of signals from satellites, and uplink jamming of signals to satellites. Downlink jamming prevents reception, but the intended receiver can still try to acquire the satellite signal by pointing its antennae to the satellite—as long as the jammer is not hovering near the line of sight to the satellite. Uplink jamming blocks communications to the satellite and can be effective so long as the jammer sits within a satellite transponder's terrestrial footprint (typically the size of a US state). Uplink jamming can therefore block two-way communications—and worse can interfere with the command and control of satellites, not merely the services that satellites provide to terrestrial users (there are countermeasures to jamming, such as spread-spectrum and frequency-hopping, but they must be provisioned in advance). Such interference may be taken far more seriously than would jamming that merely hobbles local users, especially if the failure to receive operating commands imperils a satellite's ability to maintain its orbit. So, once again, exactly where jamming a satellite's control system sits on the escalation lattice may depend on whether the other side focuses on the means used (soft-kill means, hence lower) or the ends achieved (possible hard kill, hence higher).

Dazzling a satellite hinders its ability to gather visual or other signal data—much as oncoming headlights make it difficult to see unlit objects around them. Typically, a dazzler would sit near sensitive sites. Like jamming, effects last only while the dazzler is on. Dazzling is not normally problematic when countries are under no obligation to let themselves be surveilled (compliance with arms control treaties being an exception). Countermeasures to dazzling (e.g., image-processing algorithms) exist. But too powerful a dazzler can cause long-term damage to a satellite's optical receptors, which is problematic. Both China and Russia are believed to be working on technologies for "ASAT weapons that could blind or damage sensitive space-based optical sensors, such as those used for ... missile defense."[17]

Satellites and satellite control systems can also be confused by cyberattacks on satellites—but for how long depends on what hackers can do. Many hacks have obvious effects; if discovered they can usually be neutralized. With fixes, subsequent hacks can be made much harder. But if hackers can access sensitive areas of satellite management, notably those affecting its rotation or orbit-keeping, orbital control may be hard to recover. Satellites *have* been hacked.[18] There was a flurry of incidents before and in 2011[19] plus one in 2014,[20] after which satellite owners started taking the threat more seriously (Russia interrupted Viasat's connectivity by going after receivers, not the satellite itself). Yet satellite controls can be protected by requiring that all commands to them be digitally signed by a ground terminal that is electronically isolated from the rest of the world (subject to the caveat that in cyberspace there are no ironclad guarantees against clever maliciousness).

Permanent effects can be generated by direct-ascent and on-orbit weapons. (Directed-energy weapons, such as high-powered microwaves, can destroy the satellite's electronics or thermal integrity, but there are no known antisatellite [ASAT] warheads that do so).

The standard way of killing a satellite is to send something into it at very high speed as was done in the US ASAT test of 1985, the Chinese ASAT test of 2007, India's ASAT test in 2019, the Russian ASAT test of 2021, and the US destruction of a falling satellite in 2008.[21] Direct-ascent missiles fired from earth do not even need enough energy to orbit at the requisite altitude, merely enough energy to touch the orbit. Ballistic missiles can reach apogees of 1,200 miles without exceeding 12,000 miles per hour (it takes 18,000 miles an hour to attain and maintain a low-earth orbit). The missile from the 1985 ASAT test was carried by an F-15. The 2008 interception was carried out by a shipboard missile, a modified Standard Missile–3. Russia used its System A-235, a variant of its S-500 surface-to-air missile. Antisatellite efforts that were started in the 1980s did go into hiatus when the Cold War ended: "[but] according to the Director of National Intelligence, Russia is developing and testing a new generation of direct ascent ASAT weapons, including an air-launched ASAT missile."[22] Space is now viewed as a contested environment.

ASAT missiles can work quickly (once the satellite gets within range) and are very difficult to defend against. The high cost of getting a kilogram of material into orbit means that armor is unaffordable. And because satellites are whirring around the earth at speeds from 7,000 miles per hour (in GEO) to 18,000 miles per hour (in LEO), running into something else in orbit, particularly head-on, can be extremely damaging. Several years ago, the International Space Station had to maneuver to avoid running into such particles. Mere paint flecks can hurt satellites—and would not show up on anyone's radar.

Blowing up a satellite, though, can leave harmful debris in orbit for decades or more; China's 2007 ASAT test produced at least 3,500 pieces—and that is just those large enough to be detected from earth.[23] These pieces, in turn, can hit other satellites, breaking them into pieces that can crash into other satellites and causing a chain reaction, aka the Kessler effect, overdramatically portrayed in the movie *Gravity*. The Kessler effect is more of a LEO satellite problem. If the collision is just below LEO, the debris will decelerate from air resistance and rain earthward. India's 2019 test and the US 2008 shoot-down produced nothing that stayed in orbit. But such air resistance is why satellites do not normally fly that low. And just as satellites in LEO can stay in orbit for decades, so would the debris field that was created by destroying one. The threat is lower in MEO because satellites there move more slowly. It is lowest in GEO because satellites move even more slowly and they all follow each other around the earth like train cars (so that the relative speeds between the pieces of a destroyed GEO satellite and the other GEO satellites would be low). The Kessler effect can be limited if both sides target satellites sparingly. To date, only five satellite collisions (including accidents) have produced debris. Only two satellites have been disabled by debris collisions (both were before the Chinese ASAT test). Today's debris levels are still well below that required to trigger the Kessler effect. It is unclear how much spacefaring countries would restrain themselves from fear of the Kessler effect. There is no magic number of satellites that can be destroyed before some line is crossed. In a sense the probability of a Kessler effect could play a role in modulating space warfare similar to the role the probability of Armageddon plays in modulating lethal warfare.

Several countries, notably Russia, China, and the United States, have also launched co-orbital satellites, which at least temporarily ride in the same orbits as their prey. This puts them in a position to strike if so commanded. Co-orbital satellite weapons need not destroy the satellite by collision if they can, for instance, break something internally: for example, by crushing or knocking it or smashing a projectile into a key component. Covering a satellite's solar panels with a blanket would render it powerless as its batteries depleted.

Putatively, temporary effects are less likely than permanent effects to induce reprisals, especially once reversed. Todd Harrison et al.[24] cite one analyst questioning, "whether non-kinetic and reversible actions are hostile acts or armed attacks that warrant a military response" and another one who agrees that "[t]here is no taboo against the use of many counter-space systems. The threshold for using temporary and reversible counter-space capabilities, such as electronic interference, is largely untested and likely much lower." But as with cyberattacks, rivals may place their thresholds in different places. To continue with Harrison et al.,[25] "For example, the United States may regard jamming of its satellite communications links that are used for nuclear command and control as highly escalatory, but its allies may view this form of attack as below such a threshold."

The different orbits matter because the escalation potential of attacks on satellites in different orbits are themselves different. Satellites in LEO can be attacked with only minutes of warning. It is usually impossible to distinguish, say, a ship armed with a satellite-destroying missile from one equipped only for air defense. By contrast GEO satellites are, at this point, more likely to be attacked by co-orbital satellites, maneuvers of which can give the other side hours to issue warnings against such behavior. Such warnings, if ignored, increase the credibility of retaliation, even escalated retaliation. Finally, attacking satellites in MEO and HEO present their own difficulties; they are not easily attacked by mobile platforms, and anything in the same orbit would look far more suspicious than in GEO, which hosts a plethora of satellites.

THE DEFENDER'S OPTIONS

The impetus for escalation following a space attack arises from the unsatisfactory prospects for defense. This can be seen by considering alternatives to deterrence: norms, defense/preemption, and resilience.

Peacetime norms may include not testing antisatellite weapons (especially in ways that produce debris) and not maneuvering communications satellites to interfere with the signals of nearby satellites. They could also forbid putting one country's satellites in orbit near another, but there are defendable surveillance reasons for doing so that may allow them to fly unmolested and only later ambush other satellites should war break out (likewise a norm against intrusions for purposes of illegitimate cyberattacks would also forbid intrusions for legitimate cyberespionage).[26] A wartime norm could forbid attacks on satellites, but such a norm would be unlikely unless it entailed humanitarian issues.

Defense is very difficult. Armor, as noted, is unaffordable. Satellites carry limited onboard fuel[27] to help them evade destruction by maneuvering. So-called "bodyguard" satellites[28] could protect high-value satellites by orbiting near them and engaging nearby shooters, notably co-orbital satellites. But, again, justifying preemption would be challenging if it requires proving that the satellites at issue were not there for surveillance.[29] Shooting down direct-ascent ASATs in flight is even harder than national missile defense, which is already difficult enough. Once the shooting started countries might go after assets that can host direct-ascent weapons, but hosts such as fighter jets or surface ships are many and difficult to attrite very quickly; in the meantime, satellites may disappear. Preemptively destroying manned terrestrial assets capable of hosting or supporting direct-ascent ASAT missiles (e.g., ground stations, mobile launchers, aircraft, or ships) could itself start a war.

Resilience can mitigate but not eliminate war's consequences. Substituting constellations of small satellites for large ones would make it harder to knock out space capabilities or at least do so quickly;[30] they are becoming a cost-effective way to provide some space services.[31] Commercial space satellite systems, especially those with a wide customer base, might be considered off-limits. Yet the Russians publicly threatened to target the commercial space constellation Starlink because it was supplying communications services for Ukrainian command and control.[32] That noted, each individual Starlink satellite costs far less than the cheapest *non-nuclear* ASAT missile that could take one down.

Terrestrial backup is another form of resilience. Take surveillance. UAVs can capture images at high resolution with less complex sensors (e.g., cameras) because they fly much closer to what they are looking at. And while satellites spend most of their time over uninteresting parts of the world (e.g., untrafficked oceans), UAVs can linger over the interesting parts and stare continuously at what lies below. True, UAVs often must trespass in peacetime; this creates obvious risks—but no worse than is likely for satellites in wartime. Some satellite communications could be shifted to networks of fiber optics to get messages into the theater (e.g., from CONUS) and mesh of wireless relays (perhaps UAV-mounted) to get them around the theater. Across flat terrain (e.g., oceans), two UAVs flying at 25,000 feet can be 400 miles apart and still be within each other's line of sight. Although UAVs would be targeted and their need to communicate contravenes stealth, relay UAVs (in contrast to surveillance UAVs) would sit behind the units they connect and thus would rarely fly over the other side's territory.

Ambiguity pervades operations in outer space just as in cyberspace. When satellites are attacked, what is most obvious is that they stopped working, not how—much less why or by whom. Suspicions may take time to sort out; a country's satellites are far away even as its cyber systems, which are hard enough to diagnose, are close at hand. It harms stability if the target makes a worst-case assumption, assumes an attack (rather than, say, a component failure) whenever something unexpectedly goes wrong, implicates a particular attacker, imputes a dire motive—and reacts accordingly. But it also harms stability if the attacker hides behind the certainty that its efforts can always be obfuscated enough to delay a response indefinitely and so carries on with unmerited impunity—and the target reacts, anyway.

Among the three options, norms are a long shot, defense-cum-preemption has little going for it, and resilience, while offering more hope, would take serious prewar investment and still yield a less-than-perfect substitute.

LEFT WITH DETERRENCE, WE RETURN TO ESCALATION

Can a threat to carry out reprisals for attacks on satellites keep others from using their ASAT capabilities? These reprisals would have to be serious enough to give pause to a country that already knows that destroying satellites is tantamount to an act of war. Take three types of reprisals: in-kind, lethal, and nuclear.

Deterrence-in-kind may be unpersuasive if the deterring state, such as the United States, depends far more on satellites than the attacker does (notwithstanding the role that Chinese and Russian electronic-intelligence satellites in GEO play in targeting oceangoing ships). Its only dissuasive power arises because, in a multipolar world, a country that undergoes a vigorous tit-for-tat exchange grows weaker vis-à-vis third parties.

Escalating by attacking terrestrial assets might not dissuade. The preceding scenario requires the victim to start a terrestrial war—just when the destruction of the satellites themselves would make such a war bloodier, longer, and less likely to succeed. Although the Chinese, in this scenario, would prefer not fighting, they realize that at least their *immediate* military prospects would be auspicious, and this might well inhibit the United States from starting a war. The more that the United States has emphasized beforehand that targeting satellites would lead to war, the greater the deterrence value of the warning. But if another country factored the warning into their calculations and went ahead anyway and the United States did *not* respond, ducking out would have serious reputational costs.

The credibility of a terrestrial reprisal threat may vary if attacks on satellites do not appreciably alter the military balance or at issue is a lesser scenario (e.g., a contest in the South China Sea or Russian military activity in the Caucasus). The strength of the United States would not be diminished enough to alter expected outcomes on the ground. But there still would be many reasons not to expect cross-domain reprisals. By the time attacks on satellites are characterized and attributed, the confrontation could have been resolved or its character changed. Anyway, a lethal reprisal for a non-lethal attack could seem disproportionate, and hence threats to do so not credible.

As for nuclear threats, Harrison et al.[33] observed that during the Cold War when military space systems largely supported nuclear missions, an "attack on either country's military satellites would have been regarded as either a prelude or part of a nuclear war." Yet "military satellite constellations that were once intended primarily for nuclear missions, and were thus protected by the cloak of nuclear deterrence, are now being used routinely for conventional warfighting at lower ends of the conflict spectrum."[34] US early-warning satellites, for instance, were used to predict the destinations of Iraqi Scuds in the first Gulf War. That makes them legitimate targets.

But can nuclear threats, as per the 2018 Nuclear Posture Review (NPR), suffice to preserve nuclear-related satellites? Hardened landlines can suffice for commanding and controlling ground-based nuclear missiles. Eliminating early warning capabilities would still leave over-the-horizon radar (plus whatever other secret early-warning systems might exist). For that reason, Russian coverage of nuclear events from space was allowed to lapse for a year. China lacked early-warning satellites until 2015. Nevertheless, maintaining redundancy matters. Backups to space capability might not be a given: how likely would an easy-to-hit, over-the-horizon radar go untouched while hard-to-reach GEO surveillance satellites are disabled? The only impact of disabling early-warning satellites may be to make the other side nervous in unhelpful ways. Worse, because destroying early warning satellites would make an unanswered first strike easier to pull off, those so targeted *could* react to the conventional destruction of their early warning systems as if a first strike were coming soon. It is hard to see what an aggressor gains from targeting the other side's nuclear-related satellites—apart from whatever modest help it provides to conventional warfare operations.

Granted, credible nuclear threats would give pause to any country tempted to disable nuclear command-and-control (NC3) or early-warning satellites. But the credibility of such a threat is doubtful, if losing a city to counter-reprisals would make reprisals a losing proposition even if outer space is restored as a sanctuary. So, while countries should be wary of touching another country's nuclear support satellites for fear of a neuralgic reaction, carrying out a nuclear threat is exorbitantly costly, boding ill for hopes that satellites can be protected by nuclear threats.

Finally, a caution about strategies that combine resilience and deterrence. The more resilient space-based services are in the face of attack (e.g., by virtue of large numbers or terrestrial substitutes), the less need to keep space a sanctuary. The lower the value of protecting the sanctuary of space, the less the need for catastrophic reprisals and thus the harder it would be to threaten them credibly.

Intermediate thresholds to shelter some but not all satellites may entail distinguishing attacks that leave debris (and risk the Kessler effect) from those that do not; distinguishing satellites by orbit (e.g., LEO satellites are fair game but GEO satellites are not); not touching nuclear-mission satellites (which may already be inhibited because their disruption, much less destruction, may raise the odds of Armageddon[35]); or making military satellites but not civilian satellites fair game (even as Starlink supports Ukrainian military communications). None are anywhere near international agendas, much less realization.

Space warfare lies uncertainly on the lattice. If a conventional war among superpowers results in attacks on satellites, such attacks would look like escalation (particularly if one of those satellites supported nuclear systems). Conversely a contest that starts in space but then results in attacks on ground support services (e.g., for satellite control or counter-space weapons) would also look like escalation.[36] So would it be escalation or deescalation if one side reacted to attacks on its satellites *solely* by attacking the other side's ground stations?

NONLETHAL ATTACKS MAY BE TAKEN AS PRECURSORS TO LETHAL ATTACKS

Would targets of nonlethal attacks react and stay below the threshold of violence because of what such attacks are[37] or above the threshold for what they may portend: the opening act of a lethal conflict? Similar questions, albeit with less urgency, may even be asked for particularly aggressive or disruptive (temporary) surveillance.

One factor may be how well such attacks worked and how much they shifted the military balance. The failure of a nonlethal attack that is detected, attributed, and its purpose characterized but only after time passed would also hardly justify preemption to lethal combat if nothing worse happened in the meantime. Even if attacks succeed or preparations for them are discovered, the target may infer that an attack is coming but not how or when. And what looks like an imminent attack may be surveillance undertaken for other reasons. Maneuvering a co-orbital satellite into position[38] may be preparations for an attack—or to test a capability, or again for surveillance. Nondestructive operations may also be tests—to be exploited if they work well enough or downplayed if they do not. Exploitation, however, would have to come quickly. For cyberattacks this would be measured in days. For attacks on space systems, the relevant window of opportunity would reflect how long it takes to replace the lost capability. Although the US Air Force is working on "operationally responsive space" capabilities, timelines are measured at best in weeks, even if a recent test drove the theoretical lead time down to a day.[39] A target state *could* respond preemptively to aggressive surveillance or nonlethal attacks to show resolve, especially if it warned against them. Yet doing so could also be starting a fight that was not inevitable.

Nonlethal attacks can also be used for coercive signaling. Consider a military standoff between Chinese and US forces in the South China Sea over the status of China's islands. The relative strength of both sides' forces may influence what happens next. Imbalance may predispose the stronger to stand firm and the other side to yield. Traditionally, relative strength reflected who brought what to the battle: quantity modulated by quality differences. Even if visible factors such as platforms and weapons suggest an even fight, equipment and system failure could occur and may be embarrassing if they do. But it does not take destructive attacks to shift the balance. One side could (nondestructively) interfere with external communications, compromise internal networks including RF links, sever connectivity to offboard sensors (which may result in lost sensors), or spoof sensor readings or weapons command and control. Doing so with enough success could shift the balance to where the target stands down. Of course, starting a fight would do even more to clarify who would emerge victorious, but if the goal is to preempt conflict by forcing a withdrawal, then fighting means intimidation failed.

Would matters escalate because of such hostile, albeit nonlethal attacks? If—and this is a big if—nonlethal attacks were not regarded as war, then the onus falls on the other side to start shooting to signal its resilience—or withdraw knowing that its foe full well knows the new balance of local power. But the onus is also on the attacking side to communicate that its efforts are meant to dissuade the other side, not prepare for war. The attacker would lack a clear idea about what effects were produced (visible evidence may be absent)—much less how these effects were perceived. Any strategy to show restraint by leaving sensitive systems untouched is hostage to what the other side concludes: their survival may indicate restraint—or the fact that an implant has not been activated, or that defenses were good. And unexpected effects could take down sensitive systems anyway.

IMPLICATIONS FOR THE LETHAL/NONLETHAL THRESHOLD

Might attacks on unmanned targets become a separate element of war or a distinct form of conflict? Targets include more than satellites. Some are fixed, including communications infrastructure such as radio towers, fiber-optic lines, sensors that sit on the ground or on the ocean floor, and radar dishes. Others are mobile, such as UAVs and UUVs (underwater unmanned vehicles—mooted for antisubmarine warfare). Vasily Gerasimov, Russia's chief of staff, speculates, "While today we have flying drones, tomorrow's battlefields will be filled with walking, crawling, jumping, and flying robots. In the near future it is possible a fully roboticized unit will be created, capable of independently conducting military operations."[40] Clearly a campaign against unmanned targets would matter more than one confined to unmanned satellites. Nonlethal ways to break electronic equipment—such as through short circuits caused by carbon fiber or microwave pulses[41]—add to the repertoire. But a lethal–nonlethal threshold holds only as long as the loser is willing to tolerate the pain, can implement effective countermeasures, or fears escalation into deliberate lethality. If the lethal–nonlethal distinction means that manned assets are shielded, the side that relies on unmanned assets would lose disproportionately and may not want to play by such rules.

Can a bright line between lethal and nonlethal even be maintained? Maybe not, for three reasons.

One, casualties may result anyway. Although initial reports showed no casualties from the 2020 Iranian strike on the US base in Iraq, later ones reported more than a hundred traumatic head injuries. People could easily have been killed.[42] Or a structure that was struck in the belief it was unattended was, in fact, manned.[43] Only a charitable foe will assume that the subsequent deaths were unintended and thus do not merit a lethal response. Accidents may provide excuses for escalating among those itching to do so. Mutual constraints work only if both parties really want to observe the guidelines and hope the other side does as well—and both forgive bad luck.[44]

Two, military rules of engagement that favor counterattacking attackers may hurt people as a matter of course. A submarine protecting a fiber-optic cable may react to the hostile operations of an enemy submarine no differently than if protecting a manned ship. An unmanned system equipped with automatic fire-back capabilities raises greater risks.

Three, countries that would like to respect the distinction between things and people may reconsider when things get very expensive or difficult to replace. Even if a $150 million UAV can be lost without lethal retaliation, does this guarantee the same for, say, a $1.5 billion satellite? And the secondary economic consequences of cutting enough trans-oceanic fiber optic cables (if not repaired quickly) could be in the trillions not billions of dollars.

The groundwork for distinguishing between striking people and things is yet unlaid. There are no national narratives that make that point systematically, nor have there been any proposals to embed such distinctions into norms. Countries that intend to make such distinctions[45] might be developing warheads that are lethal to electronics but not to people. These would allow manned platforms to be attacked without fear of producing casualties. But do such warheads exist? Altogether it is unclear how much any threshold between lethal and nonlethal operations will supplement or complement the war–peace distinction. Nor is it clear that a lethal–nonlethal threshold would be a good thing. It could inhibit superpowers from escalating a conflict that had seen destruction but not casualties. But for that reason, it also makes the world safer for a costly campaign of destruction. In the wake of the US shoot-down of a balloon that violated its sovereignty, some in China responded "with hints that an American surveillance satellite might be destroyed in retaliation."[46] If a lethal–nonlethal threshold reduced the perceived risks of all-out conflict, such a prospect may become even more tempting.

NOTES

1. Peter Baker, Eric Schmitt, and Michael Crowley, "An abrupt move that stunned aides: Inside Trump's aborted attack on Iran," *New York Times*, September 21, 2019, https://www.nytimes.com/2019/09/21/us/politics/trump-iran-decision.html.
2. See Indris Ali and Phil Stewart, "Exclusive: US carried out secret cyber strike on Iran in wake of Saudi oil attack: Officials," *Reuters*, October 16, 2019, https://www.reuters.com/article/us-usa-iran-military-cyber-exclusive/exclusive-u-s-carried-out-secret-cyber-strike-on-iran-in-wake-of-saudi-oil-attack-officials-idUSKBN1WV0EK.
3. See Kareem Fahim and Sarah Dadouch, "Missile strike on US targets 'did not intend to kill,' says Iranian commander," *Washington Post*, January 9, 2020, https://www.washingtonpost.com/world/middle_east/missile-strike-on-us-bases-did-not-intend-to-kill-says-iranian-commander/2020/01/09/c5c2295c-3260-11ea-971b-43bec3ff9860_story.html.
4. Michael Horowitz, "When speed kills: Lethal autonomous weapon systems, deterrence and stability, *Journal of Strategic Studies*, 42, No. 6 (2019), 772.
5. Wargames suggest that US policymakers would also consciously distinguish their responses to a UAV shootdown from the responses to the downing of a manned aircraft; see Erik Lin-Greenberg, "Wargame of drones: Remotely piloted aircraft and crisis escalation," *Journal of Conflict Resolution*, 66, No. 10 (June 6, 2022).
6. The head of Ukraine's defense intelligence agency took pains to indicate that there were "zero" civilian casualties from Ukraine's drone campaign in Russia; from *Economist*, "An interview with the head of Ukraine's defence intelligence," September 17, 2023, https://www.economist.com/europe/2023/09/17/an-interview-with-the-head-of-ukraines-defence-intelligence.
7. Jeffrey Engstrom, *Systems Confrontation and System Destruction Warfare* (Santa Monica, CA: RAND, 2018), 66.
8. Caitlin Talmadge, "Would China go nuclear? Assessing the risk of Chinese nuclear escalation in a conventional war with the United States," *International Security*, 41, No. 4 (Spring 2017), 53.
9. See, for instance, Eva Xiao, "China's WeChat monitors foreign users to refine censorship at home," *Wall Street Journal*, May 7, 2020, https://www.wsj.com/articles/chinas-wechat-monitors-foreign-users-to-refine-censorship-at-home-11588852802.
10. John Mearsheimer, *Conventional Deterrence* (Ithaca, NY: Cornell University Press, 1983).
11. *Economist*, "The siege," July 12, 2014, https://www.economist.com/leaders/2014/07/12/the-siege.
12. See Benjamin W. Bahney, Jonathan Pearl, and Michael Markey, "Antisatellite weapons and the growing instability of deterrence," in Jon R. Lindsay and Erik Gartzke, *Cross-Domain Deterrence* (Oxford UK: Oxford University Press, 2019), 121–43; and Forrest E. Morgan, *Deterrence and First-Strike Stability in Space: A Preliminary Assessment* (Santa Monica, CA: RAND, 2010).
13. Todd Harrison, Zack Cooper, Kaitlyn Johnson, and Thomas G. Roberts, "Escalation and deterrence in the second Space Age," *Center for Strategic and International Studies*, October 3, 2017, https://www.csis.org/analysis/escalation-and-deterrence-second-space-age, 11.

14. Glenn Ritchie (Bloomberg), "Why low-earth orbit satellites are the new space race," *Washington Post*, August 15, 2019, https://www.washingtonpost.com/business/why-low-earth-orbit-satellites-are-the-new-space-race/2019/08/15/6b224bd2-bf72-11e9-a8b0-7ed8a0d5dc5d_story.html.
15. See, for instance, Brandon Davenport and Rich Ganske, "'Recalculating route': A realistic risk assessment for GPS," *War on the Rocks*, March 11, 2019, https://warontherocks.com/2019/03/recalculating-route-a-realistic-risk-assessment-for-gps/.
16. If such satellites acquire military sensors as Glonass is reported to have (see Michael Weiss, "Exclusive: Western intelligence fears new Russian sat-nav's espionage capabilities," *New Lines Magazine*, July 12, 2021, https://newlinesmag.com/reportage/western-intelligence-fears-new-russian-sat-nav-espionage-capabilities/), then such satellites become more legitimate targets for attack.
17. David Majumdar, "How Russia and China would wage war against America: Kill the satellites," *National Interest*, May 14, 2017, https://nationalinterest.org/blog/the-buzz/how-russia-china-would-wage-war-against-america-kill-the-20658.
18. Lydia Leavitt, "NASA confirms satellite hacks in congressional advisory panel," *Engadget*, November 2, 2011, https://www.engadget.com/2011/11/02/nasa-confirms-satellite-hacks-in-congressional-advisory-panel/. See also Brian Barrett, "The Air Force will let hackers try to hijack an orbiting satellite," *Wired*, September 17, 2019, https://www.wired.com/story/air-force-defcon-satellite-hacking/.
19. Patrick Trucker, "The NSA is studying satellite hacking," *Defense One*, September 20, 2019, https://www.defenseone.com/technology/2019/09/nsa-studying-satellite-hacking/160009/.
20. Mary Pat Flaherty, Jason Samenow, and Lisa Rein, "Chinese hack US weather systems, satellite network," *Washington Post*, November 12, 2014, https://www.washingtonpost.com/local/chinese-hack-us-weather-systems-satellite-network/2014/11/12/bef1206a-68e9-11e4-b053-65cea7903f2e_story.html.
21. For a good assessment of the antisatellite capabilities of the major powers, see Brian Weedon and Victoria Samson, "Global counterspace capabilities: An open-source assessment," *Secure World Foundation*, April 2019, https://swfound.org/media/206408/swf_global_counterspace_april2019_web.pdf. The authors see little public evidence that on-orbit or destructive directed-energy weapons are actually in development: e.g., pages x, xiii, 1–2 (China), 2–21 (Russia), 2–24 (Russia), 3–14 (United States).
22. Harrison et al., "Escalation," 4.
23. *Aerospace Corporation*, "A brief history of space debris," November 2, 2022, https://aerospace.org/article/brief-history-space-debris.
24. Harrison et al., "Escalation," 31, citing John J. Klein, "Space warfare: Deterrence, dissuasion and the law of armed conflict," *War on the Rocks*, August 30, 2016, https://warontherocks.com/2016/08/space-warfare-deterrence-dissuasion-and-the-law-of-armed-conflict/; and Bruce W. MacDonald et al., *Crisis Stability in Space: China and Other Challenges* (Washington, DC: Foreign Policy Institute, 2016).
25. Harrison et al., "Escalation," 33.
26. See Brian Chow, "Stalkers in space: Defeating the threat," *Strategic Studies Quarterly*, 11, No. 2 (Summer 2017), https://www.airuniversity.af.edu/Portals/10/SSQ/documents/Volume-11_Issue-2/Chow.pdf, 82–116. Analysts differ on whether such satellites can be considered inherently hostile, with Brian Weeden and Victoria Samson ("Global counterspace capabilities: An open source assessment," *Secure World Foundation*,

April 2020, https://swfound.org/counterspace/) being skeptical and Todd Harrison ("Space Threat Assessment 2020") willing to entertain the notion.
27. Nuclear-powered satellites that may carry enough fuel for defensive maneuvering are still many years away, at best; see *Economist*, "Why space is about to enter its nuclear age," February 5, 2022, https://www.economist.com/science-and-technology/why-space-is-about-to-enter-its-nuclear-age/21807486.
28. See, for instance, the *Economist*, "It will soon be possible to send a satellite to repair another," November 24, 2018, https://www.economist.com/science-and-technology/2018/11/24/it-will-soon-be-possible-to-send-a-satellite-to-repair-another.
29. See, for instance, Ryan Pickrell, "A Russian satellite caught shadowing a US spy satellite earlier this year launched a mysterious space weapon, US Space Command says," *Business Insider*, July 23, 2020, https://www.businessinsider.com/russia-conducts-space-based-anti-satellite-weapons-test-2020-7.
30. See, for instance, Sandra Erwin, "STRATCOM chief Hyten: 'I will not support buying big satellites that make juicy targets,'" *Space News*, November 29, 2017, https://spacenews.com/stratcom-chief-hyten-i-will-not-support-buying-big-satellites-that-make-juicy-targets/.
31. See, for instance, Ellen Pawlikowski, Doug Loverro, and Tom Cristler, "Space disruptive challenges, new opportunities, and new strategies," *Strategic Studies Quarterly*, 7, No. 1 (Spring 2012).
32. Quoting Konstantin Vorontsov (deputy director, Russian foreign ministry), "An extremely dangerous trend [is] . . . the use by the United States and its allies of civilian, including commercial, infrastructure elements in outer space for military purposes, [which] . . . constitute indirect participation in military conflicts. Quasi-civilian infrastructure may become a legitimate target for retaliation." Cited from Eric Berger, "Russia threatens a retaliatory strike against US commercial satellites," *Arstechnica*, October 27, 2022, https://arstechnica.com/science/2022/10/russia-threatens-a-retaliatory-strike-against-us-commercial-satellites/.
33. Harrison et al., "Escalation," 3.
34. Harrison et al., "Escalation," 9.
35. E.g., "But in a fight over Taiwan, America and China would be tempted to attack each other in space, which could lead to nuclear escalation, especially if early-warning and command-and-control satellites were disabled." (*Economist*, "A new era of high tech war has begun," July 6, 2023, https://www.economist.com/leaders/2023/07/06/a-new-era-of-high-tech-war-has-begun).
36. "In a conflict, the United States could respond to an attack on a satellite in another domain of operation. American air, maritime, and land forces could target command and control infrastructure on the ground that supports adversary space systems. This would be escalatory because it would involve destroying facilities located on enemy territory and possibly include loss of life. However, this approach would deny access to space without permanently destroying satellites in orbit." From Aaron Bateman, "America can protect its satellites without kinetic space weapons," *War on the Rocks*, July 30, 2020, https://warontherocks.com/2020/07/america-can-protect-its-satellites-without-kinetic-space-weapons/. Congressman Jim Cooper ("Updating space doctrine: How to avoid World War III," *War on the Rocks*, July 23, 2021, https://warontherocks.com/2021/07/updating-space-doctrine-how-to-avoid-world-war-iii/) wrote similarly, "Even if the prior attack destroyed one of our key satellites . . . retaliating by blowing up a ground station and killing its staff seems disproportionate."

37. "PLA writings thus reflect the belief that offensive cyberspace and counterspace operations are not only advisable early in a conflict with a major adversary, but that such operations can be undertaken at a comparatively low risk of escalation." From Burgess Laird, "War control: Chinese writings on the control of escalation in crisis and conflict," *Center for New American Studies*, April 2017, https://s3.amazonaws.com/files.cnas.org/documents/CNASReport-ChineseDescalation-Final.pdf, 18.
38. Cosmos-2543, a Russian mini-satellite, had been observed tailing a US reconnaissance satellite; from W. J. Hennigan, "Exclusive: Strange Russian spacecraft shadowing US spy satellite, general says," *Time*, February 10, 2010, https://time.com/5779315/russian-spacecraft-spy-satellite-space-force/.
39. The US Space Command demonstrated that if every prerequisite was on hand, it could launch a one-ton rocket with 24 hours' notice; see Eric Berger, "The US military just proved it can get satellites into space super fast: Alpha becomes the first of the US 1-ton rockets to reach its target orbit," *Arstechnica*, September 15, 2023, https://arstechnica.com/space/2023/09/firefly-and-space-force-demonstrate-ability-to-rapidly-launch-a-satellite/.
40. Robert Coalson, "Top Russian general lays bare Putin's plan for Ukraine," *Huffpost*, September 2, 2014, https://www.huffpost.com/entry/valery-gerasimov-putin-ukraine_b_5748480.
41. See, for instance, Courtney Albon, "US Navy, Air Force running 'capstone test' of new high-power microwave missile," *C4ISRNet*, July 1, 2022, https://www.c4isrnet.com/battlefield-tech/2022/07/01/us-navy-air-force-running-capstone-test-of-new-high-power-microwave-missile/.
42. Alex Ward, "11 US troops were injured in Iran's attack. It shows how close we came to war," *Vox*, January 17, 2020, https://www.vox.com/2020/1/17/21070371/11-troops-injured-trump-iran-war.
43. See also Yuna Huh Wong et al., *Deterrence in the Age of Thinking Machines* (Santa Monica, CA: RAND, 2020).
44. See, for instance, Herbert Lin, "Escalation dynamics and conflict termination in cyberspace," *Strategic Studies Quarterly*, 7, No. 3 (Fall 2012), 46–70.
45. So-called nonlethal weapons are designed to hurt, annoy, stun, stymie, or drive away people without causing death or permanent injury. This is a separate category of limited relevance to superpower conflict. For a broader discussion see David Gompert et al., *Underkill* (Santa Monica, CA: RAND, 2009), https://www.rand.org/content/dam/rand/pubs/monographs/2009/RAND_MG848.sum.pdf.
46. *Economist*, "What America has been shooting down in the sky," February 15, 2023, https://www.economist.com/united-states/2023/02/15/what-america-has-been-shooting-down-in-the-sky. According to Flanagan, *Framework of Deterrence*, 39, "Chinese writings have taken the perspective that attacks on enemy space systems are unexceptional, readily controlled, and could be used to avoid or terminate a conventional conflict."

4

Is There a Feasible Local–Global Threshold?

How feasible is any threshold that would mark an escalation from a local to a global conflict? Local conflicts can be characterized by their restricted scope and limited goals, as well as posing little threat to the sovereignty of superpowers and the safety of their civilians. Conversely global conflict has a broader scope and broader goals—as well as greater risk.

Such distinctions, even if clear in the abstract, may be ambiguous and asymmetric. A local conflict for the United States may be more of a general conflict for those, such as China, closer to the action: for example, Korea in 1950, perhaps Taiwan in the 2020s. Conversely the asymmetry disappears if, say, the United States regarded war on its allies as war on itself—in that it is as likely to escalate after some threshold has been crossed (e.g., an attack on civilians) whether it takes place in allied lands or its own homeland.

Accordingly, this chapter explains where to look or not look for such a threshold. It does so by describing first-strike instability that can turn a local conflict into a global one. It then moots a potential homeland-sanctuary threshold.

THE RISKS OF FIRST-STRIKE CONVENTIONAL INSTABILITY

Back in the early Cold War days, first-strike nuclear instability worried strategists. If a preemptive attack on the enemy's nuclear systems was thorough and lucky, the other side's deterrent would be effectively eliminated, forcing capitulation without serious risk of a counterattack.[1] Or the losing side would make concessions for its having the far weaker force when the dust cleared. Even without concessions the side that fired first would still have a very large advantage in warfighting—albeit at great cost if the other side nevertheless retained something to retaliate with.[2] First-strike nuclear instability logic presumed the following things. *One*, each side knew where the other side's weapons lay—which they did at least until the 1960s thanks to air- and space-based reconnaissance. *Two*, such knowledge allowed them to destroy their opponent's arsenal, which was possible because of nuclear weapons. *Three*, each had the reach and the speed to strike first without giving the other side time to react effectively, which they did thanks to long-range bombers and especially missiles. First-strike instability abated over the course of the Cold War primarily through the development of second-strike capabilities and, secondarily, launch-under-attack (LUA) capabilities (whereby the detection of incoming warheads would lead to missiles being launched rather than being destroyed).

First-strike instability, though, rarely characterized potential conventional force engagements, even among the superpowers, during the Cold War (despite the example of Israel's preemptive strike on Egypt's air force in 1967). Conventional weapons platforms, being smaller, mobile, and more numerous, were harder to find. Conventional weapons had neither the warheads nor the requisite precision for a one-shot-one-kill capability. Very-long-range missiles were too expensive to waste on conventional targets.

Today none of these factors hold, reviving the specter of first-strike instability. Tremendous investments in near-real-time ISR, especially from space, have brought more of the world's conventional capabilities into precise geospatial focus. The locations of almost all fixed facilities and many mobile targets are already known with considerable accuracy. Precision munitions can strike any well-located target close enough to achieve a one-hit kill. And while ICBMs are still expensive, cruise missiles and drones are not; if their launch platforms (e.g., stealth bombers) are within several hundred kilometers of the target, the requisite munitions, being of shorter range, are even more affordable. "Sensors, global positioning, weapon guidance, digital networking, and other capabilities used to target opposing forces have advanced to the point where both US and Chinese military forces pose serious threats to each other. This creates the ability and a reason to strike enemy forces before they strike one's own, which is bound to influence both nations' war planning."[3]

Many believe that modern conventional war—or at least its heavy-weapons phase—will be quick. Speed, in turn, will reward fast starts or rapid escalation. Michele Fluornoy, President Obama's undersecretary of defense for policy, has written, "For example, if the U.S. military had the capability to credibly threaten to sink all of China's military vessels, submarines, and merchant ships in the South China Sea within 72 hours, Chinese leaders might think twice before, say, launching a blockade or invasion of Taiwan; they would have to wonder whether it was worth putting their entire fleet at risk."[4] Susanna Blume and Molly Parrish argued more generally, "To prevail in the kinds of anti-access environments that China, and to a lesser extent Russia, have created in their peripheries, the U.S. military must be able to close thousands of kill chains in tens of hours in highly contested environments."[5] And for China, James S. Johnson writes,[6]

> Chinese military doctrinal emphasis on preemptive strike tactics may hasten the decision of defense planners to employ ASMs [anti-ship missiles] during a regional crisis or conflict to seize the early initiative, sustain China's military dominance, and preserve the credibility of China's strategic deterrence. Moreover, given that U.S. countermeasures to A2/AD have also been calibrated to strike early and preemptively against Chinese military targets (especially against Chinese C^{4}ISR systems), the proclivity of Chinese strategists to view ASMs as indispensable asymmetric tools for strategic deterrence missions will likely increase.

Military technology and planning create a bias toward sharp exchange of strikes from the start, with both sides intent on gaining the upper hand. This can create first-strike *conventional* instability among the three superpowers—particularly at sea,[7] where surface assets lack cover and concealment.

On a day-to-day basis, the likelihood of any superpower launching an unprovoked conventional strike upon the other is slim. None threatens each other's existence. Conventional war is bloody and costly. Any war among nuclear powers risks escalating to the nuclear level. But when a local conflict or confrontation erupts, risks shift. After what point would a rational leader conclude that while going first would guarantee escalation, failing to go first would guarantee defeat—and then rationalize that enlarged conflict was inevitable anyway, especially if the other side was thinking similarly? If so, small wars may be hard to keep below any small-war/large-war threshold.

PRECISION WARFARE

But is conventional first-strike instability a valid fear?

This question is explored in two parts. The first reviews the technology of precision warfare against conventional targets (nuclear targets are discussed in the next chapter). The second examines the incentives created by such technologies.

A conventional conflict between two high-technology forces would illustrate a decades-long shift from force-on-force engagements to hunting-and-hiding ones.[8] In a sense, the era started with NATO's 1970s-era challenge of defeating 50,000 Warsaw Pact tanks without using nuclear weapons. This motivated the US development of a warfighting complex that used space-based and airborne sensors to see armor approaching the inter-German border, long range air power to approach the tanks, and precision weapons (such as the Hellfire and Maverick missiles) to kill them hundreds of miles behind the front line. Since then, the ability to see, the ability to reach, and the ability to strike have only improved, substantially in the case of US forces, and even faster (for their coming up from behind) for Chinese and Russian forces (notwithstanding the latter's performance against Ukraine). In the first Gulf War, a hundred hours of land conflict sufficed to drive Iraqi forces from Kuwait because they were preceded by seven weeks of air strikes. Such strikes destroyed the equipment and eroded the morale of Iraqi forces to where even Iraq's elite divisions were rendered militarily ineffective. The second Gulf War was a more efficient repeat.

The technology of hunting appears to be gaining on the technology of hiding, even in the face of tricks such as operational security and military deception. "Warfare is increasingly 'a competition between hiding and finding', noted Britain's chief of defence staff in September. The ability to find has advanced considerably. Satellites and drones gaze down, antennae-laden soldiers and vehicles hoover up electronic emissions, and amateur plane-spotters track military movements on social media."[9]

Hunting—a combination of seeking and killing—is enabled by information collection and distribution. Doing it well entails manned assets and sensors, such as UAVs and cyberespionage implants, to collect information; networks to amalgamate it; data mining and fusion to analyze it; increasingly-capable machine learning to draw inferences from it; and precision weaponry with requisite range to take advantage of it. Assisting this process are sensors in multiple domains using technologies (e.g., optical, infrared, radar, acoustic) with ever-increasing acuity, hosted on platforms that can loiter for long periods and that can relay data quickly and in bulk.[10]

UAVs exemplify the new information-collection environment thanks to advances in their navigation, guidance, and digital photography. Good software means that they can fly autonomously. Such aircraft need not attain a minimum size to hold a person. Without someone's life to defend, the need for self-defense systems in an aircraft also falls sharply. Corresponding declines in cost and weight allow for smaller airframes and less powerful engines, adding further to savings. Satellite trends are similar: the ability to cram more intelligence and signal processing power into smaller packages has led to a potential profusion in the number of surveillance satellites even before the cost of getting a kilogram of stuff into LEO fell from roughly $15,000 to closer to $2,000.[11]

The world is not yet at the point where all military assets can be found and correctly characterized. But it is getting closer.

The vulnerability of surface ships has increased greatly over the last few decades as the 2022 destruction of the Russian flagship *Moskva* dramatically illustrated. Ships have little place to hide, stand out from their background (water), and are rarely stealthy (only the United States owns low-observable ships and only a few of them). Surface ships can practice emissions control (EMCON) to avoid sensors that track electronic signatures, but with every passing year they grow more dependent on the networking they would then have to forgo to evade detection. Antiship weapons are proliferating. Ukrainians have made innovative and effective use of uncrewed sea-surface vehicles. It is hard to see many hostile surface ships surviving very long against a determined US strategy—much as German surface ships did not survive oceangoing for very long in World War I and World War II. Similarly, the consequences to US Navy ships of a determined Russian and Chinese strategy are growing daily more dire, with standing farther back (from enemy aircraft or cruise missiles) becoming the least unreliable defense. To many, the safety of US ships operating near China or Russia would rely on being able to first degrade their sensor-and-engagement systems. But that would still leave them visible until such a campaign nears completion.

Trends toward greater visibility have affected submarine-hunting only in evolutionary ways[12] in part because hunting and hiding has been the leitmotif of undersea warfare from its pre–World War I origins. This created a long history of measures and countermeasures. Furthermore, making information technology work in the water is more expensive than doing so on land. Salt water is a tough environment for electronics. Freestanding sensors need careful battery management. Long-distance communications from submarines, for the most part, are carried out by satellite, very-low-frequency means, or not at all. Despite growing scientific interest in looking beneath the high seas, notably to understand climate change, commercial interest in doing so is modest; finding seabed mineral deposits does not necessarily mean that mining them pays off. Thus, the potential for sensor networks that are illuminating the man-made world is unlikely to extend to the high seas without a deliberate military attempt to do so. Correspondingly, advantages held by US submarines should persist if carefully tended. A Russian or a Chinese attrition strategy against US submarines is likely to proceed slowly—and the assets required to prosecute such a strategy are, in turn, vulnerable to US counterstrikes. A US attrition strategy against open-ocean Russian and Chinese submarines might well succeed, but hardly instantly, and not necessarily even faster than what might have been true during the heyday of the 1980s US maritime strategy.

Aircraft have three levels of vulnerability. They are easy to target but hard to find when airborne, particularly if stealthy or operating farther back. They are easy to hit and find when on runways. They are hard to hit, even if easy to find, if sheltered in sturdy bunkers. An attrition campaign against aircraft in the air but over friendly territory is feasible but also costly as it usually requires the aggressive use of the hunter's own air power. At a minimum the targeted aircraft may hunker down. A campaign that waits until an aircraft is back on the runway but before heading into shelter requires a great deal of staring and the near-instant exploitation of a very short window of opportunity.

Campaigns against most ground warfare assets are somewhat more difficult than against floating or flying assets because such assets can be hidden or at least disguised amongst man-made and natural clutter. What cannot be hidden can be entrenched or even buried in shelters and tunnels, which hinders both searching and killing. Many military assets—most notoriously unarmored but armed vehicles (such as the "technicals" in Somalia) look civilian from a distance. But other military assets—tanks, helicopters, artillery, and missile batteries—look nothing like their civilian counterparts.

Above-ground facilities are easy to target (they do not move) and hard to protect (steel reinforced concrete makes for a hard structure but, as pictures from Syria prove, not an invulnerable one). Burying facilities can be expensive and still provide no guarantee against bunker-busting bombs. Disguising them as civilian facilities can inhibit attacks on them but brings defenders into war crimes territory.

AI (artificial intelligence) *qua* machine learning can help hunting as sensor systems are trained to recognize patterns of adversary assets, such as mobile missiles, by learning from huge data sets.[13] But predictions are iffy. Machine learning requires matching the data (e.g., imagery) to what it indicates (e.g., a mobile missile). With faces and speech, the data are out there, often on the Web, and humans can classify it using natural intelligence. But with enemy assets, the data are not out there, and there may be little confirmation on whether something was characterized correctly. The enemy has every incentive even in peacetime to use cover, camouflage, and deception to foil such classification. Learning may therefore be slow and sometimes misleading. Training software on one's own assets may be used as a substitute—but the other sides' systems may not look like one's own systems. Their tactics, techniques, and procedures (TTPs) may also differ. If those TTPs are key to recognition, the AI may be misled. AI can be brittle; poor characterizations that are not corrected will recur indefinitely. Modest changes in an image can lead machines to make big errors in classification: buses have been subtly manipulated to register as ostriches, and turtles as rifles.[14] If an agile adversary can find instances in which its own equipment inexplicably drew no or the wrong reaction (or if it uses cyberespionage to steal the algorithms directly), it can present the AI edge cases to fool it. To wit, AI can be hacked.

So while hunting is getting better, it is a long way from perfect.

US over-optimism about the ability to strike and kill targets from stand-off goes back to interwar and World War II–era promises[15] about the precision and efficacy of strategic bombing. Proponents of the Vietnam War's Operation Igloo White believed that the vigorous use of sensors could detect, locate, and hence quash the smuggling of men, machines, and supplies southward along the Ho Chi Minh trail. It did not.[16] During the 1991 Gulf War, the United States "launched about 1,500 sorties against Scud launchers ... not a single mobile launcher was confirmed destroyed."[17] NATO operations against Serbian tanks, which seemed productive during the 1999 campaign over Kosovo, looked less so in postwar analyses: "NATO analysts were unable to confirm the destruction of a single VJ [Serbian Army] tank or military vehicle, owing to the success of enemy ground units at dispersing and concealing their armor. That disappointment underscored the limits of conducting air operations against dispersed and hidden enemy troops in conditions in which weather, terrain, and tactics all favored the enemy and where no friendly ground combat presence was on hand to compel those forces to concentrate and expose themselves."[18] Although Israel was able to use ISR and precision strike in its 2006 war in southern Lebanon to knock out roughly three out of the four mobile missile launchers, doing so had little impact on the number of missiles that hit Israel, in part because most launchers were not meant to be reused.[19]

Threats to strike platforms can widen the disconnect between seeing and killing a target. US forces operating against Iraq and Serbia worked in a lightly contested environment. They could approach close enough to their target to ensure short and secure flight-times for the weapons. Superpowers have tougher defenses, though. As a result, missile-launching platforms (aircraft but also ships) must work from farther away, and even subsonic nonstealthy cruise missiles risk being intercepted. The war in Ukraine has demonstrated that even supersonic cruise missiles can be shot down, particularly if they are aimed at a predictable point target (e.g., to take out an air defense missile launcher).[20]

The longer the flight time of the weapon, the harder it is to strike a target that is exposed only for brief periods of time. This may explain some of the enthusiasm for hypersonic missiles, which can not only give targets less time to flee and hide but may defeat terminal defenses. Reaching from farther away permits attacking a target without putting missile platforms in so much danger.[21] Clearly, having hypersonic *cruise* missiles makes the success of a *conventional* bolt-from-the-gray strategy more likely, but how much more likely depends on several factors, not least being how many will be afforded, given their expected price tags (currently tens of millions of dollars each).

Nevertheless, mutually hostile superpowers are increasingly capable of keeping their adversaries' assets under continuous long-run surveillance. The greater the odds of a general war, the greater the incentive to prosecute as many sightings as possible preemptively. Local wars increase the odds of a general war. The fear of going second makes one even more likely. Any threshold between local and global wars thus could be unstable.

NEED COUNTRIES PANIC INTO ESCALATION WHEN SHOTS ARE FIRED?

Not necessarily.

All three superpowers are geographically extensive to the point where a large share of their military assets lies beyond easy reach. Wide oceans coupled with naval superiority give the United States the most depth. Russia is next by dint of its size. Even China can keep assets thousands of miles from US strike forces. The big exception is naval forces, which must be ocean-accessible to be useful.[22] The best any country can do with a first conventional strike is to eliminate assets that are deployed at or near the equivalent of front lines—which can buy itself a few weeks before the other side brings its untouched assets forward. Even if all conventional assets are within reach of the other side's very long-range missiles, such missiles (e.g., ICBMs) are scarce: America's and Russia's numbers are limited by the NEW START treaty, and China only has a few hundred, so far. And like hypersonic missiles, they are costly in comparison to many of their targets.

The US motivation for preemption when it can look forward to ultimately prevailing in a conventional war would be a narrow one. The notion that it would squelch the possibility of a general war (especially one that might go nuclear) runs into the problem that superpowers suddenly on their back foot may overreact. It is not as if US allies will be pushing for pre-emption; they are warier of war because they have less power of their own and sit closer to either Russia or China. Conversely, for Russia or China to attack first must presume the United States can be persuaded to quit early—but then see the persistence of the US commitment after Pearl Harbor and 9/11. Attacks that land on US bases in South Korea or Japan are also more likely to pull the latter into armed conflict regardless of how it started—and further reduce the odds that a preemptive attack will, in fact, preempt rather spur conflict.

Lastly the balance of conventional forces among superpowers is important but not existential. A country stripped of the ability to defend itself with conventional arms can nevertheless protect its existence and sovereignty with nuclear threats. By contrast World War I's rush to mobilize reflected the use of forces at the top of 1914's escalation ladder. Ditto, of course, for Cold War nuclear forces. Granted, a country disarmed of conventional power and forced to fall back on its nuclear capabilities faces a dismal choice between surrender or threatening mutual suicide. Winners have more attractive options. Even in the earlier outer-space scenario the prospect facing Japan was not that Japan would be occupied, become a Chinese puppet, or even see its citizens suffer much—just that it would be neutralized.

Any global conflict that escalated from a local one would not, by definition, be a bolt from the blue. The major powers all have intelligence services and run sensors (e.g., on satellites) that were unavailable to, say, the United States circa Pearl Harbor. Prior to Russia's invasion of Ukraine, for instance, the United States had not only detected its preparations but broadcast its likelihood. Once even a small crisis or confrontation starts, the other side is unlikely to be naïve, hence surprised. One side's mobilization for a crisis far broader in scope (e.g., to conduct a broad antiaccess area denial campaign) than the initial source of tensions (e.g., the status of islands in the South China Sea) may well be detected. It could thus spark parallel preparations by the other side. Carrying out a first strike against mobile or at least moveable targets, however, requires being able to track them precisely and continuously. Nontrespassing sensors—such as satellites, seismic or acoustic detectors, and submarines—can do this without acting in ways that set off alarms. But using air-based assets, surface ships, proliferated ground-based sensors, and perhaps even cyberespionage to augment what comes from distant sensors would be more noticeable and may well trigger suspicion by the other side—leaving it a less naïve target.

For small conflicts of the sort to presage a large conflict, such warning could make a real difference by reducing the odds of a successful attacks. Land assets can be hidden; aircraft can be moved to the rear or launched; and ships and submarines can steam out to sea. Network penetration in peacetime would be more likely to work than if attempted only after target systems have tightened up security in the face of war. Electronic equipment can use war reserve modes in the face of potential electronic warfare. That noted, buildings and runways cannot up and move, nor can ports where ships and submarines would sit. Moving assets to shelter would make them safer but harder to use.[23] Pulling back one's own forces would also make *executing* a first strike more difficult. This may reduce the other side's fears of falling victim to a first strike and, with it, some of its motive to preempt with its own first strike. Greater attention to the arts of operational security, military deception, electronic warfare, and even cyberattack would also complicate the other side's hunting. Of comparable importance, the other side's confidence that it is seeing what it should see would be reduced, perhaps to where it doubts that a first strike can succeed.

A variant of a first-strike strategy is to focus on the other side's sensors in the hope that quickly disabling them would disarm the other side's ability to execute its own first strike without itself generating a large war. It helps that many sensors are unmanned or lightly manned; many can be destroyed without the other side necessarily escalating into lethal operations. Sensors that are fixed (e.g., over-the-horizon radar), on predictable paths (notably satellites), or not easily maneuverable (e.g., wide-bodied aircraft, large UAVs, balloons) are easier to target. Shipboard sensors (e.g., Aegis systems) may be an important exception. Mass destruction of such sensors may not necessarily return one's own platforms to obscurity. Surviving sensors may include those mounted on maneuverable or stealthy platforms, those too well-hidden to find or too widely distributed to target efficiently, and seekers that are part of weapons themselves. People (especially if outfitted with electronics) are also sensors. Circumstances and the character of both side's leaders would influence whether such a campaign would represent a satisfactory middle ground between doing nothing—and chancing a bolt from the gray—and throwing such a bolt itself. And, of course, the other side would determine if such a half-strike would lead to a half-strike or a full-strike back.

On net, if the ambiguity and imprecision associated with creating a threshold between a small and a large war were not discouraging enough, fears of preemption add potential for escalation over and above any motives associated with prevailing in a small conflict. Escalation is not inevitable but likely enough to frustrate maintaining a local–global conflict threshold in crises where one is most needed.

COULD THERE BE A HOMELAND THRESHOLD?

The need for a homeland threshold among superpowers may reflect the ability to do with conventional warfare what previously required strategic nuclear warfare. After 1945 destroying cities and national infrastructures has been considered the job of strategic *nuclear* operations. But precision allows conventional operations to effectively turn cities off without escalating to nuclear weapons and mass casualties. When used against well-identified nodes in infrastructures (e.g., power grids, pipelines, telecommunications networks, and transportation systems) what used to take huge fleets of bombers now takes a volley of missiles. Infrastructures themselves are increasingly important to the economic life of economically advanced civilizations, even Russia and China. The Internet is a prime example, one absent 50 years ago. So is the electric grid, which although having been around for over a hundred years, grows more vital with every electronic device. In August 2003 a one-day blackout affecting fifty million people in North America cost roughly $5 to $10 billion of lost GDP, essentially by eliminating most income-producing activities in the affected areas.[24] A blackout that would last until new equipment were installed to replace damaged equipment could wipe away most of a modern economy's income in the interim. And although transportation systems and other energy networks (e.g., natural gas) are also nearly a century old, today's logistics practices, notably just-in-time manufacturing, have exacerbated the disruptive effect of taking them out. A strategic bombing campaign using precision weapons against a well-wired city can reduce its income far more effectively than a similar effort using the same quantity of dumb bombs against a less-well-wired city.

Russia's attacks on Ukrainian cities may exemplify what it calls a campaign of special operations to destroy critical infrastructure targets (SODCIT). Early in the war Russia attacked Ukrainian cities primarily to instill terror and encourage refugee flows. After the partial destruction of the Kerch bridge on October 8, 2022, and simultaneous appointment of General Sergei Surovikin as commander of Russian forces in Ukraine, Russia embarked on a more systematic campaign against Ukrainian infrastructure. The electrical grid was the first goal, with substations (rather than the larger and better-hardened power stations) being the primary target. The density of its electrical grid allowed Ukraine to restore power expeditiously at first, but the pace of recovery waxed and waned.[25] Later the Russians added Kyiv's water supply to their list of infrastructure goals.[26] As World War II should have taught, Ukraine did not buckle under Russia's campaign, even if it prompted evacuations (e.g., from Kherson, where nearly all infrastructure was destroyed). By the springtime, services were largely restored. Neither the 2022–2023 campaign nor the 2023–2024 campaigns made a strong case for the efficacy of conventional strategic attack. But such attacks continue.

The more persuasively conventional attacks can damage a developed economy, the stronger the argument for small yet advanced states to invest in conventional deterrence rather than solely in defense. Rather than focusing entirely on a "porcupine defense," Taiwan may be thinking about a strategy of strategic, albeit non-nuclear, warfare against Chinese cities as a deterrent strategy.[27] Perhaps Taiwan assumes that China is going to do similarly to Taiwan—and so executing its own strategy would not be escalatory. But would (a nuclear-armed) China regard it that way? Similarly a desire to hold a nation's infrastructure at risk might explain why Iran's president-elect declared that while he was willing to sign away Iran's nuclear program, there would be no such concession involving the country's increasingly accurate ballistic missiles.[28]

Conventional strategic warfare among the superpowers would be asymmetric, thanks again to differences in geography, alliances, and the reach of each side's weapons systems. Oceans and allies mean that the United States can keep enemies from striking the homeland with many conventional weapons. The most Russia or China could threaten (Alaska and Hawaii aside) would be a few cruise missiles[29] into coastal US cities (e.g., naval bases in San Diego, Honolulu, and Bangor, Washington, as well as Vandenberg Air Force Base's space launch facilities). Even *that* would require being able to maintain submarines within cruise-missile range of the US coastline, no small feat (unless hostile countries such as Cuba or Venezuela host Russian or Chinese force elements[30]). The DoD fears, however, that China is developing conventionally armed ICBMs.[31] By contrast the ability of the United States to start from its allies' territory or, lacking that, to project power from the sea makes it far easier for the United States to strike Russia and China. The US strategy against China's area-denial/antiaccess strategy putatively calls for attacks on China's ports, air bases, missiles, and command centers[32]—all in China's homeland. The US strategy against Russia's threat to its neighbors assumes operations against air defenses systems that would, at least initially, sit within Russia itself. Thus, any homeland threshold favors Russia or China vis-à-vis the United States.

This makes it unlikely that the United States would adhere to, much less advocate, any threshold associated with refraining from hitting the other side's homeland. Conversely, if the United States *did* treat homeland attacks as crossing a threshold, hence forbidden, it is hard to imagine Russia or China not wanting to declare likewise.[33]

One analyst[34] argued that the United States can complicate the other side's targeting choices by placing its conventional C⁴ISR assets in the lower forty-eight states, thereby forcing them to attack the rest of the US homeland if they want to reduce US information superiority. Given their difficulty in physically reaching the US homeland, they may be tempted to go for cyberattacks on the US homeland to seek similar effects. If these worked, would it be in the US interest to indicate that a cyberattack on a homeland facility is tantamount to a kinetic attack on it (even if it is hard to tell where a virtual system physically sits)? Such a question further highlights why the United States may lack interest in a homeland threshold.

When allies in Europe or Asia—which *are* more easily reached by Russian or Chinese precision weapons—are included, though, a quasi-homeland threshold could be more symmetric. Whether such a threshold would enjoy US support may depend on how it regards Russian or Chinese threats to attack US allies in retaliation for US attacks on their homelands. On the one hand the United States is pledged to defend its allies, and kinetic attacks on them would raise expectations that the United States would strive to disarm Russia's or China's ability to carry out such attacks and perhaps also attack back in kind. The more the United States cares about its allies—or the more that allies object to a homeland threshold that differentiates their cities from United States cities—the greater the credibility of any threat to hit back. But it may be hard to persuade either friend or foe that the United States cares as much about those on allied homelands as it does on its own. During the Berlin crises of 1958–61, the US officials could contemplate taking out all Soviet nuclear delivery systems capable of hitting the United States. That such actions would leave the Soviet Union with the much larger inventory of weapons that could hit European cities did not seem to affect how US officials hoped to stare down or, if they had to, preemptively knock down long-range Soviet nuclear weapons.[35] The less the United States cares about what happens to allied economies, the less Russia could coerce the United States by putting European cities at risk (ditto for China and Asian cities).

To what extent would Russia or China make credible *nuclear* threats to ward off *conventional* attacks on their territory? A threshold that deems civilian targets off-limits (per LOAC) to forestall such a reaction crumbles at the fuzzy border between dual-use and civilian targets. And accidents are likely from errors in intelligence and aiming. Declarations made after the homeland has been struck—thus far but no farther—may look desperate and thus lack credibility, especially if earlier homeland attacks drew no disproportionate response. Although Russia complained that Ukrainian attacks on its homeland were an act of escalation, no obvious counterescalation resulted.

Russia and China may threaten tactical rather than strategic nuclear weapons in response to a homeland violation. Because the tactical nuclear weapons would not fall on the United States but on its allies' homeland(s), they may calculate that the United States would hesitate before responding with anything that raises the probability of all-out nuclear war. But Russia and China would know that such a strike raises the same risks for them. If the threat does not deter, the credibility reserved for future threats diminishes.

China relies less on drawing explicit red lines than on conveying that a particular situation has become intolerable.[36] But such signals are easily misread—otherwise the United States would have anticipated China's entry into northern Korea in late 1950. A version of that signaling may be for China (or Russia) to indicate that if its population becomes sufficiently enraged because of being struck, its leaders would not be able to resist demands to retaliate against the US homeland, even with nuclear weapons. Such a threat could provide a plausible basis for near-suicidal threats not otherwise credible. But such a threat is more believable coming from a democratic society whose narrative emphasizes popular rule rather than an autocratic society whose narrative emphasizes wise central leadership.

Decisions by the United States to strike an adversary's homeland require determining what red lines they are trying to establish and how credible the associated threats are (especially when encoded as signals and subtexts). Can, for instance, the United States signal to China that using assets in its homeland to support warfighting directly removes such assets from sanctuary status? If so what kind of assets would qualify as eligible targets: weapons only? including C^4ISR? including logistics? If the needs of war preclude the United States from promising not to hit the Chinese homeland, can a lesser threshold—to avoid hitting critical infrastructure—be a more credible promise? Any definition of critical infrastructure—particularly one that allows attacks on infrastructures (e.g., ports) that directly support China's war effort—may be hard to define; conformance may be harder to ascertain.

As a rule, any potential homeland target can be evaluated by, first, the extent to which its destruction adds to the fight and, second, the extent to which the other side has a neuralgic overreaction to its destruction. High-gain low-neuralgia-risk homeland targets would be attractive targets; the opposite quadrant would be avoided. But if the two metrics are correlated—a target is sensitive to the other side to the degree that its destruction affects the military balance—then there are no good trade-offs. Nevertheless, some targets may be particularly sensitive if freighted with symbolism or key to regime survival. And while these are the very targets whose sensitivity makes them ideal to hold at risk for deterrence and coercive purposes, it also makes them the worst targets if the goal is to modulate the other side's escalation while pursuing military victory.

WHAT IS A LOCAL FIGHT TO A SUPERPOWER MAY BE EXISTENTIAL TO ITS FRIENDS

Wars in which one or more superpowers help one side may be considered local by the superpower and existential, and thus tantamount to global, for those at war. This, too, can complicate the observation of thresholds, whether or not there is a superpower on the other side. When one superpower is directly involved, the other one may for that reason hold off. The United States pretended that the "North Korean" pilots it faced were not, in fact, from the Soviet Union when as many as 90 percent of them were.[37] The possibility that US strikes on North Vietnam's SAM sites may have generated Russian or Chinese casualties was also downplayed. In 2018 the war in Syria featured an intense firefight between US commandos and Russian "mercenaries."[38] But the latter's not being official forces gave Russia an excuse for not escalating in response. Nevertheless if interventions in other country's wars become more common among superpowers,[39] associated escalation paths need to be explored. In a stereotypical conflict in which the local combatant is less militarily capable than its superpower friend, the ability of the former to escalate beyond the latter's comfort zone would run out when the local combatant has no escalation options but the superpower still does.

Proxy conflicts have two characteristics of note: high levels of asymmetry and at least one escalation path that does not necessarily entail overall greater conflict intensity.

Asymmetries can arise even if both superpowers avoid direct participation in the fighting. Differences such as material endowments, the stakes, and strategies between the two local combatants exacerbate asymmetries already present between the superpowers. Another asymmetry arises if only one side is a coalition (e.g., Egypt and Syria in the October 1973 war). Although conflict generally takes place where the local combatants are (rather than where superpowers collide), battle may be close to one superpower and far from another—who may therefore be more sensitive to interference with its supply lines. Lastly the relationship between the local combatant and the superpowers may be unequal: one side may welcome the superpower's troops on its soil, and the other may prefer all its help be in the form of materiel.

Superpowers and local allies will have different stakes in the conflict, leading to different trade-offs in what and how hard to push. In a Taiwan fight, the United States might want to avoid strikes on China's dual-use infrastructure in tacit return for China's doing likewise within the United States. But Taiwan, whose infrastructure may well be shredded by China, might find China's infrastructure fair game. Would China then still respect any such arrangement with the United States, or would it instead see Taiwan as America's cat's paw—using US armaments and intelligence support to do what the United States is technically not doing? Conversely Taiwan's actions could be used to test China's red lines. If China pushes back hard enough, the United States can disavow direct responsibility.

LARGE WARS ARE NOT JUST LARGE VERSIONS OF SMALL WARS

Prospects for establishing a threshold between small localized conflicts and large general wars are weakened whenever there is no marked difference between the two. Inherent in the phrases "small localized" and "large general" is whether intensity or breadth defines the threshold—another example of points on a lattice rather than a ladder. The possibility that the United States may be better off responding to a Chinese attack on Taiwan not by a local defense but a global economic blockade[40] (particularly of oil and other resource inputs) suggests a US interest in *not* recognizing a simple small–large threshold. Indeed one analyst[41] argues that "Distant naval blockades preserve two key escalation thresholds: the nuclear threshold and the homeland sanctuary. They avoid the use of nuclear weapons. They also avoid threatening an adversary's nuclear retaliatory capability advertently or inadvertently in a way that could trigger nuclear escalation. Blockades do not violate the homeland sanctuary. They avoid attacks that could signal an expansion in conflict aims to completely defeat the adversary, conquer it, and impose regime change."

Keeping a war local is hard (even setting blockades aside). In a fight over Taiwan, the United States, for instance, would have to judge which Chinese-based assets are eligible targets. Could it discriminate between warships and warplanes that *could* become involved in fighting from those that *were*, in fact, involved? What about C^{4}ISR assets? What about logistics assets? Would cyberattacks on these assets be judged by the same standard that kinetic attacks are? Could the United States maintain that it was not expanding the conflict if such cyberattacks jeopardize some of China's infrastructure? Would the Chinese—whose cyberattacks can reach as far as US cyberattacks can—see things likewise? Even if attacking US military assets in Guam that support the fight over Taiwan crossed no local–global threshold, attacking

US bases in Japan and South Korea would clearly broaden the conflict. At what point would US military goals shift away from a local reckoning over Taiwan and toward a global reckoning with China? Antisatellite operations could provide another crossover between local and global conflict. The United States depends on GEO satellites for trans-Pacific military communications. The Chinese depend on other GEO satellites for ocean surveillance. GEO satellites (whose footprints can easily cover a third of the globe) are deemed regional assets, but LEO and MEO satellites clearly fly global orbits.

But if there is no first-order threshold between small and large wars, there are several second-order thresholds. They involve commerce, space, and nuclear issues.

Start with commerce. Two superpowers can support opposite sides in a proxy fight or engage in a limited confrontation and yet both participate in world commerce (even if direct trade between the two falls sharply). Third parties, even allies, may not be persuaded to abandon otherwise large markets (India, a Quad partner of the United States, still buys oil and weapons from Russia). But with more general conflict such pressures will increase to where third parties will have difficulties trading with both. From, say, China's view a US "request" that neutral countries stop trading with China may cross a threshold. A blockade *forcibly* stops trade with third parties; its imposition would cross an even more widely recognized threshold. Granted, a country that is already autarkic (e.g., the old Soviet Union, today's North Korea) will be harmed less than one dependent on world trade (e.g., China) and, correspondingly, may make less of a deal about the other side's trade-war escalation except as a *post hoc* justification for crossing unrelated thresholds. In a general war, though, attacks on the homeland may be used to reinforce an embargo (e.g., destroying oil pipelines), hobble industrial mobilization, or devastate rear-area military bases.

A large war is also far more likely than a small war to see satellites disabled—as distinct from being jammed, dazzled, or hacked. Antisatellite operations, as noted, touch nuclear issues; many nuclear command-and-control as well as early warning assets (NC3/EW) are in orbit. But even if a conflict limited to antisatellite operations lies below a lethality threshold, the introduction of antisatellite operations into terrestrial lethal conflict may be viewed as crossing a threshold.

A large war among nuclear powers is likely to feature the risk of Armageddon as a dark cloud overhead rather than one off on the horizon. An incremental rise in the odds of Armageddon is inherently not a threshold event (except if defined arbitrarily). But the shift between "it cannot be ruled out" to "we need to plan for its happening" might be. The latter may include a shift of nuclear assets from bunkered to operational stations, raised alert levels (e.g., US DEFCONs), higher operational tempos for nuclear-capable aircraft, and the redeployment of theater missile defense assets, such as Aegis ships with loadouts of antiballistic (SM-3) missiles. Most actions that make nuclear weapons (or antinuclear weapons) more usable raise the odds of accidents, inadvertent attacks, and misinterpretations (e.g., exaggerated expectations of being attacked).

CONCLUSIONS

There may no longer be any such thing as a small war among great powers. Everyone can both see and strike farther. Distance makes no difference to cyberspace operations. A small crisis or conflict among superpowers *could* create fears that feed on themselves and build to a large war. As one side sees the odds of a more general conflict rising, it may accelerate its hunt for enemy assets, the better to take them out quickly if tasked. The decision would reflect the harm from escalating a war when a larger war was not a certain prospect versus the cost of going second if war ensues—the odds of which would depend in part on similar calculations by the other side. The growth of ISR and long-range precision strike could convert escalation into a self-fulfilling prophecy, echoing, albeit less catastrophically, the classic first-strike nuclear dilemma of the Cold War. First strike instability is a function of weapons precision and ISR on one side, and consequent platform vulnerability on the other. It also requires that both sides have such a capability: if one does and the other does not, the first need not escalate out of fear, and the second cannot escalate even if afraid.

No homeland threshold employed as a barrier between local and global conflict can be counted on. Excluding US allies, it is highly asymmetric. There is very little in it for the United States, which is too hard to hit in quantity with conventional weapons. And because the distinctions rest on multiple criteria, it is unclear which one matters. It may also be difficult to discourage a country from nuclear escalation after its homeland has been struck by conventional weapons that take out critical infrastructures.

NOTES

1. See Daryl Press, *Calculating Credibility: How Leaders Assess Military Threats* (Ithaca, NY: Cornell, 2005), 80–116.

2. See, for instance, Albert Wohlstetter, "The delicate balance of terror," *Foreign Affairs*, 37, No. 2 (January 1959), 211–234. For the 1970s argument see Paul Nitze, "Assuring strategic stability in an era of détente," *Foreign Affairs*, 54, No. 1 (January 1976) as well as Report of Team B, "Intelligence community experiment in competitive analysis," December 1976, https://www.cia.gov/library/readingroom/docs/LOC-HAK-545-28-1-5.pdf.
3. David C. Gompert, Astrid Stuth Cevallos, and Cristina L. Garafola, *War with China: Thinking through the Unthinkable* (Santa Monica, CA: RAND, 2016), 2–3.
4. Michele Fluornoy, "How to prevent a war in Asia: The erosion of American deterrence raises the risk of Chinese miscalculation," *Foreign Affairs*, 98, No. 3 (May/June 2020).
5. Susanna Blume and Molly Parrish, "Investing in great-power competition," *Center for Naval Analyses*, July 9, 2020, https://www.cnas.org/publications/reports/investing-in-great-power-competition.
6. James S. Johnson "China's 'Guam Express' and 'carrier killers': The anti-ship asymmetric challenge to the U.S. in the Western Pacific," *Comparative Strategy*, 36, No. 4, 319–33.
7. "[Thibault] Lavernhe and [François-Olivier] Corman [authors of Vaincre en mer au XXIe siècle: La tactique au cinquième âge du combat naval] develop an insight that seems self-evident but bears reflection: in naval warfare the clear advantage goes to the side that fires first (assuming they hit their target) because those first hits will likely be decisive. Indeed, that is a if not the primary objective of ships at war: scoring a knockout blow with the first strike. This has become more pertinent with modern warships and modern anti-ship weapons." Michael Shurkin, "Plus ça change: a French approach to naval warfare in the 21st century," *War on the Rocks*, October 13, 2023, https://warontherocks.com/2023/10/plus-ca-change-a-french-approach-to-naval-warfare-in-the-21st-century/. See also Stephen Biddle & John Severini, "Military Effectiveness and Naval Warfare," *Security Studies*, 33, 3 (published online: 08 Aug 2024), 325–347.
8. The theory of hunting and hiding preceded such technology. See, for instance, Amron Katz, *Hiders and Finders: An Approach to Inspection and Evasion Technology* (Santa Monica, CA: RAND, 1961), https://www.rand.org/pubs/papers/P2432.html. Stephen Biddle (*Military Power: Explaining Victory and Defeat in Modern Battle* [Princeton, NJ: Princeton University Press, 2006]) argues that this dynamic was present as far back as World War I as well.
9. *Economist*, "Democracies need to relearn the art of deception," December 16, 2020, https://www.economist.com/christmas-specials/2020/12/16/democracies-need-to-re-learn-the-art-of-deception.
10. Keir Lieber and Daryl Press, "The new era of counterforce: Technological change and the future of nuclear deterrence," *International Security*, 41, No. 4 (Spring 2017).
11. After 2015, SpaceX's Falcon demonstrated a path to get such costs below $10,000 per kilogram. Harry Jones, "The recent large reduction in space launch cost," 48th International Conference on Environmental Systems, July 2018, https://ttu-ir.tdl.org/bitstream/handle/2346/74082/ICES_2018_81.pdf.
12. See, for instance, *Economist*, "Mutually assured detection," March 8, 2018, https://www.economist.com/technology-quarterly/2018/03/08/mutually-assured-detection.
13. The ur-paper in this field is J.J. Hopfield, "Neural networks and physical systems with emergent collective computational abilities," *Proceedings of the National Academy of Sciences*, 79, No. 8 (April 1, 1982), 2554–8.

14. Dave Gershgorn, "Your computer thinks this turtle is a rifle," *Quartz*, November 2, 2017, https://qz.com/1117494/theres-a-glaring-mistake-in-the-way-ai-looks-at-the-world/. See also Kevin Hartnett, "Machine learning confronts the elephant in the room," *Quanta Magazine*, September 20, 2018, https://www.quantamagazine.org/machine-learning-confronts-the-elephant-in-the-room-20180920/.
15. See the discussion about Giulio Douhet, Hugh Trenchard, and Billy Mitchell in Stephen Budiansky, *Air Power* (New York: Penguin, 2004), especially Chapter 5, "Lessons Learned and Mislearned."
16. See, for instance, John Prados, *The Blood Road: The Ho Chi Minh Trail and the Vietnam War* (New York: John Wiley, 1999), 267–86.
17. James Acton, "Managing vulnerability," *Foreign Affairs*, 89, No. 2 (2010), 146–8.
18. Benjamin S. Lambeth, *NATO's Air War for Kosovo: A Strategic and Operational Assessment* (Santa Monica, CA: RAND, 2001), https://www.rand.org/pubs/monograph_reports/MR1365.html.
19. Uzi Rubin, "The rocket campaign against Israel during the 2006 Lebanon War," Begin-Sadat Center for Strategic Studies, Bar-Ilan University, June 2007, https://besacenter.org/wp-content/uploads/2007/06/MSPS71.pdf, 20–21. Much of what was hit may have been decoys.
20. Gleb Garanich and Sergiy Karazy, "Kyiv says it shoots down volley of Russian hypersonic missiles," *Reuters*, May 16, 2023, https://www.reuters.com/world/europe/air-defence-systems-repelling-attacks-ukraine-early-tuesday-officials-2023-05-16/.
21. See for instance Dean Wilkening, "Hypersonic weapons and strategic stability," *Survival*, 26, No. 4 (October–November 2010), 129–48.
22. But in 2022 Russia launched cruise missiles from vessels in the Caspian Sea into Ukraine (*Reuters*, "Russia strikes Ukraine with cruise missiles from two seas," March 20, 2022, https://www.reuters.com/world/europe/russia-strikes-ukraine-with-cruise-missiles-black-sea-caspian-sea-2022-03-20/).
23. Albert Wohlstetter, "Delicate balance," argued that basing strike aircraft close to the Soviet Union to maximize operational efficiency also made it easier for the Soviets to nullify the US deterrence. Preserving a second-strike capability required pulling assets back from the Soviet border.
24. The Electricity Consumers Resource Council, "The economic impacts of the August 2003 blackout," Report, 2004, http://www.elcon.org/Documents/Profiles%20and%20Publications/Economic%20Impacts%20of%20August%202003%20Blackout.pdf.
25. Michael Birnbaum, David L. Stern, and Emily Rauhala, "Russia's methodical attacks exploit frailty of Ukrainian power system," *Washington Post*, October 25, 2022, https://www.washingtonpost.com/world/2022/10/25/russias-methodical-attacks-exploit-frailty-ukrainian-power-system/. By springtime, indications were that Ukraine had proven very resilient: see Marc Santora, "How Ukraine's power grid survived so many Russian bombings," *New York Times*, April 11, 2023, https://www.nytimes.com/2023/04/11/world/europe/ukraine-war-infrastructure.html.
26. Marc Santora and Matthew Mpoke Bigg, "Russian missiles deliver new woe to Kyiv, knocking out tap water," *New York Times*, October 31, 2022, https://www.nytimes.com/2022/10/31/world/europe/russia-ukraine-kyiv-water.html.
27. Michael A. Hunzeker, "Taiwan's defense plans are going off the rails," *War on the Rocks*, November 18, 2021, https://warontherocks.com/2021/11/taiwans-defense-plans-are

-going-off-the-rails/. See also Raymond Kuo, "The counter-intuitive sensibility of Taiwan's new defense strategy," *War on the Rocks*, December 6, 2021, https://warontherocks.com/2021/12/the-counter-intuitive-sensibility-of-taiwans-new-defense-strategy/.

28. See Isabel Debre and Jon Gambrell, "Iran's hard-line president-elect says he won't meet Biden," *Associated Press*, June 21, 2021, https://apnews.com/article/iran--president-elect-ebrahim-raisi-biden-63db1fbbdb1ff9fe40aca40f3f8046a2.

29. See, for instance, Bruce M. Sugden, "Nuclear operations and counter-homeland conventional warfare: Navigating between nuclear restraint and escalation risk," *Texas National Security Review*, 4, No. 4 (Fall 2021). But also see Josh Rogin, "The most shocking intel leak reveals new Chinese military advances," *Washington Post*, April 13, 2023, https://www.washingtonpost.com/opinions/2023/04/13/china-hypersonic-missile-intelligence-leak/, which suggests Chinese advances.

30. Troianovski, "Russia issues": "when a Russian reporter asked Mr. Ryabkov in an interview broadcast on Thursday whether Russia was considering deploying military infrastructure in Venezuela or Cuba, he responded: "I don't want to confirm anything or rule anything out."

31. Department of Defense, "Military and security developments," 2023, 66–67.

32. From Eric Gomez, "The future of extended deterrence: Are new U.S. nuclear weapons necessary?" in Caroline Dorminey and Eric Gomez, *America's Nuclear Crossroads* (Washington, DC: CATO Institute, 2019), 62, "American war plans are classified, but they most likely involve deep strikes against Russian and Chinese air defenses, command and control nodes, and logistics facilities to destroy the latter's 'anti-access/area denial' (A2/AD) zones."

33. Russia had announced many times that the use of long-range weapons supplied by the United States to Ukrainian forces that, in turn, used them against Russian cities would be escalatory, but the stated consequences would essentially be an intensified attack on Ukraine (the capacity of Russia to do that is another issue). See John Leicester and Hanna Arhirova, "Russia claims advances in Ukraine amid barrages, troop boost," *Associated Press*, June 7, 2022, https://apnews.com/article/russia-ukraine-kyiv-moscow-411ca8f38524e0d2b120479accf4ad56.

34. Chris Dougherty, "More than half the battle: Information and command in a new American way of war," *Center for Naval Analyses*, May 2021, https://www.cnas.org/publications/reports/more-than-half-the-battle. See also Chris Dougherty, "Confronting chaos: A new concept for information advantage," *War on the Rocks*, September 9, 2021, https://warontherocks.com/2021/09/confronting-chaos-a-new-concept-for-information-advantage/.

35. Press, "Calculating credibility."

36. Paul H.B. Godwin and Alice L. Miller, *China's Forbearance Has Limits: Chinese Threat and Retaliation Signaling and Its Implications for a Sino-American Military Confrontation* (Washington, DC: NDU Press, April 2013).

37. Austin Carson, "Facing off and saving face: Covert intervention and escalation management in the Korean War," *International Organization*, 70, No. 1 (Winter 2016), 103–31.

38. Thomas Gibbons-Neff, "How a 4-hour battle between Russian mercenaries and U.S. commandos unfolded in Syria," *New York Times*, May 24, 2018, https://www.nytimes.com/2018/05/24/world/middleeast/american-commandos-russian-mercenaries-syria.html. See also Neil Hauer, "Russia's favorite mercenaries," *The Atlantic*, August 27, 2018,

https://www.theatlantic.com/international/archive/2018/08/russian-mercenaries-wagner-africa/568435/.
39. See for instance Dominic Tierney, "The future of Sino-U.S. proxy war," *Texas National Security Review*, 4, No. 2 (Spring 2021), https://tnsr.org/2021/03/the-future-of-sino-u-s-proxy-war/.
40. See for instance T.X. Hammes, "A military strategy to deter China," *Real Clear Defense*, December 1, 2013, http://www.realcleardefense.com/articles/2013/12/01/a_military_strategy_to_deter_china_106987.html.
41. Cunningham, "Maritime rung."

5

Conventional Operations against Nuclear Systems

Striking nuclear systems during a conventional war—something facilitated by information technologies—offers both great military potential and great escalation risk. Here we examine how such capabilities can challenge the conventional/nuclear threshold.[1] Would the deliberate targeting of nuclear systems be regarded as a serious escalation of a conventional conflict? Would that also hold for inadvertent attacks? Would it spur the other side to escalate? The point of using conventional rather than nuclear weapons to attack nuclear systems, after all, is to leverage the nuclear taboo and shift the onus to the target to break it. The choice, for instance, between using a ten-ton conventional bomb (e.g., a so-called MOAB, mother of all bombs [it's a conventional bomb with an explosive power of roughly ten tons of TNT]) and a nuclear weapon with equivalent blast effects (e.g., the Davy Crockett) requires understanding that using the latter would cross into a very different war. But could that taboo survive the forced attrition of one side's nuclear deterrent?

Our assumption, which we next explain, is that this capability is currently asymmetric; it is for United States to choose to go down that road and for China or Russia to defend or deter it.

Technology and political geography explain the asymmetry. Well-funded US conventional warfare capabilities developed for stand-off precision attacks in conventional campaigns can be turned to the similar problem of going after nuclear assets. Even as China and Russia bring their hunting technologies toward US levels, the time and expense required to convert such capabilities into militarily useful form that can work at speed and at range will delay convergence by years. The same geographical advantage that lessens the risk to US homeland assets—oceans and allies—would also facilitate such a campaign. China's and Russia's remote sensing of US nuclear forces is limited to whatever it can get from satellites (which, as argued, are vulnerable) and cyberespionage (which is difficult against usually isolated classified systems). Striking US nuclear systems with conventional weapons would require considerable reach on their part. US submarines patrol closer to Chinese or Russian borders than theirs do to ours. A serious counternuclear campaign working from the oceans would require China to have a large, robust, and very quiet submarine force that could run some very tight gauntlets past the first island chain formed by Japan, the Ryukyus, Taiwan, and the Philippines and then sustain itself in the open oceans. Russia's problem is somewhat easier but the Atlantic Ocean is still large and the US Navy has long practiced listening for Russian submarines moving around Norway out to the ocean. By contrast, stealthy US aircraft, both manned and unmanned, could probably roam over most of the Earth's entire landmass (except maybe central Asia) looking for mobile nuclear missiles (which the United States lacks).[2]

HOW SUCH A CAMPAIGN MIGHT WORK

Any conventional counternuclear campaign would be shaped by the fact that most nuclear weapons are either hardened or hidden. Hardened weapons—ICBMs in silos or deep shelters—are difficult to destroy except by using nuclear weapons.[3] By dint of being findable, they can be considered first-strike targets as well as first-strike weapons. Hidden (or at least hidable) weapons include mobile missile launchers, long-range cruise missiles, submarines, and aircraft in flight. Any of them can be destroyed with a well-aimed conventional weapon, but most can be made hard to find except when they sit in obvious locations: aircraft on runways (or unhardened hangers), ships at port, and mobile missiles in known sheds. Countries raise alert levels when they need to move these vulnerable assets into the air, out to sea, or into the countryside, thereby making them harder to find.

Although Russia and the United States have ICBMs in hardened silos, and China originally did not, news reports point to two sets of silos under construction in its northwest.[4] Some believe that China is dropping its minimal deterrence posture in favor of nuclear dominance or at least is seeking parity.[5] Others, pointing to China's lack of fissile material, argue that China's goal is to complicate US targeting by creating far more silos than missiles.[6] The latter could suggest that China is not confident in the survival of its mobile missiles—which is to say, its ability to keep them hidden. China also maintains many tunnels—even more than the several hundred ICBMs it owns.[7] If their tunnels are deep enough, their ICBMs could be protected from conventional attack to the extent that their location within these tunnels is unknown.[8] The Chinese counter that their tunnel system is man-rated rather than missile-rated. Those used to hide mobile missiles are not particularly well hardened. Finally, entrances and exits associated with such wide tunnels can be closed by attack. Thus, China has more grounds than Russia to fear that conventional counternuclear operations, *if successful*, could whittle down its deterrence.

Correspondingly, a conventional counternuclear campaign is likely to leave US and Russian first-strike weapons (ICBMs) alone because they sit in hardened siloes. Second-strike weapons are those at risk because the latter survive by being able to hide. It is hiding, not hardening, that would erode over time under the pressure of war.

Counternuclear campaigns using conventional weapons are not entirely a new idea. The 1980s-era US maritime strategy took it as a matter of course that if US submarines found Soviet submarines in wartime, they would attack them without attempting to differentiate those without nuclear weapons (SSNs) from those with nuclear weapons (SSBNs). Austin Long and Brendan Green[9] go further to argue that US policy in a general war would have been to hunt for the USSR's submarines—which is to say the country's second-strike capability. The authors observed that the difficulty of targeting Soviet strategic nuclear forces in the 1950s (jet bombers on runways) had been overestimated by analysts who were not given access to highly classified intelligence on the location of Soviet airfields. Today's doubts on the possibility of targeting second-strike nuclear capabilities are likewise, they argue, overstated. With the aid of SOSUS (a sea-bed acoustic network), US submarines circa 1970 were able to keep nearly continuous track of Soviet nuclear-missile submarines. Even after Soviet submarines grew quieter there were ways to track them (especially if detected leaving port) using wiretaps on seabed communication links. The lack of radical change in technology underseas suggest it may still be a plausible campaign.

Paul Bracken argued in 2016[10] that cyberspace operations and "the new technologies of cell phone, package, and vehicle tracking, as well as technologies for distributed car services such as Uber, Lyft, mobile social nets, customer tracking in retail stores, fleet management, distributed sensors on drones and highway cameras, and automated license plate readers ... [coupled with] pattern recognition, system visualization, and predictive analytics"[11] mean that "mobile systems are not nearly as survivable as was believed a decade ago." Mobile missile batteries, he writes, are complex organizations with multiple vehicles suffused with electronics—not least being cell phones in the hands of their operators and support crew—that permit tracing, tracking, and geolocation by the other side. And while such cell phones may well be turned off in a crisis, operational habits developed in peacetime exercises create patterns that hunters can look for in wartime.

Maneuver may not defend such assets. As one Chinese observer has pointed out: "the mobility of China's land-based missiles is constrained by some factors, which make China's missiles more vulnerable. First, the launch units of mobile missiles are composed of a large number of service trucks, which 'makes the weapon more visible to detection by foreign intelligence assets.' For example, the DF-21 launch unit includes six service trucks, for TEL, fire control, power, power distribution, aiming, and inspection respectively."[12] Some caution against reading too much from the complete failure to find Iraq's Scuds in the Gulf War, arguing[13] (1) there was very little prewar intelligence on their deployment patterns; (2) Scud command-and-control was carried out via landlines, but such techniques would be too slow for more modern and mobile (especially nuclear) forces; (3) Scuds are smaller than mobile ICBMs; and (4) the stakes were lower because the Scuds were conventionally armed. Since then, they argue, for more precise geolocation, the United States has developed stealthy UAVs, better signals intelligence, and new types of unattended ground sensors.

A surprise conventional attack on nuclear systems could sharply reduce enemy nuclear inventories. Satellites, side-looking air sensors, surreptitious ground sensors, or SIGINT may provide the location of ships in port, some mobile missiles, or parked aircraft. Even if submarines can get to sea in a crisis, knowing when and from where they launched helps in tracking their subsequent movements. But to execute that strategy, a country must have a culture that permits a no-warning war, an ability to mask preparations for the onset of such war, and a determination to go after nuclear systems from the outset of a conventional conflict despite its escalation risk. By contrast, expanding a conventional conflict to include nuclear assets among its targets could be done gradually from inadvertent strikes to targets of opportunity to a deliberate campaign.

Once nuclear weapons become targets, a counternuclear operations campaign would then largely depend on prosecuting fleeting opportunities that may arise when, say, operational security slips[14] or when assets leave shelters. A measure–countermeasure contest is likely. Shifts in this contest—whether by hunters or hiders—could be sudden, sharp, and substantial. When the difference between hiding and finding is human skill, diligence, discipline, and luck, then unexpected faults that favor hunters or hiders are limited to the individuals and their weapons (although their revelation ought to warn others). But when success is a matter of systemic vulnerabilities (e.g., leaked RF emissions, characteristic infrared signatures, tell-tale acoustics) discerned and exploited, large shifts in success rates can take place—particularly when exploiting faults that are present in *classes* of systems rather than this or that particular system. Whenever each system contains much of the same software code, for instance, a specific vulnerability could pervade all of them.[15] Electronic warfare tricks work similarly. Granted, vulnerabilities in every instance of a class of systems can arise in hardware, not just software: US torpedoes circa 1942 were almost all failures. During the Cold War some in the United States feared losing many systems at once. "If the Soviets were to find a way to locate, identify, and trail our *Polaris* submarines 'on station' around the Soviet periphery, they might be able to destroy them all nearly simultaneously."[16] Yet the ability of one side to *predict* such failures by exploiting known vulnerable software in peacetime (e.g., via hacking) is novel.

Because hitting a target as soon as it is found might teach the other side where it is vulnerable and thus what faults must be repaired, hunters may hold off striking targets until they can take many out at the same time.[17] Until that point, the other side may be lulled into thinking such assets are well-hidden. It may thus hold off threatening nuclear escalation until shocked by unexpected losses.

Predicting the outcome of a hunt-and-hide contest is iffy. Physical parameters (e.g., the acuity of one's satellites) are only one factor behind success and often not the most important one, compared to the quality of data assessment. Exercises in which their hunters go after their own hiders (e.g., the US National Training Center) only hint at how well their hunters will find your hiders and vice versa. If nothing else the stakes in exercises are less than life-and-death. But some peacetime activities *can* provide good hints. Every country's access to the ocean allows each to practice searching for and tailing the other's submarines. This can foretell outcomes—assuming highly sensitive hunting or hiding techniques are not withheld in an effort to forestall countermeasures against them. Similar contests may yet come to outer space. Offenses and defenses vie constantly in cyberspace.

Even if finds are hard to verify in peacetime, searching then can still help to gather indications and warning; develop correlated indicators of a target (e.g., finding a target using visual leads and then detecting other, say infrared or electronic, signatures of the target); discover facilities associated with a particular weapon, which could then be added to a broader target list;

understand how a target behaves (e.g., maneuvers); and strike targets if war suddenly breaks out.

Yet too vigorous a peacetime search program can warn the other side and even create its own escalation risks. The 1960 Soviet shoot-down of a US U-2 spy plane wrecked a presidential summit. The 2023 discovery of a Chinese spy balloon persuaded the US secretary of state to cancel a visit to China. Conversely as noted, aggressive tracking of Soviet submarines by US submarines was normalized as peacetime activity. Also, unless hunters are stealthy, watching them may reveal how *they* work and hint at their leaders' strategic intentions. This may teach the target to hide or mask its assets better. Lastly efforts to improve the finding and geolocation of nuclear assets may cause the other side to react in ways that complicate monitoring their quantity to verify arms control treaties.

Opinions vary on how successful any conventional counternuclear campaign can be. Russia's Vice Prime Minister Dmitry Rogozin declared,

> [even though it is said that] three to four thousand US high-precision weapons could during six hours destroy 80 to 90 percent of Russian strategic forces 'and deprive [them] of any resistance capability.' . . . research by some independent Russian experts demonstrates that, for the foreseeable future, the threat [was] . . . grossly exaggerated, especially in terms of their capability to implement a preemptive strike against Russian strategic forces. Such a strike would involve lengthy preparations and a long campaign of repeated massive strikes, lasting days or even weeks.[18]

Li Bin, a Chinese nuclear expert, estimates that "that the United States likely cannot develop the capability to find all of China's mobile missiles, as long as China undertakes some basic efforts at deception and dispersal."[19] Such confidence may keep the Chinese from rapid nuclear retaliation if it loses a few. But as operations continue, a lot would depend on "whether China believes it can hide a couple of dozen mobile missiles from the United States—or, more precisely, whether China believes that the United States believes that China can hide these missiles. That story may become progressively harder for Chinese leaders to tell themselves as more and more of their conventional and nuclear or nuclear-relevant assets come under threat during a conventional war."[20]

WHY NOT USE NUCLEAR WEAPONS TO STRIKE NUCLEAR WEAPONS?

The point of not using nuclear weapons to destroy nuclear weapons is to place the onus on the other side to cross the nuclear threshold—with all its risks—rather than tolerating whatever attrition it cannot prevent. But once the nuclear threshold is crossed, the other side has far fewer reasons not to cross it as well.

In 2006 Lieber and Press argued that countries may nevertheless gamble on a nuclear first strike as a counterforce option. Deterrence, they argue, is not what it was because "hardening... already been largely negated by leaps in the accuracy of nuclear delivery systems... [and] concealment, is being eroded by the revolution in remote sensing."[21] Against a missile silo hardened to 3,000 pounds-per-square-inch (psi) overpressure 1980s-era ICBMs could get close enough to destroy it half the time; 1980s-era SLBMs, only 10 percent of the time. With today's missiles the odds are near certain.[22] Inasmuch as accuracy never gets worse, nuclear weapons with smaller warheads and less fallout can become just as effective as larger ones against hardened ICBM sites. Conversely, since 2006, both China and Russia have improved the survivability of their mobile nuclear forces perhaps to where attempting a disarming nuclear first strike has become too dangerous.

Might using weapons that create fusion reactions without using fissile material (aka fourth-generation weapons)[23] lower the odds of nuclear retaliation? For low-lethality nuclear weapons to avoid a response that would follow using high-lethality nuclear weapons, the target would have to respect such a distinction. Yet no country has voiced any inclination to do so. It is unclear why any would want to. The notion that a country hoping to face no messier weapon would calibrate its reaction according to the fallout such a weapon produced is also curious. It would require the target state be able to determine that a low-fallout weapon was used; reason that a high-fallout weapon could have been used instead; infer that the attacker is thus sensitive about enemy casualty levels (thus giving it credit for moral reasoning); and conclude that its citizens would be better off if it withheld nuclear retaliation even though losing the power to protect its sovereignty. Only by using conventional weapons does the attacker force the target to be the one to make the decision to cross the nuclear threshold.

RATIONALES FOR A COUNTERNUCLEAR OPERATIONS STRATEGY

Given the manifest risks involved in going after the other side's nuclear weapons even with conventional weapons, why might countries do so?

One reason would be to reduce the other side's destructive capabilities. The fewer nuclear weapons that survive such a campaign, the less the expected damage they can inflict—even if the destroyed weapons were second-strike weapons. How much this matters depends on the odds that destroyed nuclear weapons would have been used. After all, the situations under which *second-strike* weapons would be used (for lack of enough first-strike weapons) are a subset of the situations under which *any* nuclear weapon would be employed. And if only *some* of the second-strike weapons are erased by a counternuclear campaign, the odds are even lower that not having *those* weapons makes a difference in scenarios short of emptying out all the nuclear barrels. Removing those weapons would have even less impact on deterrence, the quality of which depends on many factors apart from inventory levels.

The attacker may also believe that whoever has more surviving weapons would prevail in a face-off. Matthew Kroenig,[24] having analyzed nearly twenty nuclear confrontations, concluded that countries with larger nuclear arsenals can and do stare down countries without them. But their doing so would seem to require that the confrontation has escalated to where there is a nontrivial prospect of nuclear use (beyond a few for signaling purposes). Only two crises qualify: the 1962 Cuban missile crisis and the 1969 Sino-Soviet confrontation over the Ussuri River.[25]

The next set of reasons all assume an ongoing conventional conflict. Otherwise, a counternuclear campaign looks prefatory to a first strike—making nuclear reprisals by the other side more urgent, hence more likely.

Two is to force the other side to the bargaining table while it still has some nuclear weapons left. As its strategic disadvantage grows under the weight of attacks, it would lose the credibility to threaten escalation. A related advantage—more relevant to mobile missiles than submarine-launched missiles—is that an active counter-nuclear campaign can complicate the other side's being able to get off a nuclear shot because it is vulnerable in the minutes required to set up nuclear operations. That noted, if the United States is carrying out such attacks, everyone but Russia starts off with far fewer weapons than the United States has. China's *current* nuclear strategy necessarily presumes that it can induce enough fright even with its smaller stockpiles to get the United States to back down. Only Russia can plausibly believe that its surviving inventories *might* give it any advantage, for whatever that would be worth, in a counterforce nuclear exchange with the United States.

Three is to reduce the other side's ability to use tactical nuclear weapons for combat. Once used or even positioned for use, they are legitimate targets and cannot plausibly be understood as deterrents any more. If both sides believe that their use is being held back, then each side may refrain from striking the other's assets lest the other side react as if it would otherwise lose them. But if one side fears they might be used later in combat, it might strike them preemptively to limit how many of them are used—thereby also making it harder for the other side to use them to deter escalation. If the other side considered tactical nuclear weapons to instead be primary deterrents, it could react to their being targeted as if its entire deterrent force were at risk. And a country deprived of tactical nuclear weapons may resort to using strategic nuclear weapons for battlefield purposes.

Four is to affect the outcome of conventional combat. Consider the 1980s-era US plans, as noted, to move its submarines into the Barents Sea, a bastion for Soviet SSBN nuclear-armed submarines (SSBNs), if war broke out.[26] Soviet SSBNs would have been protected by attack submarines rather than by hiding (as US SSBNs do). The greater the threat to the Soviet SSBNs, the more attack submarines would have been dedicated to SSBN protection. Thus the fewer they would allocate to threaten the sea lines of communications (SLOCs) used by the United States to reinforce NATO. Similarly, a counternuclear campaign may persuade the other side to invest in protecting their deterrence—much as air threats to Nazi Germany and the (1980s-era) Soviet Union persuaded both countries to invest heavily in air defenses. Similarly mounting a credible cyberattack threat against dual-use command-and-control systems (or indications-and-warnings systems) may persuade the other side to secure their command and control by limiting the connectivity of those systems (to leave fewer routes for malware to enter or fewer people authorized to touch the system). But connectivity is what makes command-and-control systems useful. Thus anything that limits such connectivity reduces the quality or timeliness of adversary decision-making for conventional warfare.

Five, even though threatening nuclear use to deter conventional attacks might lack credibility because of its suicidal nature, threatening the other side's nuclear weapons to dissuade it from starting a conventional war could be quite credible. Aaron Friedberg has argued, "If PLA planners believe that the US would respond to a [conventional] first strike with a blinding campaign, and if they recognize that this could force them to contemplate using or losing their own nuclear weapons, their desire to avoid being put in such a situation might cause them to refrain from launching an [antiaccess/area-denial] campaign in the first place."[27] Because it is hard to build shelter capacity for mobile missiles or harden network architectures against cyberattacks *after* a counter-second campaign has started racking up successes, the side under threat must divert resources to protect nuclear assets in peacetime.

Conversely fears of a conventional counternuclear campaign may convince the other side to build a larger inventory of nuclear weapons in anticipation. Might the US or Russian development of counternuclear options (in conjunction with its fears over the US national missile defense, despite its 50:50 track record[28]) further persuade China that it had far too few nuclear weapons? Perhaps yes.[29] The United States and Russia, even if currently constrained by the New START treaty, could build weapon components as a hedge.

Attrition campaigns that work too slowly may be inherently self-defeating. Maybe both superpowers in a conventional war would conspicuously not add to their nuclear inventories to signal that they intend the conflict to stay non-nuclear. But once nuclear weapons are targeted, such restraints would likely disappear. Countries would at least want to replace the weapons they lost. Having gone that far, they may well adjust their production schedules to hedge against future attrition and then reason that if the attacker thinks the size of their nuclear weapons inventories matter enough to motivate a nuclear attrition strategy, then they, too, should think so—and act accordingly.

Any sustained conventional warfare would complicate nuclear weapons operations even without specific counternuclear operations. The crippling of dual-use seaports will hamper the ability of nuclear submarines to return for servicing. Attacks on road or rail networks carried out to impede conventional forces can also impede the movement of mobile missiles and thereby restrict their getting to prepared launch areas[30] or other hiding places. Unless NC3 systems have their own links and nodes, they will be damaged by attacks on conventional command-and-control systems. Jamming communications frequencies used by conventional forces will also jam communications on the same frequencies used by nuclear forces.

ESCALATORY CONSEQUENCES OF A COUNTERNUCLEAR CAMPAIGN

Assume that a conventional counternuclear campaign attrites nuclear systems and threatens to attrite more. Will the target escalate to the nuclear level—and when? The longer a country delays raising nuclear threats to deal with counternuclear operations, the greater the damage to its deterrent, the harder it would be to win a staring contest, and the more a newly made threat to go nuclear would smell desperate. The attacker observing the other side's declining nuclear capabilities may attempt complete annihilation of its foe's second-strike deterrent if confident that the other side will not use its own nuclear weapons. This confidence, however, may be fatally misplaced if the other side *does* reach for its nuclear weapons.

Leaders worried about their dwindling deterrence are apt to be increasingly watchful for the other side's *coup de grace*, and their reliance on a LUA posture would rise. So would their urge to have every sensor reading and intercept scrutinized for signs of an incoming nuclear attack. The implications of twitchiness can be inferred from the 1983 crisis when aging Soviet leaders were tempted to preempt US nuclear warfighting capabilities thanks to their perception of declining Soviet power. The latter was exacerbated by troubling incidents, such as the Korean Airlines 007 shoot-down and a NATO command-post exercise (Able Archer).[31] Had NATO and the Soviet Union been fighting a conventional war, particularly with military operations that could mask nuclear preparations (as the Soviet Union feared during the Cold War), the urge to preempt would have been greater. Twitchiness by one side does not help the other.

Or the target country may react in ways that look as if it were going nuclear even if it was only trying to protect assets. For nuclear-missile submarines, for instance, that would mean deploying them out to sea—which, in turn, is exactly what countries contemplating their imminent use would also do. According to James Acton,[32] "The likelihood of misinterpreted warning would probably increase if... China had dispersed or alerted nuclear-armed missiles. Although this step could be a standard defensive precaution to protect the missiles' survivability in a major conflict, it might also exacerbate concerns in Washington about the possibility of Chinese first use."

Since the odds of Armageddon arising from a conventional war between two nuclear powers would be high to begin with, would counternuclear operations raise such odds enough to discourage such a campaign? Many hold that the target of a counternuclear campaign would use nuclear weapons early. But would the target be motivated by use-it-or-lose-it fears[33] or, instead, the need to back up threats made to ward off attacks on its nuclear weapons? The odds should also reflect whether the target thinks its deterrent would be effectively disarmed otherwise—which should then reflect its need for nuclear weapons. Those that need but a handful *in extremis* will be more relaxed. Those who think they need large nuclear inventories to win a showdown would be more anxious.

Lieber and Press[34] argued that during "peacetime, almost any course of action is better than starting a nuclear war against a superpower. But during war—when that superpower's planes are bombing command and leadership sites, and when its tanks are seizing territory—the greatest danger may be to refrain from escalation and let the war run its course. Leaders of weaker states—those unlikely to prevail on the conventional battlefield—face life-and-death pressures to compel a stalemate. And nuclear weapons provide a better means of coercive escalation than virtually any other."

Thomas J. Christensen[35] concluded,

> Secure second strike ... does not necessarily posit that the same state can or will stand idly by while its key strategic assets, including relevant weapons and command and control systems are degraded during a conventional or tactical nuclear war. ... [Said] one 'high-ranking military officer' [in 2006] ... China would likely begin a 'nuclear-counterattack of some sort' if the United States were inadvertently to strike with conventional weapons an important nuclear command and control node for China's nuclear forces.

Fiona Cunningham and Taylor Fravel[36] observed in 2015 that "the People's Liberation Army (PLA) has been planning to protect its nuclear forces and its command and control facilities from conventional attacks for at least a decade ... even as China has sought to maintain the smallest possible force capable of surviving a first strike and being able to conduct a retaliatory strike."[37] But China's fears have less to do with a long attrition campaign and more to do with a bolt-from-the-blue attack—especially using hypervelocity vehicles that Chinese experts fear would be used on their country (if the United States had them). Although such experts discount US counternuclear operations against China, its *Science of Military Strategy* holds that such operations would "place us in a passive position, greatly influence our nuclear retaliatory capability, and weaken the effectiveness of our nuclear deterrent ... [yet signaling] to increase the effectiveness of nuclear deterrence and to carry out the actions of preparing for nuclear combat ... [could] push the nuclear adversary to escalate the conflict and ultimately give rise to a nuclear crisis."[38] They believe that the Chinese "government has decided how to respond, but that it will not make that decision public."[39]

Caitlin Talmadge takes a different tack by maintaining that if China's leaders conclude that the United States *were* conducting a deliberate counternuclear campaign, they "might see limited nuclear escalation as their least bad option, using nuclear weapons for purposes of military advantage or coercive leverage or both."[40] She adds, "the danger stems less from the purely military-technical threat that a US conventional campaign would pose to China's nuclear arsenal, which pessimists may at times overestimate, than from what China is likely to believe these military technical developments signal about broader US intentions once a conventional war is under way, which optimists too often overlook." If China's posture reflects a world in which conventional war is highly unlikely, war's outset would indicate that China had erred—forcing it to rethink its other strategic postures. Leaders would listen more to hawks who had been proven right rather than doves who had been proven wrong.[41] The prospect of escalation derived from peacetime experience would have to reflect the more hostile environment that must have been in place for war to break out. By contrast the prospect of escalation from accidental or third-party actions would not necessarily reflect higher hostility levels between the superpowers.

Underestimating a nation's willingness to fight based on peacetime indicators has a history. The Oxford Pledge of 1933 ("This House will under no circumstances fight for its King and country") reflected a low-threat atmosphere of the time and the difficulty of imagining how someone like Hitler could imperil the British way of life. When these Oxford students had to fight, they did. Those who read too much into the pledge were mistaken. Polls in which Americans and Europeans hesitate to honor NATO commitments[42] reflected a world in which the consequences of *current* threats were muted. Russia's war in Ukraine then changed a lot of minds.

Russia, according to Olga Oliker and Andrey Baklitskiy, would limit itself to conventional weapons unless it received a nuclear strike or its leaders feared for the continued existence of the Russian state.[43] Russian nuclear doctrine itself also indicates that it could respond to "attack by adversary against critical governmental or military sites of the Russian Federation, disruption of which would undermine nuclear forces response actions" with nuclear weapons.[44] Right after Ukraine was invaded, Dmitry Medvedev, Russia's former president, reiterated those tenets, arguing that "an attack on a critical infrastructure that will have paralyzed our nuclear deterrent forces" and "an act of aggression . . . which jeopardized the existence of the country itself" would entitle Russia to use nuclear weapons first.[45] In recent years, senior Russian military officers threatened that any ballistic missile launched at Russian territory will be presumed to be a nuclear missile and will be responded to accordingly (even though long-range ballistic missiles on fixed trajectories are not the best way to engage mobile targets). As one analyst (CSIS's Vladimir Isachenkov) has speculated, a nuclear response could follow any sufficiently damaging conventional strike whether or not it jeopardized the state.[46] John K. Warden (together with the DoD, he adds) argued,[47] "Russian capabilities, exercises, and publicly available strategy and doctrine point to a willingness to consider limited nuclear strikes in a broader range of circumstances, potentially early in a conflict." Bruce M. Sugden responded that because Russia's 2014 military doctrine "does not list the criteria by which Russian leaders would assess threats to the state, there may be multiple US-NATO conventional courses of action—including rolling back the Western Military District's integrated air defense system or launching an air-missile raid against the Northern Fleet's naval facilities on Russia's Kola Peninsula—that could create perceptions of a growing threat against the Russian state and elicit different types of Russian military reactions."[48]

Arguably Russia's incorporation of nuclear weapons into its doctrine, war plans, and exercises means that if it sees an opportunity to use nuclear weapons—for operational, retaliatory, or escalate-to-deescalate purposes—it will take it. "Granted, if plans are not developed, then executing them suddenly is more difficult, hence less likely. But, when the stakes are potentially existential, it would take an extraordinarily feckless leader to yield the decision on nuclear use to whatever is written in military doctrine."[49]

According to Alexei Arbatov et al.,[50] Russia's strategy for "solving air-space defense tasks . . . should be based on deterring the enemy from large-scale airspace attacks by implementing an operation of nuclear deterrence at a scale that would avoid escalation but force the enemy to refrain from further airspace attack." But like Li Bin, they argue there are defenses against counternuclear operations, such as moving mobile ICBM launchers frequently, using decoys, protecting SSNs with other naval forces, dispersing bombers, and developing missile defenses ("highly effective Pantzir-S2 close-range antiaircraft gun and missile complexes, as well as by other air- and missile defense systems").[51] Nevertheless, "Moscow might retaliate early with a limited strategic nuclear strike in the event that the United States launched a conventional counterforce operation against Russia's nuclear forces (in accordance with Russia's launch-under-attack doctrine). Alternatively, Moscow might even preempt the United States with selective strategic nuclear strikes to thwart US naval and air forces that were engaged in a conventional conflict."

Dave Johnson observes[52] that to Russians,

> conventional precision weapons are seen not as a way to raise the nuclear threshold, but as a more credible deterrent in the early stages of conflict—because of their usability—without excluding the utility of nuclear weapons beyond the early stages. . . . The nuclear threat is not in the background, casting a shadow, but is front and center, posing a clear and present danger . . . [and that is why] Russia has implemented a program of ostentatious strategic bomber flights in proximity to NATO European and North American air space as well as in the Asia-Pacific region.

So, does Russia brandish such bombers to indicate that they would be used or just to exacerbate what they see as European fears that they might be? Given its multiple veiled threats to use nuclear weapons in Ukraine if the West (or even Ukraine[53]) crossed some threshold, all Russian statements made before the invasion of Ukraine should be viewed judiciously.

The issue is not limited to superpowers. Experts argue that Pakistan's "fear of having [its] small nuclear arsenal destroyed" by an Indian conventional first strike could lead it to "delegate launch authority to military leaders in the field" during a crisis. A subsequent "conventional Indian attack that severed Pakistani command and control might lead a Pakistani military officer to launch a nuclear attack on his own."[54] In Jeffrey Lewis's 2018 speculative novel,[55] North Korea uses nuclear weapons on the United States (having already used them against South Korea and Japan) as the United States *begins* hunting, with conventional weapons, for nuclear launchers in North Korea.

Now, what would the United States do if China or Russia attacked US nuclear assets with conventional weapons (during a conventional war)? Perhaps "Russian experts know that if they attacked a US SSBN base (including with non-nuclear weapons) the United States would take it as an extreme form of escalation and could respond accordingly. As the 2018 NPR states, 'Significant nonnuclear strategic attacks include, but are not limited to ... attacks on US or allied nuclear forces.'"[56] But it is unclear which US assets might be promising targets for Russia or China. US nuclear weapons are difficult to hit because they are well-hidden (submarines on patrol), hardened (ICBMs), or easily dispersed (aircraft). Striking NC3 assets (to include early warning) and not immediately following up with nuclear weapons would only leave the United States twitchier.

China and Russia—which currently lack serious national missile defenses (NMDs)—may well try to disable US NMD systems to increase their confidence in their own nuclear deterrents. Any clue to a plausible US response would reflect two factors. Attacks on an iffy NMD system that is anyway sized for smaller nuclear powers may not merit US nuclear escalation. Likewise, some assets—notably Aegis ships with NMD-capable Standard Missile Block IIAs—are already legitimate targets of conventional warfare, especially if used for offense or for stand-off theater missile defense. Striking a ship that sits farther back from the fight and is more clearly being positioned for national missile defense could be another matter.

When the only way to disarm a country's nuclear capability was a bolt-from-the-blue nuclear attack, there was logic to a LUA posture. But when hardened ICBMs are only one part of a country's nuclear capability, then conventional weapons can put everything but such weapons (and deeply buried NC3 sites) out of commission. The logic of LUA, driven by a scenario in which every minute counts, does not apply to threats from conventional weapons, particularly if it takes time to find hidden nuclear assets and most conventional weapons, anyway, serve conventional roles (so that an incoming volley may not necessarily be aimed at the target's deterrent). It is not the is-it-conventional-or-is-it-nuclear characteristic of the weapon that merits a LUA response, but whether one is facing a mass attack or a few-at-a-time attack. A mass attack with conventional weapons against nuclear weapons assumes considerable preparation because it takes time to find hidden targets. Because the other side can only guess the goal of such weapons, a LUA response would offer more risks than rewards. The case against building dual-warhead delivery vehicles lest they trigger a LUA response[57] is thus weak.

INADVERTENT COUNTERNUCLEAR ATTACKS

Risks of nuclear escalation may persuade both sides to avoid targeting anything that *could be* associated with the other side's nuclear establishment. But exercising discretion requires being able to discriminate among targets and being willing to give many important conventional targets a pass because they just might be nuclear. Any selective policy will need rules of engagement, ways to determine if these rules are being followed, and ways to credibly tell the other side that there *are* rules and what they are.

Several considerations arise. *First*, if dual nuclear–conventional assets are off-limits, then which ones and why? What about targets that are central to their other side's conventional operations but peripheral to their nuclear ones? *Second*, how much effort will be put into distinguishing ineligible from eligible targets: for example, what confirmation will be required to distinguish a hunter-killer submarine (eligible for attack) from a ballistic missile submarine (if deemed ineligible for attack)—or missiles with conventional warheads from those with nuclear warheads? Assessment procedures would have to be translated into mission orders and some allowance made for when attackers do not know exactly what they have hit—even afterward. *Third*, the time and attention required to control forces with the requisite fidelity may degrade military efficacy; legitimate targets may thereby go unmolested or be engaged only after a delay. Exercising forbearance may require reworking standard rules of engagement (e.g., traditional US naval actions during the Cuban missile crisis quarantine). Although the US military has, through long inculcation, imbued its forces with the willingness to make LOAC distinctions in combat, humanitarian considerations are easy to grasp. But military officers may well question why they may hit conventional forces that can do limited damage to their country but not strategic forces that can do unlimited damage to it. Will operators interpret the rationale for blunting their conventional campaign as *political*—so as not to upset foes disinclined to show much gratitude? Disciplining commanders that do overstep the line will be complicated by having to ascertain what they understood under the stress of war and at the time they struck nuclear systems.

Actions of the sort that could hit nuclear systems by accident will draw considerable oversight. President Johnson was widely criticized for overseeing every air strike package against North Vietnam—which lacked nuclear weapons. When stakes are much higher, the president (or at least command-level DoD officials) may feel even more impelled to review every missile strike to assess its effect on the risk of nuclear escalation. Doing so for confrontations at sea can be difficult when combatants maintain the kind of radio silence necessary to avoid being detected. Conversely if the information revolution has achieved anything, it has multiplied the amount of information collected by machines and made available to anyone authorized to see it. So, there will be plenty of Monday-morning quarterbacks available.

Communicating one's own restraint to the *other* side is also hardly trivial.

First, if the other side has credibly threated to escalate if *any* of its nuclear systems are touched for any reason, the one side's intention to restrain operations could be secondary compared to its actions. To hold its retaliatory fire, the other side must believe that the one side was restraining itself even though something nuclear was struck. If, for instance, one side says it hit a nuclear asset because it could not be distinguished from a conventional asset, would the other side think this was reasonable or an excuse? Would there be ways to convey such a message? Such questions might be easier to answer if preceded by some norms-making process under which countries could agree to or at least understand the case for some rules. A plausible and prompt narrative that an attack was accidental or inadvertent—and thus is unlikely to recur—may allow the other side to back off without losing face (for not fulfilling its threats). But to some, even talking about counternuclear activities would legitimize them as tools of armed statecraft (in contrast to having each side respect the other's deterrent as long as it is not used).

Second, the other side may not be inclined to believe *anything* its foe says that is at all self-serving, especially if it smells self-congratulatory ("did you see with what self-restraint we wage war?"). Wartime leaders are more likely to see their counterparts as evil rather than moral individuals pursuing their own self-interest under the constraints of the security dilemma.[58] Asking, "How are they trying to manipulate me?" may precede asking "How do I know that they can keep their word?"

Third, a country that promises to not target dual-purpose military assets thereby motivates the other side to protect conventional warfighting assets by admixing them with nuclear assets—or claiming as much in order to lend them protected status. Doing so could raise the military consequences of exercising restraint.

Unless the single attack is gravely consequential or a response is urgently needed, the target of such an attack could ask itself whether the attacker understood the sensitivity of what was hit and, if so, what the attacker's intentions were. The target could warn: we will not regard a similar strike as ignorance on your part. The attacker then can ask itself: Is it credible: will the target carry out its threats? Is it fair: are we being asked to refrain from doing what the other side itself does? It can also dispute the victim's right to red-line a set of targets or challenge the inferences that victim drew about the first side's objective. Stanislav Petrov's 1983 decision to not report an incoming (albeit erroneously perceived) nuclear strike rested on his mental model that "one missile would not mean the all-out attack they were expecting."[59] Similar reasoning would not lead to a LUA response to a one-off inadvertent attack.

Those whose nuclear assets are struck bear the onus of deciding whether it was (1) an accident (e.g., poor aim, bad intelligence) or (2) inadvertent (i.e., the limits were real but poorly implemented), (3) considered allowable thanks to different interpretation of what was off-limits, or (4) a violation of limits that the other side, despite its words, had no intention of following. If the latter, it must decide whether to retaliate with nuclear weapons, make new threats, complain, or just suffer.

Countries that believe that adversaries will respect the nuclear/nonnuclear distinction *could* separate the two types of systems more clearly to protect nuclear assets—and test whether the attacker is serious about exercising restraint. If so accidents are less likely to be excused. But *would* countries make the effort—particularly since doing so costs resources? A state would have to make it clear what it was doing and why (it would likely indicate that the other side would respect the distinction or else). It might have to accept the other side's use of espionage, notably cyberespionage, to verify that such a separation exists. The attacker, in turn, would have to trust that what is labeled nuclear or nuclear-support (especially sensors) truly lacks serious nonnuclear capabilities. By contrast it is not so hard to stick a general-purpose sensor or transponder on an NC3-supporting satellite.

Conversely, as per Cunningham and Fravel,[60] "the United States could state that it mistook a Chinese nuclear weapon for a conventional missile, and that it could keep making such 'mistakes' to attrite China's nuclear deterrent." Much depends on the plausibility of such mistakes. The authors assert,[61] "Open-source materials indicate that the majority of China's nuclear missiles are not co-located with conventional ones." Others are skeptical that conventional-nuclear distinctions can be made in combat.[62] But while one or at most a handful of strikes could be so explained, a deliberate strategy under the guise of successive mistakes is implausible—while using claimed mistakes to test China's reaction *is* quite plausible. According to retired Admiral Dennis Blair, "rather, before even considering violating their long-held 'no first use' doctrine, Chinese leaders would wait to see a concerted, sustained US campaign against their nuclear arsenal was under way."[63] Avery Goldstein argues, conversely, that even an inadvertent sinking of one Chinese SSBN in the belief that it was an SSN would invite Chinese nuclear retaliation.[64]

Postures for managing risk could range from deliberate avoidance (taking pains to ascertain there are no nuclear systems in the damage zone) to incidental avoidance (not targeting nuclear systems but taking no pains to avoid them), instrumental targeting (of systems if they are dual-use), opportunistic targeting (striking nuclear systems if found while looking for something else), and deliberate targeting (looking for and striking nuclear systems as a priority).

But if the other side believes that its systems are at risk and threatens nuclear war to underline its belief, the one side is down to just two options: either go after nuclear assets (if worthwhile) or take pains to avoid doing so and thereby forgo striking some conventional targets.

In the 1980s Barry Posen[65] argued that NATO could prevail against a non-nuclear Warsaw Pact invasion even if it took pains not to hit Soviet nuclear systems. But why would the Soviet Union entertain the serious use of nuclear weapons (and thereby risk Armageddon), as distinct from a warning shot, just because a NATO strike inadvertently destroyed some of its nuclear weapons? Would it be from (1) fears that it would be denuded of its deterrence, despite the bulk of its deterrence sitting in hardened ICBM silos far from any European front line; (2) a lesser fear that some of the Soviet's nuclear weapons could not be used for battlefield purposes so easily; or (3) the belief that a *conventional* strike by NATO on Soviet nuclear weapons meant that NATO would use nuclear weapons first? Maybe the Soviet Union would feel itself impelled to respond with nuclear weapons because it had to maintain its credibility after telling NATO not to touch them (even if the Soviets never made that distinction).

Matthew Kroenig and Mark Massa[66] argue that states who face attrition in their nuclear capabilities have a plethora of choices besides either doing nothing or starting a nuclear war. Conversely while starting a nuclear war can be suicidal, exemplary use of nuclear weapons, even if answered in kind and quantity, may be a rational way to raise fears of all-out use and thereby introduce caution into the other side (as well as your own). If things ended there, the risks of great escalation would be modest—but once the nuclear threshold is breached then all further thresholds, as argued subsequently, have lesser power.

James Acton's "Entanglement" article argues that co-mingling of NC3 and conventional C4ISR capabilities (often in the same equipment) risks inadvertent nuclear conflict.[67] NC3/EW systems are often more vulnerable than nuclear weapons because they are neither hardened nor hidden. Chinese writing "appears to endorse attacks against U.S. early-warning radars as a way of suppressing missile defenses in a conventional conflict. Moreover, Chinese experts have openly advocated for the ability to attack U.S. early-warning satellites. In a similar vein, Russian experts have stated that, in a conventional conflict, Moscow would consider attacking U.S. C3I assets, including ground-based early-warning radars." The same works in reverse. China's early-warning over-the-horizon radars, for example, look for nuclear missiles *and* ocean-launched air-breathers such as aircraft and cruise missiles. That makes them obvious targets in a purely conventional campaign—something they must already know. But how large is such a risk? The point of a deliberate attack is to prevent the other side from launching nuclear weapons quickly, notably in a LUA response. Paradoxically, the target may take strikes on NC3/EW assets to be the attack that they launch under (defeating the purpose of striking them) or not launch under (in which case, did they even have a LUA response?). Even if the other side holds its nuclear fire, it could lose the confidence that it can see a nuclear strike *not* coming and would reasonably become dangerously nervous. Leaders who lack confidence that they can communicate launch orders are more apt to predelegate launch authority. This would raise the odds of nuclear use—particularly if conflict is going on—by removing a national-level check on field commanders.

WOULD CYBERATTACKS ON NUCLEAR SYSTEMS LEAD TO ESCALATION?

Cyberattacks can be another non-nuclear way to jeopardize nuclear deterrents.[68] Their uncertainty (will they work, and even *did* they work?) and ambiguity (who did what?) point to different escalation implications than conventional attacks do. The placement of such cyberattacks on the escalation lattice depends on what criteria are used to judge them. If measured by means, they would be grouped with other cyberspace operations, toward the bottom. If measured by ends, they would be grouped with counter-nuclear operations, towards the top.

Although no cyberattacks have even hindered the ability to *use* nuclear weapons, no nuclear system with at least some electronics can be guaranteed as safe from such intrusions.[69] As one analyst[70] wrote, "Even with a 'modernized' NC3 system, survivability in the face of hypersonic glide vehicles, *cyber operations*, electro-magnetic pulse, and low-observable conventional or nuclear cruise missiles remains a major concern [emphasis added]." Another argued, "cyberweapons could be used to disable a nuclear command and control system ... potentially generating preemptive pressures similar to those kinetic forces can create ... [but] it is impossible, at least on the basis of publicly available information, to know whether cyberweapons could actually be used in this way."[71] To paraphrase General Robert Kehler, the former commander of the US Strategic Command, while one can have high confidence in the security of a system against knowns and even known unknowns, the security of a system against unknown unknowns from cyberspace is another matter.[72]

The odds that hackers can wreak mischief on nuclear systems[73] successfully—and there are many degrees of success—are unknown. However, we do know that experts have examined the dependencies of nuclear systems on digital systems and worried that they would work as they should when called upon.[74] Similarly faults have been discovered in the integrity and availability of US NC3 systems—although not (as far as known) from hacking. Faults have also been discovered in the integrity of US and Russian indications and warnings systems—although not (as far as known) from hacking. Lastly Stuxnet has proven that nuclear *production* processes can be hacked.[75]

The importance of nuclear systems to national survival creates a strong incentive to painstakingly hacker-proof them. When a system has multiple locks, finding a weakness in one does not necessarily spell disaster. Arguments that the vulnerability of nuclear systems to hacking calls for dealerting nuclear systems[76] depends on the likelihood, not just the possibility, of a consequential hacking event. Furthermore, just because something has failed from internal causes does not prove that it can fail from externally induced causes, especially if hackers have no paths by which they can reach the vulnerability. A random temporary internal fault cannot be exploited by someone else who cannot know that it just appeared—and thus not without some mechanism that looks for and reports faults to hackers.

Potential mischief from cyberattacks can come in three types.[77]

Premature detonation or launch is possible but unlikely.[78] Machines do not launch nuclear weapons (*War Games* notwithstanding); people do. Hackers must either fool the highly trained people who command nuclear weapons or fool the nuclear weapons themselves. Fooling a nuclear weapon is difficult. Many warheads predate the digital era. All are air-gapped. Launching a missile or making a nuclear weapon go off—especially at a time of the hacker's choosing—requires that errant circuitry was inserted in the highly guarded production process and that the system has an electronic connection to the rest of the world to signal that it is time (preset launch times are possible, but then how would they be synchronized with events the launch was meant to exploit?). Fooling people into launching on warning from hacked early-warning systems requires many very different systems be corrupted in the same way at the same time. Finally, those thought most interested in *starting* an "accidental" nuclear war are likely to be third parties such as terrorists, deranged hackers, and evildoers. Those with the requisite cyberspace capability are sophisticated nation-states with little to gain and literally everything to lose if one starts.

Disabling a weapon by corrupting its controls is more possible. It requires a supply-chain attack, though, because the missile at launch is the missile as it leaves the factory. Although missiles are assigned aimpoints (and, in some cases, bomb yields) after the factory, the process is largely manual. If the malware is to lurk undetected, it must be designed not to activate itself during tests. Again nuclear planners on all sides have given other sources of failure—accident, weather, bad design, sabotage, rogue operators—a great deal of time and attention. Many countermeasures to overcome anticipated faults (e.g., lost communications links) apply regardless of what caused the fault.[79] Furthermore disabling a single weapon is of limited relevance in the context of a larger deterrent capability. But disabling a large class of systems at once—which is possible in principle if each runs the same software—has serious strategic ramifications. This is particularly so if the attacking state understands and has enough confidence in its success to leverage the other side's newly created impediment.

Delaying a nuclear launch by corrupting the NC3 or early-warning system is the least implausible consequence of cyberattack. The chain of command can be broken by going after links, nodes, or authentication mechanisms. False messages can be inserted into the system to override or at least cast doubt on true messages. Countries that authenticate a commander's orders by using *only* human recognition of their commander's voice delivered over a network can be fooled by deepfakes of such voices if hackers can access such networks.[80] The failure to receive early-warning sensor information (or to act on it because of too many prior false alarms) could mean that retaliation is launched after incoming nuclear weapons have detonated rather than having been detected. Again NC3 systems are built with the redundancy necessary to sustain the ravages of *nuclear* attack.

The value of delaying the other side's launches depends on context. If nothing critical needs to happen while the system is restored, then inducing delay does nothing but dent the other side's confidence in the instant usability of its deterrent. If each side is racing to limit the damage from the other side's nuclear attacks or to preserve its edge in a nuclear confrontation, then even a 30-minute delay could mean the difference between seeing missiles, aircraft on runways, and submarines in port destroyed and seeing them launched or at least dispersed. Using cyberattacks to delay a nuclear launch may be useful to stall a nuclear response to a conventional or nuclear counterforce strike. By the time systems are restored, the other side may decide against initiating nuclear use after becoming palpably weaker.

The escalatory potential of a cyberattack on nuclear systems would reflect not the cyberattack *per se*, but how it affects the other side's view of the nuclear balance and reflects the one side's intentions. But undetonated cyberattacks have their own escalation implications. Typically, hackers first implant malware in target systems before detonating them. If implants in nuclear systems are discovered, defenders may infer that someone is trying to disable their nuclear systems (rather than simply eavesdropping on them). So thinking, they may conclude that the implant's creator is planning an imminent nuclear attack, and they must try violently preempt it.[81] "Unlike official US documents, PLA texts do not recognize the danger of the OPE [operational planning of the environment]-espionage distinction problem and the risk of escalation if an intrusion is discovered in a crisis."[82] A variant of this reaction—they must turn up the sensitivity of monitoring—can lead to indicators, previously overlooked, driving a misleading narrative of imminent nuclear attack.[83] In 2023 the discovery of a Chinese spy balloon persuaded the United States to recalibrate its radar to find more balloons, leading to three innocent balloons being shot down in quick succession.

That noted, discovering an implant is the first step not in its activation but its eradication. Discovery indicates that nuclear systems *had been* compromised rather than *will be* compromised. Furthermore, the worst time to start a war is when one's systems are compromised or are taken offline to fix the compromise. And when systems are finally cleaned out, enough time may have passed to persuade defenders that the implant did not portend imminent attack. If a discovered implant signifies that one's nuclear systems may be vulnerable, a panicked reaction may be a public admission that one's deterrent has flaws. Even if the immediate flaw is fixed, owners of nuclear systems may not want to advertise that flaws were possible.

Cyber-induced nuclear instability cannot be completely dismissed. Erik Gartzke and Jon Lindsay[84] argue,

> If... one side knows, but the other does not, that the attacker has disabled the target's ability to perceive an impending military attack, or to react to one when it is underway, then they will not have a shared understanding of the probable outcome of war.... The cyber attacker... cannot reveal the advantage to the target, lest the advantage be lost. The target does not know that it is at a disadvantage.... The attacker perceives an imbalance of power while the target perceives a balance.... The first side knows that it does not need to back down. The second side feels confident that it can stand fast.

But this argument must confront a big difference between a conventional and a nuclear standoff. In the former, tilting the scales (e.g., with a cyberattack) can improve the war's outcomes. But in a nuclear confrontation, both sides lose if war ensues. The ability of the stronger to stare down the weaker is reduced when the weaker side does not feel weaker. The attacker may reason: I know I have compromised their systems and because they are closer to their own systems, they obviously know—and so their resistance is a bluff and can be called. But the success of a cyberattack often depends on the target being none the wiser. Arguably,[85] "Perhaps what is most destabilizing is that these adversaries are incentivized to hide their capabilities until they are ready to be used, so the true extent of the cyber-nuclear threat is unknown." But that is exactly why a successful cyberattack—except in the brief gap between discovery and reversal—might not influence a nuclear confrontation.

The link between cyberspace operations and nuclear stability may be indirect. Cyberattacks during war, for instance, might cripple port operations at a facility that handles only conventional submarines. The attacks are detected, eliminated, and their damage reversed. But the fact that the other side penetrated network barriers in the first place suggests that they had invested in finding vulnerabilities—and may know of others yet unexploited. Can the defender be confident in its ability to move submarines into their roaming areas if need arise? If not, it may pay to move them out sooner. How then would the attacker interpret such submarine movements—especially if unaware that the hack was discovered?

So just as the atomic queens, at rest,[86] throw a shadow over the chessboard of war, so might the cyber rooks. Surprises from cyberspace have eroded anyone's easy assurance that systems have not been compromised somewhere along the line. Even when the legacy nuclear weapons of superpowers are analog, decisions to use or move them are increasingly supported by digital information systems—whose reliability thus becomes critical. This creates opportunities for one or both sides to manipulate the other side's fears in a crisis. Nevertheless, well-briefed leaders would recognize that a cyberattack on their nuclear systems may mean, at very worst, temporary discomfort as the integrity of their systems is restored. Nuclear war could be put off. Cyberattacks are far less likely to induce nuclear escalation than the kinetic attacks bruited previously.

CONCLUSIONS

Nuclear weapons these days can be destroyed without using nuclear weapons and thus without *necessarily* starting a nuclear war. Yet if the other side cannot make credible nuclear threats to stop the attrition, it may end up using nuclear weapons. Even exemplary use breaks the nuclear taboo and thereby takes the conflict to a new level.

Ultimately, there are three stable end-states when counternuclear targeting is at issue. *One*, Armageddon, is stable, but in the worst possible way. *Two* is a consensus that no one be the first to use nuclear weapons regardless of what is happening to them.[87] Although China and India, for instance, have adopted a no-first-use (NFU) policy, would they really restrain themselves as their deterrents were eroded by a counternuclear campaign? So the second state might not be stable. *Three*, no one strikes a nuclear system, something that may be difficult to achieve if a general conventional war is raging unless attackers exercise great forbearance even at the expense of conventional warfighting. It also requires the target to recognize when mistakes are made and forgive them. Such a condition may, therefore, also not last long.

Does nuclear war also mean attacks *with* nuclear weapons? Or does it mean attacks *on* nuclear weapons? If the Russians, for instance, used tactical nuclear weapons in Ukraine, and the United States responded by using conventional weapons to sink Russian SSBNs, would the Russians claim that the US response escalated conflict from the tactical nuclear to the strategic nuclear level—even though it responded to nuclear use with conventional use? Or did the United States try to deescalate the contest by not following suit? Those conducting counternuclear operations may argue that they have not crossed the nuclear taboo. Those on the receiving end may argue that attackers have crossed the nuclear taboo and that their own retaliation did not break anything already broken. The problem, again, is one of threshold definition in a lattice world.

NOTES

1. South Korea is also developing conventional counter-nuclear capabilities against North Korea. See Ian Bowers and Henrik Stålhane Hiim, "Conventional counterforce dilemmas: South Korea's deterrence strategy and stability on the Korean Peninsula," *International Security*, 45, No. 3 (Winter 2020/21), 7–39.
2. India is believed to enjoy similar advantages over Pakistan. From Ben Barry, "Pakistan's tactical nuclear weapons: Practical drawbacks and opportunity costs," *Survival*, 60, No. 1 (2018), 76: "Pakistan's missiles, warheads and dedicated nuclear command and control can be expected to be a high priority for Indian intelligence-gathering in peacetime. In crisis and war, . . . [once] these were found, India would likely apply a high proportion of its airpower, ballistic missiles, long-range artillery, attack helicopters, air-assault forces and special forces to striking them." According to Dinshaw Mistry ("Complexity of deterrence among new nuclear states: The India-Pakistan case," cited in T.V. Paul, *Complex Deterrence* [Chicago, IL: University of Chicago Press, 2009], 196), "India's satellites could detect Pakistan's air and missile delivery systems. Its aircraft with precision-guided munitions could target Pakistan's mobile missiles, while its missiles with improved accuracy could target Pakistan's airfields. Missile defenses also could provide protection against retaliatory strikes by the limited number of Pakistan's nuclear delivery systems that survive an Indian preemptive strike."
3. A well-hardened ICBM silo can withstand roughly 10,000 psi (pounds per square inch) overpressure. If a 1 megaton nuclear weapon can deliver 10 psi at a distance of 10 kilometers, then it can deliver 10,000 psi at a distance of 300 meters. A 1 ton conventional warhead must detonate within 3 meters to create a similar effect, and while really good guidance systems might get a weapon within similar levels of precision, there are ways of keeping a conventional weapon from detonating that close. Over 30 years ago, *Discriminate Deterrence* (Fred Iklé and Albert Wohlstetter, co-chairs, *Report of the Commission on Integrated Long-Term Strategy*, January 1988, https://www.airforcemag.com/PDF/DocumentFile/Documents/2008/DiscriminateDeterrence_010188.pdf) argued that conventional weapons could substitute for nuclear weapons for *some* targets that were on the nuclear list.
4. Steven Lee Myers, "China bolsters its nuclear options with new missile silos in a desert," *New York Times*, July 2, 2021, https://www.nytimes.com/2021/07/02/world/asia/china-missile-silos.html. For the second set of discovered silos, see William Broad and David Sanger, "A 2nd new nuclear missile base for China, and many questions about strategy," *New York Times*, July 26, 2021, https://www.nytimes.com/2021/07/26/us/politics/china-nuclear-weapons.html.
5. William Schneider Jr. "China sees its nuclear arsenal as more than a deterrent; Beijing is adding warheads, missiles and subs at an alarming rate. The goal is global dominance," *Wall Street Journal*, September 7, 2021, https://www.wsj.com/articles/china-nuclear-arsenal-deterrent-navy-new-start-proliferation-national-security-11630524535. In November 2021 the Pentagon predicted that China would have a thousand nuclear weapons by 2030; US Department of Defense, "Military and security developments involving the People's Republic of China," November 3, 2021, https://media.defense.gov/2021/Nov/03/2002885874/-1/-1/0/2021-CMPR-FINAL.PDF.

6. See James Cameron, "China's silos: New intelligence, old problems," *War on the Rocks*, August 12, 2021, https://warontherocks.com/2021/08/beijings-silos-new-intelligence-old-problems/; and *Economist*, "China is rapidly building new nuclear-missile silos," July 31, 2021, https://www.economist.com/china/2021/07/31/china-is-rapidly-building-new-nuclear-missile-silos.
7. In 2013 Wu Riqiang ("Certainty of uncertainty: Nuclear strategy with Chinese characteristics, *Journal of Strategic Studies*, 36, No. 4, 579–614) countered the claim of Phillip Karber and Russian general Viktor Yesin that Chinese nuclear inventories were grossly underestimated by arguing that their numbers would be greatly in excess of Chinese stockpiles of fissile materials.
8. See, for instance, Office of the Secretary of Defense, *Annual Report to Congress: Military and Security Developments Involving the People's Republic of China 2017*, 61: "The PLA continues to maintain a robust and technologically advanced underground facility (UGF) program protecting all aspects of its military forces, including C2, logistics, missile systems, and naval forces."
9. Austin Long and Brendan Green, "Stalking the secure second strike: Intelligence, counterforce, and nuclear strategy," *Journal of Strategic Studies*, 38, Nos. 1–2 (2015), 38–73.
10. Paul Bracken, "The cyber threat to nuclear stability," *Orbis*, 60, No. 2 (February 12, 2016), 188–203.
11. Bracken, "The cyber threat," 193.
12. Riqiang, "Certainty of uncertainty," 587.
13. Long and Green, "Stalking," 57–58.
14. This is a growing leitmotif taken from how professional hackers penetrate systems. "We'll poke and we'll poke and we'll wait and we'll wait and we'll wait . . . looking for an opportunity to finish that mission . . . persistence and focus will get you in," from Rob Joyce speaking at the USENIX Enigma 2016 conference: https://www.youtube.com/watch?v=bDJb8WOJYdA.
15. See, for instance, Bruce Schneier, "Class breaks," *Schneier on Security*, January 3, 2017, https://www.schneier.com/blog/archives/2017/01/class_breaks.html.
16. Glenn Snyder, *Deterrence and Defense: Toward a Theory of National Security* (Princeton, NJ: Princeton U. Press, 1961), 88.
17. The influence of countermeasures on the timing of deployment has been long-understood. From John Stillion and Bryan Clark, "What it takes to win: Succeeding in 21st century battle network competition," *Center for Strategic and Budgetary Analysis*, July 10, 2015, https://csbaonline.org/research/publications/what-it-takes-to-win-succeeding-in-21st-century-battle-network-competitions: "It is generally better to wait until innovative airborne systems can be fielded in sufficient numbers to achieve significant operational results during their relatively short 'unopposed' operational lives than to introduce them piecemeal and risk early compromise."
18. Alexei Arbatov, "Challenges of the new nuclear era: The Russian perspective," in Linton Brooks, Francis J. Gavin, and Alexei Arbatov, *Meeting the Challenges of the New Nuclear Age: US and Russian Nuclear Concepts, Past and Present* (Cambridge, MA: American Academy of Arts and Sciences, 2018).
19. Talmadge, "Would China," 85.
20. Talmadge, "Would China," 87.
21. Lieber, "Counterforce"; Keir A. Lieber and Daryl G. Press, "The end of MAD? The nuclear dimension of US primacy," *International Security*, 30, No. 4 (Spring 2006), 7;

and Keir A. Lieber and Daryl G. Press, *Coercive Nuclear Campaigns in the 21st Century: Understanding Adversary Incentives and Options for Nuclear Escalation*, US Naval Postgraduate School, March 2013, http://www.dtic.mil/dtic/tr/fulltext/u2/a585975.pdf.
22. Lieber, "Counterforce," 21.
23. Keir Lieber ("Counterforce") makes a similar argument but posits highly accurate 0.3 kiloton weapons instead of today's 300 kiloton weapons; the argument does not require evoking fourth-generation nuclear weapons. Eldridge Colby ("Against the great powers: Reflections on balancing nuclear and conventional power," *Texas National Security Review* 2, No. 1 [November 2018]) argues, "Accordingly, nuclear weapons that could significantly damage or impair such targets, but with lessened collateral damage ... [e.g.,] those with a lower yield, those that could be employed in ways that would create less radioactivity, and those that would travel on trajectories and from platforms that would be less likely to generate an opponent's fear that they were part of or precursor to a general or attempted disarming attack." Mark Ambinder ("How Obama made it easier for Trump to launch a nuke: Maybe we should talk about this?," *Politico*, September 14, 2018, https://www.politico.com/magazine/story/2018/09/14/barack-obama-nukes-donald-trump-219912) argued, "The big problem is that the technology we use to deliver nuclear weapons has advanced to the point where a president might not find all that much reason to worry about using a nuclear weapon in a real conflict. If she or he can be assured that the radioactive fallout would be minimal, the threat to civilians basically zero and the scope of the destruction precisely tailored, then many of the disincentives fall away." In 2010, President Obama ordered the development of a nuclear weapon (the B-61 Model 12) with a 0.2 kiloton warhead that used precision to achieve its battlefield effects. The first was produced in 2021.
24. Matthew Kroenig, *The Logic of American Nuclear Strategy* (Oxford UK: Oxford University Press, 2018).
25. For a contrasting view of who won that confrontation, see Hyun-Binn Cho, "Nuclear coercion, crisis bargaining, and the Sino-Soviet border conflict of 1969," *Security Studies*, 30, No. 4 (2020), 550–577.
26. See, for instance, John J. Mearsheimer, "A strategic misstep: The maritime strategy and deterrence in Europe," *International Security*, 11, No. 2 (Fall 1986), 3–57.
27. Aaron Friedberg, *Beyond Air-Sea Battle: The Debate over US Military Strategy in Asia*, Adelphi Paper No. 444 (London UK: International Institute of Strategic Studies, April 2014), 89–90.
28. Union of Concerned Scientists, "US ballistic missile defense timeline: 1945-today," March 29, 2019, https://www.ucsusa.org/resources/us-missile-defense-timeline. See also Theresa Hitchens, "No US missile defense system proven capable against 'realistic' ICBM threats," *Breaking Defense*, February 22, 2022, https://breakingdefense.com/2022/02/no-us-missile-defense-system-proven-capable-against-realistic-icbm-threats-study/.
29. "Beijing ... [is] intending to at least double the size of its nuclear stockpile during the next decade and to field a nuclear triad," Office of the Director of National Intelligence, "Annual Threat Assessment of the US Intelligence Community," April 9, 2021, https://www.dni.gov/files/ODNI/documents/assessments/ATA-2021-Unclassified-Report.pdf. That point is made explicitly in Henrik Stålhane Hiim, M. Taylor Fravel, and Magnus Langset Trøan, "The dynamics of an entangled security dilemma: China's changing nuclear posture," *International Security*, 47, No. 4 (Spring 2023), 147–87.

30. Talmadge, "Would China," 75, "The PLARF [PLA Rocket Force] relies heavily on surreptitious circulation of nuclear warheads along road and especially rail networks to improve survivability in a crisis or war, but this approach raises the risk that US efforts to stymie movements of the conventional missile brigades could have a similar effect on the nuclear brigades."
31. Even though US forces shipped to Europe were typical for such exercises: only 16,000 troops. See, for instance, Dmitry Adamsky, "The 1983 nuclear crisis—Lessons for deterrence theory and practice," *Journal of Strategic Studies*, 36, No. 1 (2013); and President's Foreign Intelligence Advisory Board report, "The Soviet 'war scare'," February 15, 1990, https://nsarchive2.gwu.edu/nukevault/ebb533-The-Able-Archer-War-Scare-Declassified-PFIAB-Report-Released/2012-0238-MR.pdf.
32. James Acton, "Escalation through entanglement: How the vulnerability of command-and-control systems raises the risks of an inadvertent nuclear war," *International Security*, 43, No. 1 (2018), 56–99.
33. For example, "Believing that their nuclear forces are under attack and might soon become unusable, the enemy might escalate to nuclear use." From Madison Estes, "Prevailing under the nuclear shadow: A new framework for US escalation management," *Center for Naval Analyses*, September 2020, https://www.cna.org/CNA_files/PDF/DRM-2020-U-027973-Final%20(003).pdf.
34. Keir A. Lieber and Daryl G. Press, "The new era of nuclear weapons, deterrence, and conflict," *Strategic Studies Quarterly*, 10, No. 5 (USSTRATCOM 2016 issue).
35. Thomas J. Christensen, "The meaning of the nuclear evolution: China's strategic modernization and US-China security relations," *Journal of Strategic Studies*, 35, No. 4 (2012), 447–487.
36. Fiona Cunningham and M. Taylor Fravel, "Assuring assured retaliation: China's nuclear posture and US-China strategic stability," *International Security*, 40, No. 2 (Fall 2015), 10. See also M. Taylor Fravel, *Active Defense: China's Military Strategy since 1949* (Princeton NJ: Princeton University Press, 2019), especially pp. 236–269: "China's nuclear strategy since 1964." See also Hans M. Kristensen and Matt Korda, "Chinese nuclear forces," *Bulletin of the Atomic Scientists*, 75, No. 4 (2019), 171–8, who argue, "Chinese officials privately say that China would respond with nuclear weapons if its nuclear forces were attacked with conventional weapons."
37. Cunningham and Fravel, "Assuring assured," 14.
38. Cunningham and Fravel, "Assuring assured," 27.
39. Cunningham and Fravel, "Assuring assured," 20–21.
40. Cunningham and Fravel, "Assuring assured," 51.
41. Similarly, research that deprecates the influence of deterrence on the outcome of militarized crises overlooks the fact that countries enter militarized crises precisely because they are not deterred from doing so; see James Fearon, "Selection effects and deterrence," *International Interactions*, 28, No. 1 (2002), 5–29.
42. Linley Sanders, "How does America feel about NATO? Support for alliance falls across key Western nations," *Yougov.com*, April 4, 2019, https://today.yougov.com/topics/politics/articles-reports/2019/04/04/how-does-america-feel-about-nato.
43. Olga Oliker and Andrey Baklitskiy, "The nuclear posture review and Russian 'de-escalation': A dangerous solution to a nonexistent problem," *War on the Rocks*, February 20, 2018, https://warontherocks.com/2018/02/nuclear-posture-review-russian-de-escalation-dangerous-solutionnonexistent-problem/.

44. Amy Woolf, "Russia's nuclear weapons: Doctrine, forces, and modernization," *Congressional Research Service*, April 21, 2022, https://sgp.fas.org/crs/nuke/R45861.pdf citing Ministry of Foreign Affairs of the Russian Federation, *On Basic Principles of State Policy of the Russian Federation*, Moscow, June 2, 2020, https://www.mid.ru/en/web/guest/foreign_policy/international_safety/disarmament/-/asset_publisher/rp0fiUBmANaH/content/id/4152094. The CRS report also quotes Putin to the contrary, saying Russia "will use nuclear weapons only when we know for certain that some potential aggressor is attacking Russia, our territory [with nuclear weapons]," p. 11.
45. From *The Guardian*, "Russia reasserts right to use nuclear weapons in Ukraine," March 26, 2022, https://www.theguardian.com/world/2022/mar/26/russia-reasserts-right-to-use-nuclear-weapons-in-ukraine-putin.
46. From Brennan Deveraux, "Why intermediate-range missiles are a focal point in the Ukraine crisis," *War on the Rocks*, January 28, 2022, https://warontherocks.com/2022/01/why-intermediate-range-missiles-are-a-focal-point-in-the-ukraine-crisis/. "Section III on 'Conditions under which the Russian Federation Transitions to the Use of Nuclear Weapons,' especially Clause 19, specifies four conditions that could lead to nuclear use ... the third condition has to do with actions taken against Russian critical government or military installations by an adversary that would have the effect of disrupting Russia's capacity for nuclear retaliation." From Cynthia Roberts, "Revelations about Russia's nuclear deterrence policy," *War on the Rocks*, June 19, 2020, https://warontherocks.com/2020/06/revelations-about-russias-nuclear-deterrence-policy/.
47. John K. Warden, "Limited nuclear war: The 21st century challenge for the United States," Lawrence Livermore National Laboratory Center for Global Security Research, *Livermore Papers on Global Security*, No. 4 (July 2018), 15.
48. Bruce Sugden, "A primer on analyzing nuclear competitions," *Texas National Security Review*, 2, No. 3 (July 16, 2019), 124.
49. See, for instance, Michael Kofman and Anya Loukianova Fink, "Escalation management and nuclear employment in Russian military strategy," *War on the Rocks*, June 23, 2020, https://warontherocks.com/2020/06/escalation-management-and-nuclear-employment-in-russian-military-strategy/.
50. Alexei Arbatov, Vladimir Dvorkin, and Petr Topychkanov, "Entanglement as a new security threat: A Russian perspective," *Carnegie Moscow Center*, November 08, 2017, https://carnegie.ru/2017/11/08/entanglement-as-new-security-threat-russian-perspective-pub-73163, 6.
51. Arbatov et al., "Entanglement," 11.
52. Dave Johnson, "Russia's conventional precision strike capabilities, regional crises, and nuclear thresholds," *Livermore Papers on Global Security*, No. 3, February 2018, https://cgsr.llnl.gov/content/assets/docs/Precision-Strike-Capabilities-report-v3-7.pdf, 78.
53. "Russia's Medvedev warns of nuclear response if Ukraine hits missile launch sites," *Reuters*, January 11, 2024, https://www.reuters.com/world/europe/russias-medvedev-warns-nuclear-response-if-ukraine-hits-missile-launch-sites-2024-01-11/.
54. From Muhammad Irshad, "Crisis of nuclear neighbors," *Defense Journal*, 6, No. 2 (2002), 120–25; the paraphrasing comes from Paul Kapur, *Dangerous Deterrent*, 42.
55. Jeffrey Lewis, *The 2020 Commission Report on the North Korean Nuclear Attacks against the United States: A Speculative Novel* (Boston, MA: Mariner Books, 2018).

56. George Perkovich and Pranay Vaddi, "Proportionate deterrence: A model nuclear posture review," *Carnegie Endowment*, 2020, https://carnegieendowment.org/files/Perkovich_Vaddi_NPR_full1.pdf, 68.
57. See, for instance, Christine Parthemore and Catharine Dill, "Paint the B-52s brightly: Reducing confusion between conventional and nuclear weapons is essential," September 18, 2024; https://warontherocks.com/2024/09/paint-the-b-52s-brightly-reducing-confusion-between-conventional-and-nuclear-weapons-is-essential/.
58. See for instance, Robert Jervis, "Cooperation under the security dilemma," *World Politics*, 30 No. 2 (January 1978), 167–214.
59. *Economist*, "Obituary: Stanislav Petrov was declared to have died on September 18th," September 30, 2017, https://www.economist.com/obituary/2017/09/30/obituary-stanislav-petrov-was-declared-to-have-died-on-september-18th.
60. Cunningham and Fravel, "Assuring assured," 22.
61. Cunningham and Fravel, "Assuring assured," 43.
62. But the two systems may be more difficult to distinguish than it seems. So argues Wu Riqiang, "Sino-U.S. inadvertent nuclear escalation," Renmin University (2016), 6, 10, 13–17, 30, 33–35 (available from the author upon request).
63. Dennis Blair's letter to the editor in *Foreign Affairs*, 98, No. 1 (January/February 2019), 218–19.
64. Avery Goldstein, "First things first: The pressing danger of crisis instability in U.S.-China relations," *International Security*, 37, No. 4 (Spring 2013), 49–89 (especially 70–72, 88).
65. Barry Posen, *Inadvertent Escalation: Conventional War and Nuclear Risks* (Ithaca, NY: Cornell University Press, 1991).
66. Matthew Kroenig and Mark Massa, "Are dual-capable weapon systems destabilizing? Questioning nuclear-conventional entanglement and inadvertent escalation," *Atlantic Council*, June 2021, https://www.atlanticcouncil.org/in-depth-research-reports/issue-brief/are-dual-capable-weapon-systems-destabilizing/. They add, "In sum, on closer examination, it appears that US strikes on China's nuclear-related forces would not make deliberate nuclear use an obvious or attractive choice for China's leaders."
67. David C. Logan ("Are they reading Schelling in Beijing? The dimensions, drivers, and risks of nuclear-conventional entanglement in China," *Journal of Strategic Studies*, 46, No. 1 [2023], 5–55) argues that "Chinese entanglement was not a deliberate strategic choice," perhaps because, "Chinese writings are notable for their lack of attention to the potential risks of entanglement."
68. See, for instance, James M. Acton, "Cyber warfare & inadvertent escalation," *Daedalus*, 149, No. 2 (Spring 2020), 133–49.
69. For a thorough treatment see Andrew Futter, *Hacking the Bomb: Cyber Threats and Nuclear Weapons* (Washington, DC: Georgetown University Press, 2018). See also Beyza Unal and Patricia Lewis, "Cybersecurity of nuclear weapons systems: Threats, vulnerabilities and consequences," *Chatham House*, January 2018, https://www.chathamhouse.org/publication/cybersecurity-nuclear-weapons-systems-threats-vulnerabilities-and-consequences. For evidence that the quest to hobble nuclear weapons production is recurrent, see David Sanger and William Broad, "U.S. revives secret program to sabotage Iranian missiles and rockets," *New York Times*, February 13, 2019, https://www.nytimes.com/2019/02/13/us/politics/iran-missile-launch-failures.html.

70. Adam Lowther, "The big and urgent task of revitalizing nuclear command, control, and communications," *War on the Rocks*, October 4, 2019, https://warontherocks.com/2019/10/the-big-and-urgent-task-of-revitalizing-nuclear-command-control-and-communications/. See also *Economist*, "Why nuclear stability is under threat," January 25, 2018, https://www.economist.com/special-report/2018/01/25/why-nuclear-stability-is-under-threat.
71. David Ochmanek and Michael Sulmeyer, *Challenges in U.S. National Security Policy: A Festschrift Honoring Edward L. (Ted) Warner* (Santa Monica CA: RAND, 2014) 112–114.
72. From Futter, *Hacking the Bomb*, citing Aliya Sternstein, "Officials worry about vulnerability of global nuclear stockpile to cyberattack," *Global Security Newswire* (March 14, 2013) and Eric Schlosser, "Neglecting our nukes," *Politico*, September 16, 2013, https://www.politico.com/story/2013/09/neglecting-our-nukes-96854_Page2.html.
73. For an earlier working of this material see David C. Gompert and Martin Libicki, "Cyber war and nuclear peace," *Survival*, 61, No. 4 (August–September 2019), 45–62.
74. As expressed in US Defense Science Board, "Resilient military systems." See also Bruce Blair, "Why our nuclear weapons can be hacked," *New York Times*, March 14, 2017, https://www.nytimes.com/2017/03/14/opinion/why-our-nuclear-weapons-can-be-hacked.html. For a comprehensive examination see Herbert Lin, *Cyber Threats and Nuclear Weapons* (Palo Alto, CA: Stanford University Press, 2021).
75. Hackers may have compromised the production of North Korea's Musudan medium-range ballistic missile; see Sanger and Broad, "Trump inherits."
76. Bruce Blair in the *Global Zero Commission on Nuclear Risk Reduction, De-Alerting and Stabilizing the World's Nuclear Force Postures*, April 2015, https://www.globalzero.org/wp-content/uploads/2018/09/global_zero_commission_on_nuclear_risk_reduction_report_0.pdf, 31: "If we cannot fully assess the risks, it would seem prudent to keep nuclear missiles off of high alert status at all times. This would be a sure-fire way to mitigate foreseeable risks as well as those that have not yet been imagined."
77. A longer list sketches 21 possible routes between cyberspace operations and nuclear crises; see Jon Lindsay, *Cyber Operations and Nuclear Weapons*, Nautilus Institute: NAPSNet Special Reports, June 20, 2019, https://nautilus.org/napsnet/napsnet-special-reports/cyber-operations-and-nuclear-weapons/.
78. Ockmanek, "Challenges," 112–14.
79. See Ross Anderson, *Security Engineering: A Guide to Building Dependable Distributed Systems, Second Edition* (Hoboken NJ: Wiley, 2008), Chapter 15, "Nuclear command and control," 529–48. Michael Pillsbury ("The sixteen fears: China's strategic psychology," *Survival*, 54, No. 5 [October–November 2012], 149–82) has written, "training exercises [of China's strategic missile force] have emphasized strategies to counter air attacks, attacks by special forces, electromagnetic jamming, live-troop reconnaissance, and network attacks using hackers and computer viruses."
80. See Jesse Damiani, "A voice deepfake was used to scam a CEO out of $243,000," *Forbes*, September 3, 2019, https://www.forbes.com/sites/jessedamiani/2019/09/03/a-voice-deepfake-was-used-to-scam-a-ceo-out-of-243000/#61b8d9002241. Multifactor authentication can defeat these threats, but see Aja Romano, "Jordan Peele's simulated Obama PSA is a double-edged warning against fake news: This deepfaked warning against deepfakes almost makes its point too well," *Vox*, April 18, 2018, https://www.vox.com/2018/4/18/17252410/jordan-peele-obama-deepfake-buzzfeed.

81. For instance, James Miller and Richard Fontaine ("A new era in US-Russian strategic stability: How changing geopolitics and emerging technologies are reshaping pathways to crisis and conflict," *Center for a New America Security*, September 19, 2017, https://www.cnas.org/publications/reports/a-new-era-in-u-s-russian-strategic-stability, 30) wrote, "The vulnerability of both U.S. and Russian military forces to cyberattack generates classic 'first use' pressures. In other words, in the event of a crisis, knowing how vulnerable it is to a potential impending cyberattack, each side is incentivized to use its cyber-vulnerable capabilities first or lose them."
82. Ben Buchanan and Fiona Cunningham, "Preparing the cyber battlefield: Assessing a novel escalation risk in a Sino-American crisis," *Texas National Security Review*, 3, No. 4 (Fall 2020), 54–81.
83. E.g., Taylor Downing, *1983: Reagan, Andropov, and a World on the Brink* (New York: Hachette, 2018), 142.
84. Erik Gartzke and Jon R. Lindsay, "Thermonuclear cyberwar," *Journal of Cybersecurity*, 3, No. 1 (2017), 37–48.
85. Johnathan Falcone et al., "Prove it before you use it: Nuclear retaliation under uncertainty," *War on the Rocks*, June 1, 2023, https://warontherocks.com/2023/06/prove-it-before-you-use-it-nuclear-retaliation-under-uncertainty/.
86. Paul H. Nitze, "Atoms, strategy, and policy," *Foreign Affairs*, 34 No. 2 (January 1956), https://www.foreignaffairs.com/articles/1956-01-01/atoms-strategy-and-policy, 195: "The atomic queens may never be brought into play; they may never actually take one of the opponent's pieces. But the position of the atomic queens may still have a decisive bearing on which side can safely advance a limited-war bishop or even a cold-war pawn. The advance of a cold-war pawn may even disclose a check of the opponent's king by a well-positioned atomic queen."
87. Joshua Rovner, "A long war in the east: Doctrine, diplomacy, and the prospects for a protracted Sino-American conflict," *Diplomacy and Statecraft*, 29, No. 1 (2018), 129–42: "A low-risk approach would keep the conflict off the mainland to the extent possible and assiduously avoid targeting China's deterrent force. It would err on the side of caution, steering clear of targets that Chinese officials might construe as part of an attack on its nuclear complex. It would also avoid the kind of blinding attacks that have become commonplace in American military operations. Instead of inhibiting China's intelligence capabilities, it would ensure that the PLA had enough situational awareness to feel confident that its nuclear force was secure."

6

The Putative Tactical–Strategic Nuclear Threshold

The Russian military establishment has spent decades thinking and arguing about escalation management, the role of conventional and nuclear weapons, targeting, damage, etc. In the United States, precious little attention has been paid to the question of escalation management, which is overshadowed by planning for warfighting. Thinking on escalation management and limited nuclear war should take priority, because the political leadership of any state entering a crisis with a nuclear peer will inevitably wish to be assured that a plausible strategy for escalation management and war termination exists.[1]

In 1957 Henry Kissinger argued[2] that NATO countries could use tactical nuclear weapons to hold off Warsaw Pact armies—and still not make strategic nuclear war inevitable—thereby presuming a threshold between tactical and strategic nuclear war.[3] In the 1980s Robert McNamara (the Secretary of Defense in the 1960s), conversely, concluded that no NATO plans to use tactical nuclear weapons (in particular nuclear artillery) could improve military outcomes without creating a very high risk of Armageddon.[4] Yet the INF controversy of 1979–85, during which the United States decided to upgrade its theater nuclear missiles, was fueled by the fear that the Soviet Union *could* exploit the gap between tactical and strategic nukes, undermining NATO's escalation threat and thus undermining deterrence.

Can a tactical–strategic threshold slow the ascent to Armageddon even after nuclear use? Maybe not. *First*, it is not obvious what distinguishes tactical and strategic nuclear weapons. Is it warhead yield range (the reason why certain weapons fall within New START limits), destination (e.g., in the homeland of a nuclear state versus an allied state versus the immediate battlefield), command arrangements (civilian leadership versus military), or the type of target (military or civilian)? *Second*, no nuclear country has declared or even intimated that it would respect the difference between tactical and strategic nuclear weapons use. Therefore none has pledged to *not* answer a tactical nuclear strike with a strategic nuclear strike. Beyond that it is unclear whether any other post-nuclear-use threshold has purchase. The exemplary use of nuclear weapons only works if it is understood that matters might not stop there.

THE LOGIC OF TACTICAL NUCLEAR USE

Tactical nuclear weapons have both warfighting and warning roles. Both can lead to escalation but in different ways.

In the early Cold War nuclear weapons were mooted for many roles—such as antiship, anti-air, anti-armor, as well as anti-infrastructure. With greater weapons precision, though, there was no need to waste blast power on such targets, leaving far fewer appropriate aimpoints: concentrated armies, runways (because rapid runway repair kits limit the long-term damage conventional weapons can do), spread-out infrastructures (concentrated ones can be taken out with conventional weapons), and high-value targets whose location is only approximately known. The military usefulness of tactical nuclear weapons has correspondingly declined—but not to zero. The side that is struck by nuclear weapons may resent not only that the nuclear taboo is breached, but that doing so could also reap serious military advantages. Anger could overtake the fear of Armageddon of the sort that retaliation in kind could bring. Perhaps the other side can even the score by using tactical nuclear weapons itself, but it sees no reason to adhere to the exact parameters that characterized the nuclear blow that it suffered—especially if doing so would fail to turn the tide. So it escalates. Neither side was making any decision blithely. Both sides know what unrestrained escalation would bring. But both had other important values for which they were already fighting and dying. Avoiding Armageddon was just one of them.

The use of tactical nuclear weapons also draws force from the fact that it was *not* just a battlefield weapon. Escalating to tactical nuclear weapons would concentrate minds on the prospect of Armageddon—and might induce the other side to settle before it was too late. No conventional weapon could do that. The escalate-to-deescalate notion is not merely some recent invention of

Putin but was explicitly mooted as a rationale for nuclear use as far back as 1967 even by Bernard Brodie, he of "no other useful purpose" fame.[5] Here, one side uses tactical nuclear weapons to signal that things have gone too far; the other side gets the message, realizes that retaliation in kind would serve only to deliver the same message—and settles. But the side that saw reason and sued for peace rather than upped the ante would thereby reveal itself as less powerful or at least less pain-tolerant—thus also prey to being intimidated again and correspondingly less intimidating to its rivals. Even in the face of disaster, people can convince themselves that the cost of trying to edge out the other side would be small and the rewards would justify the expected pain.

Threats to use tactical nuclear weapons may be more credible, hence more usable, than threats to use strategic nuclear weapons; they can be the "threat that leaves something to chance."[6] To see how, consider a scenario (familiar to students of the war in Ukraine) in which Blue fears that something it does could lead Red to use nuclear weapons but Red says nothing. How does Blue play this? What is "the danger that they may inadvertently cross a threshold of escalation"?[7] Every action Blue could take can be placed on a spectrum from those with no risk (maybe it had been done before); to those of medium risk because they involve acts that Red might want to raise a serious scare to deter; and to those of great risk where Red prefers nuclear war to seeing Blue carry them out (again). Even if nuclear war is mutual suicide, maybe Red feels nuclear war is inevitable—so why not go first? Or maybe Red thinks some outcomes are worse than Armageddon (e.g., "death before dishonor"). If the trigger point is unspoken, Blue can only guess where it lies. Inching forward might seem to be Blue's best strategy,[8] but if Red's only response is nothing or nuclear war, then the odds of stumbling into a nuclear "land mine" by taking small steps to a goal are the same as if taking one large leap to the goal. Red's silence, though, means that its own survival is entirely in Blue's hands. So perhaps Red should warn Blue if it gets close. The more that Red can raise Blue's estimate of the odds of Armageddon for a given action, the less likely Blue will act. But extending the trigger point too far down the intensity curve raises the odds that Blue will test Red in an area where Red really does not want to react and cannot credibly threaten to as a result. Blue's crossing some stated line says it thinks that the trigger point lies farther away—and that the next steps are also fairly safe to take. For example, if supplying the High Mobility Artillery Rocket System (HIMARS) to its ally seemed risky, Blue did it anyway, and no nuclear weapons fell, then try the Army Tactical Missile System (ATACMs) next. Because a do-not-or-we-all-die trigger point does not serve Red's interest as there are no second moves, such a threat provides the wrong traction. This is why Red is better off threatening tactical nuclear use, which is more credible by dint of its lower risk to Red if carried out.[9] Blue can believe that Red can use such weapons and Blue can still come out ahead. Paradoxically this may help Blue. If threatened with Armageddon, every Blue action carries risk, and Blue may hold back well before it reaches Red's trigger point. With tactical nuclear use on the line, the cost of guessing wrong would be not Armageddon, but an outcome between having to back down or continuing with high tension levels plus suffering grave but not existential damage from nuclear use. Blue can afford to run closer to Red's true red lines.

Small nuclear weapons still have their adherents. Mark Fitzpatrick offers, "The immediate moral stigma attached to nuclear use might be less if the nuclear weapon(s) used were very small, accurate bombs with minimal collateral damage and civilian casualties for which the 'just war' criteria of necessity, proportionality and discrimination could be said to apply."[10] In principle, everyone would see the "small" in small nuclear weapons and not overreact. Yet even that would require at least a rough consensus on the definition of "small," lest one or the other side find advantage in using weapons of successively greater power and range while claiming that they were tactical even as the other side felt otherwise. Hence the search for clear boundaries in the hope that once leaders understood that they were about to cross from tactical into strategic conflict, they would think deeply about their doing so. It would not be a line that they would see only in their rearview mirrors. As one analyst argued, "Tactical nuclear weapons are designed to be used within a defined theater of operations and against military, not civilian, targets. It's not that hard."[11] But is it so easy?

WHAT DOES TACTICAL MEAN?

Compared to strategic nuclear weapons, tactical nuclear weapons are said to have less powerful warheads, shorter ranges, military uses, and land elsewhere than in superpower territory. Range and warheads were correlated in that the greater range of strategic weapons meant that, at least initially, each missile needed to carry a large warhead to overcome its inaccuracy and still destroy its objective.[12] But that still leaves a fuzzy tactical–strategic threshold. Consider several possible definitions.

One distinction may be the size of the weapon's warhead—for which there is no consensus on where to draw the line. According to one observer, "What the Russians believe are tactical nuclear weapons are roughly as powerful as to what the United States believes are strategic nuclear weapons (roughly several hundred kilotons of TNT equivalent); thus, what the

Russians may regard as variation within the broad category of tactical weapons may strike the United States as a dire escalation from tactical to strategic weapons."[13] There is not even a clean distinction in the US inventory. The obviously strategic Minuteman III (the mainstay of the US ICBM fleet since the mid-1990s[14]) carries a 170 kiloton W62 warhead. The warhead for tactical cruise missiles (the W80 and W84 types—ones not counted as part of New START) could reach 150 kilotons. Initial post-detonation measurements of warhead sizes—and thus whether a weapon crossed a threshold—may vary. Even as recently as 2009, North Korea's nuclear test was measured at 2 to 7 kilotons[15] (a later paper concluded 2.35 kilotons).

A weapon's range could be another distinction. Putatively tactical nuclear warheads arm delivery vehicles whose range is smaller than those carrying strategic warheads. Weapons covered under the SALT and the later New START treaty[16] observe that distinction, in part because these were bilateral treaties between two countries far away from one another, and in part because strategic missiles are easier to see and hence count than tactical missiles. Even if nuclear cruise missiles look like non-nuclear cruise missiles, every deployed ICBM and SLBM these days is nuclear. But how relevant is the range distinction? It does not limit destruction. And while the United States can reach Russia or China with tactical cruise missiles launched from sea, the reverse is harder. Moscow and Beijing may be therefore reluctant to observe a threshold so defined. In South Asia, where two nuclear powers share a border (and neither has great strategic depth behind it), tactical–strategic distinctions are even harder to draw.[17]

A third distinction is that tactical nuclear weapons would hit the area of immediate military operations; strategic weapons land beyond it. The official DoD definition[18] does distinguish between the strategic ("the purpose of progressive destruction and disintegration of the enemy's warmaking capacity and will to make war") and the tactical ("in support of operations that contribute to the accomplishment of a military mission of limited scope, or in support of the military commander's scheme of maneuver, usually limited to the area of military operations"). But such a distinction requires agreement on what the area of military operations is. The US military strategy to defend western Europe in the 1980s called for interdicting follow-on forces (albeit with conventional weapons) as they were crossing Poland, several hundred miles east of where forces would be clashing. NATO's air bases and ports hundreds of miles westward were also considered legitimate military targets by the Soviets. Indeed it is hard to imagine any territory of a US ally in Europe or Asia being deemed outside the area of military operations.

A closely related distinction is who the weapon hits. Tactical nuclear weapons would be those used on allies. Strategic weapons would be those used on superpowers. This distinction has the merit of being easy to measure, but it is highly asymmetric. Accepting that a nuclear attack on a US ally sits at a lower level of escalation than a nuclear attack on the United States breaks the promise of extended deterrence built into NATO and US mutual-defense treaties in the Pacific. Both Russia and China, by contrast, have few allies to worry about. The superpower–allies distinction also protects military assets in Russia from being targeted by tactical nuclear weapons while those across the border in NATO can be struck. So unless the United States intends to bomb only naval targets or the occupied territory of its allies, no nuclear weapon it employs against Russia or China can be tactical by this definition.

Lastly the release of strategic nuclear weapons is likely to be the prerogative of the National Command Authority (here the US president). If tactical nuclear weapons are deployed to field units, their commanders may also have the authority to decide when to use them. But detecting whether a threshold was crossed based on who authorized it requires knowledge of the other side's command arrangements, which is hardly obvious.

Some nuclear uses are clearly strategic (e.g., a nuclear strike on missile silos in North Dakota); others are clearly tactical (e.g., a neutron bomb dropped on advancing Russian tank forces). But there is a large zone in between. If nuclear operations in that zone matter to outcomes (rather than being some weird edge case), the temptation by one side to call its nuclear weapon use there tactical may overcome the risks of fudging prevailing tactical–strategic distinctions. Tactical nuclear weapons use by one side thinking that it would not escalate war to the strategic level—for example because the warhead was delivered on a cruise missile—may nevertheless lead there because the other side held to a different distinction—such as the warhead size or where it landed. A state that needed a threshold could select and promote *one* criterion that distinguishes tactical from strategic nuclear weapons. If potential adversaries agree on that criterion as a threshold, the other potential criteria can be ignored. But this has not happened yet (apart from what is implicit in the New START treaty and its predecessors).

A serious tactical–strategic threshold would *lower* the odds that a tactical nuclear exchange would lead to Armageddon by inserting one more barrier to cross before it happens. It makes the world safer for tactical nuclear war and makes Russia's (say, escalate-to-deescalate) tactical use less risky. If the United States, however, lacked effective inventories of tactical nuclear weapons, such a threshold would not matter as much because the United

States would have no convincing option between doing nothing nuclear or using strategic nuclear weapons. Politically, "the U.S. interest in adding nuclear rungs to escalation ladders feeds a Russian perception that their smaller-yield nuclear weapons make Americans nervous. This perception, in turn, increases a Russian belief in the coercive power of nuclear threats and strengthens voices within Russia that see value in additional nuclear escalatory steps."[19] A threshold thus increases the need for the United States to have an adequate tactical nuclear response.

The refusal of Russians and Chinese to even talk about the possibility of a threshold that admits of *some* nuclear use bodes ill for any attempt to recognize a threshold that either would accept. This despite claims[20] that "in contrast with Soviet thinking, the Russian military does not believe that limited nuclear use necessarily leads to uncontrolled escalation." Even mulling the prospect that nuclear use can be managed raises the odds that it will take place. Yet if it *does* take place anyway, then finding a stopping point before Armageddon would require some prior understandings. Once nuclear weapons are used, requisite conversations could easily be drowned in the noise of war.

In the nearly eighty years of the atomic age, no country has offered to make any tactical–strategic distinctions, much less assert where the distinction may lie and indicate how such distinctions might be measured in the heat of nuclear combat. There have been mutual conclusions only that nuclear war should be so scary to the other side that their leaders will sweat hard to avoid one. Anything to make certain types of nuclear war merely semi-scary defeats the deterrence purpose. To give the last word to former Secretary of Defense James Mattis, "I don't think there is any such thing as a 'tactical nuclear weapon.' Any nuclear weapon used any time is a strategic game-changer."[21]

EXEMPLARY NUCLEAR USE AS A THRESHOLD

Other nuclear-related thresholds may fare no better than the tactical–strategic one. In the early 1960s Robert McNamara declared that in a nuclear war, the United States would start with counterforce use (against Soviet nuclear capability), pause, and then threaten countervalue use (against cities) if the Soviet Union targeted US cities. Such a pause would mark a threshold between a nuclear war that killed millions and one that killed tens of millions. The Soviets rejected the notion, arguing that the United States policy was trying to normalize and sanitize nuclear war by moving it from unthinkable to thinkable, perhaps usable.[22] They argued that nuclear war was nuclear war, period.

Can Armageddon be avoided if there *were* a threshold that separated the exemplary use of nuclear weapons from their instrumental use? That way, nuclear weapons could be used only to signal the other side to, for instance, stop its counternuclear campaign. One or at most a few nuclear weapons could suffice—and may be worthwhile even if the other side retaliated in like measure. Or such a move could backfire by cracking the nuclear taboo.

Incremental nuclear use—not only demonstration shots but smallish warheads or limited use (e.g., avoiding cities)—may serve serious purposes when a large escalation raises the odds of Armageddon too high and a refusal seems like giving up. As Schelling wrote,[23] "When the act to be deterred is inherently a sequence of steps whose cumulative effect is what matters, a threat geared to increments may be more credible than one that must be carried out either all at once or not at all." Many small steps provide better opportunities to learn before it is too late than would one large step that takes place before anyone has learned anything. Three jumps, each of which raises the odds of Armageddon by 10 percentage points, may *each* assure people that Armageddon is not inevitable better than one large jump that raises the odds by 30 percent. One analyst has written, "Since the 1980s, Chinese strategists have expressed a clear preference for tactical nuclear weapons (especially dual-capability ballistic and cruise missiles) as a way to build rungs on the 'nuclear ladder' to enhance the credibility of China's nuclear deterrence."[24] In the Cold War, as another analyst wrote,

> Deterrence required making it as hard as possible for any adversary to form the view that NATO would shrink from decisions on raising the conflict's breadth or severity, or to dare to act on such a view. The range of options available must therefore be an unmistakable continuum without huge gaps. That, in turn, mean that there had to be nuclear forces, backed by will and doctrine for their possible use, intermediate between conventional forces ... and the ultimate strategic nuclear capability.[25]

Likewise some analysts[26] have concluded from steadily increasing US aid to Ukraine coupled with Russia's failure to respond that the boiling frog rules apply. The speed rather than extent of escalation is what makes it escalatory.

Those who would want to use nuclear weapons for psychological effects may elect a strategy that limits the odds of Armageddon in their own mind but still signals resolve. But can it do both? States signal to alter (or anchor) the other side's decision calculus. Raising the specter of nuclear use should, by rights, indicate that the value of the stakes to them is greater than others believe (or that the cost to themselves of nuclear weapons use is less). So they are more prepared to run nuclear risks.

Signaling has always had many well-understood problematic features. Signals are often misread,[27] in part because different leaders, states, and cultures frame a confrontation and its elements differently, and in part because of the human tendency for people to misunderstand what their counterparts know (e.g., "We see and understand this; therefore, they also do. So if they act this way, it must be because ..."). Sometimes signals seem to appear when totally absent. The August 2014 discovery of a hack into the servers of JPMorgan Chase was read by the Obama administration as a signal from Putin that intervening into Ukraine would imperil the Western financial system—until it was discovered that the hackers were criminals (most from Israel).[28]

But the logic of signaling also explains why you cannot win, you cannot break even, and you cannot get out of the game.

You Cannot Win

To quote Schelling,[29] "The impressive demonstrations are probably the dangerous ones. We cannot have it both ways.... There is no cheap, safe way of using nuclears that scares the wits out of the Russians without scaring us too." This observation survived the Cold War's end: "The risk of escalation to large-scale nuclear war is inescapably present in any significant armed conflict between nuclear-capable powers.... If the risk of escalation, whatever its degree of probability is to be regarded as absolutely unacceptable ... a state attacked by a substantial nuclear power must forgo military resistance.... But ... the risk of escalation is an inescapable burden also on the aggressor."[30] An asymmetric threat—nuclear use hurts them more than you—hardly solves the problem. The other side, in assessing the signal's strength, could ask: how much risk does the *signaler* think it runs by this move? If the signaler threatens a confrontation to its advantage, a smart adversary will infer little new about how much the signaler values victory. Running a low risk but sending a strong signal only works if the other side overestimates the risk the signaler *believes* it is running. But how often can that be counted on?

You Cannot Break Even

The more that an action is seen as a deliberate signal, the less of a signal it is. If an action is *not* read as a deliberate signal, others must compare the value of the goal to the costs and risks in achieving it; a signaling action implies a more serious goal. If the action *is* read as a signal, one must compare the value of the goal *plus* the benefits of signaling resolve versus the cost and risks. The more that an action looks like signaling, therefore, the less can be inferred about the value of the goal being signaled (so a less valuable goal can still make this equation work). This applies, in particular, to third-party signaling. The UK's visible commitment to the liberation of the Falklands not only underlined that the Falklands would be defended but signaled to the Russians that Britain would use force to defend its interests in Europe. Thus signaling to Russia reduced the power of the signal to Argentina (even if it was too late to signal Argentina at that point anyway).

More to the point, assume there *is* a threshold between the use of nuclear weapons to signal resolve and the use of nuclear weapons to generate effects. One side uses nuclear weapons to send a signal. The other side could well read exemplary use as signaling a willingness to use nuclear weapons to send a signal rather than a willingness to use them for effect. The very thing that makes signaling safe also weakens it.

Signals raise attention to themselves in another way. Consider a capability meant to impress the other side. In a world of force-on-force, bringing out, say, a Dreadnought-class battleship would make the point without revealing too much about the ship in ways that would spur specific countermeasures to its capabilities. But when wars are won by the ability to hunt and hide, revealing a capability in a particularly impressive way begins to suggest *how* it works and thus where to look for countermeasures. Revelations that the NSA could do truly impressive feats (as per Edward Snowden) may have contributed to cyber-deterrence—but also jeopardized NSA's access to systems it would target. The decision to signal capabilities is a trade-off: sometimes it is worthwhile to show people capabilities the better to dissuade them from challenging you, and sometimes it is worthwhile to hide such capabilities the better to fend off such a challenge if it arises. Demonstrating capabilities suggests that dissuasion is more important than defeat, perhaps because the side doing the signaling believes it is unlikely to use the capability in war. In other words signaling a capability connotes that it might not be used—and thus should be deemed *less* influential than earlier thought.

Another paradox of signaling arises from what narrative to emphasize. Leaders who are worried about a crisis getting out of hand would emphasize thresholds and mutual self-control. Those who more want to deter the other side would instead indicate that their reaction would be unbounded. Which narrative gets employed should correspondingly reflect how close one is to crossing a threshold. If one is far, emphasize deterrence; if one is near, emphasize the threshold. Correspondingly emphasizing deterrence suggests that one is far from the breach; emphasizing thresholds signals one is close. In 2022 Russian spokespersons would moot scenarios that Ukraine would try to take Crimea with NATO support; Russia's back would be against the wall, forcing them to respond with nuclear weapons.[31] But the better conclusion is counterintuitive: Russian leaders are talking about overreacting only because they are confident that the nuclear threshold is unlikely to be approached. Here, nuclear bluster signals low odds of nuclear use.

You Cannot Get Out of the Game

Both sides start with presumptions about the other; signals amend such perceptions but rarely create them. Signaling that you are seven feet tall may be self-defeating if the other side thought you were eight feet tall. Likewise using only a few nuclear weapons could persuade the other side to reassess one's stake in the matter either upward (because nuclear weapons were used) or downward (because only a few were used when many could have been). Is an exemplary nuclear shot a warning to deescalate or an indication that, regardless of what is being said, war has henceforth tipped from conventional to nuclear and will not tip back?

CONCLUSIONS

Those looking for thresholds to modulate nuclear use after the first detonation face long odds of finding them. The boundaries between tactical and strategic nuclear use are far from clear-cut, and the very idea that there *is* a distinction is hardly universal. Any nuclear use breaks the nuclear taboo for everyone. Their use for signaling is fraught, especially if the signal fails to move the other side toward deescalation. Interwar nuclear deterrence could yield to intrawar nuclear deterrence, aka escalation management. But it would require that communications, after having failed in the quiet, work in what has then become a nuclear din.

By way of distinction but little balm, nuclear use is where the lattice thins out. Simply put, nuclear weapons are so efficient at killing quickly that nothing competes with them (even if some *contagious* biological weapons may kill more people, the unpredictability of a lethal contagion makes a poor choice of weapons). So escalation pathways once nuclear weapons are used are almost entirely nuclear themselves.

NOTES

1. Kofman and Loukianova, "Escalation management."
2. Henry's Kissinger, *Nuclear Weapons and Foreign Policy* (New York: Harper and Brothers, 1957). He had withdrawn the argument by 1961.
3. For instance, see the talk by James Miller, former undersecretary of defense for policy (Obama administration) at the Lawrence Livermore Lab's Center for Global Security Research: https://www.youtube.com/watch?v=LKzp-WX4p_s (17:18 to 17:27), "During the Cold War, in a sense, we have had, I think, two key firebreaks. One is between conventional and nuclear systems; second, between so-called theater and strategic systems or strategic attacks."
4. See Robert S. McNamara, "The military role of nuclear weapons: Perceptions and misperceptions," in *Foreign Affairs*, 62, No. 1 (Fall 1983), 59–80.
5. *Strategy in the Missile Age* (Princeton, NJ: Princeton, 1967). The quote comes from Bernard Brodie (ed.), *The Absolute Weapon: Atomic Power and World Order* (New York: Harcourt, 1946). The full quote is, "Thus far the chief purpose of our military establishment has been to win wars. From now on its chief purpose must be to avert them. It can have almost no other useful purpose." Even today, analysts (e.g., see Vincent Manzo, "Managing escalation in northeast Asia," *Joint Forces Quarterly*, 77 [2015], https://ndupress.ndu.edu/JFQ/Joint-Force-Quarterly-77/Article/581877/after-the-first-shots-managing-escalation-in-northeast-asia/) argue that escalation can be "calibrated to convince an adversary that the conflict is spiraling out of control, but not to the point where nuclear escalation is a better option than negotiating a peaceful off-ramp" (94). Conversely the refusal to do so "could signal that the United States is unwilling to take risks to contest" (96) and reinforce allied concerns about decoupling. See Michael Eisenstadt, "Iran's gray zone strategy," *PRISM*, 9, No. 2 (2021), 92: "Escalation dominance—embodied by America's unmatched power-projection and precision-strike capabilities—constitutes one of its most potent asymmetric advantages vis-à-vis adversaries like Iran, and escalating in order to de-escalate may sometimes be necessary." See also Bryan Clark, Mark Gunzinger, and Jesse Sloman, "Winning in the gray zone: Using electromagnetic warfare to regain escalation dominance," *Center for Strategic and Budgetary Assessments*, 2017, https://csbaonline.org/research/publications/winning-in-the-gray-zone-using-electromagnetic-warfare-to-regain-escalation; and Matthew Kroenig, "Deterring Chinese strategic attack: Grappling with the implications of China's strategic forces buildup," *Atlantic Council*, November 2021, atlanticcouncil.org/in-depth-research-reports/report/deterring-chinese-strategic-attack-grappling-with-the-implications-of-chinas-strategic-forces-buildup/, "to reliably deter Chinese strategic attack . . . Washington must maintain a favorable balance of power over China at each rung of the escalation ladder."
6. Schelling, "The threat."
7. Janice Gross Stein, "Escalation management in Ukraine: 'Learning by doing' in response to the 'threat that leaves something to chance,'" *Texas National Security Review*, 6, No. 3 (Summer 2023), https://tnsr.org/2023/06/escalation-management-in-ukraine-learning-by-doing-in-response-to-the-threat-that-leaves-something-to-chance/, 23–50.
8. From Stein, "Escalation management," 33: "Incremental learning, a strategy that reduces uncertainty, seems to offer more promise. At first glance, the strategy seems

prudent because each step is small and calibrated. However, I argue that this promise of prudence may be exaggerated because leaders could overlearn from prior successes. When early actions do not provoke escalation, leaders could become overconfident that they can keep taking small steps."

9. Less costly does not mean free. In autumn 2022, when fears of Russian nuclear use spiked, strong opposite was conveyed by both China (Stuart Lau, "China's Xi warns Putin not to use nuclear arms in Ukraine," *Politico*, November 4, 2022, https://www.politico.eu/article/china-xi-jinping-warns-vladimir-putin-not-to-use-nuclear-arms-in-ukraine-olaf-scholz-germany-peace-talks/) and India (Tahir Qureshi, "India warns Russia against use of nuclear weapons in Ukraine: Indian Defence Minister Rajnath Singh on Wednesday warned his Russian counterpart Sergei Shoigu that nuclear weapons should not be used by any side in the Ukraine war." *India.com*, October 26, 2022, https://www.india.com/news/india/india-warns-russia-against-use-of-nuclear-weapons-in-ukraine-5707075/). Sufficient opposition from them could make Western sanctions bite much harder.

10. Mark Fitzpatrick, "The world after: Proliferation, deterrence and disarmament if the nuclear taboo is broken," *Proliferation Papers, IFRI* (Spring 2009), 17–18, as quoted in Warden, "Limited nuclear war."

11. Al Mauroni, "Tearing down the nuclear firewall," *War on the Rocks*, October 15, 2019, https://warontherocks.com/2019/10/tearing-down-the-nuclear-firewall/.

12. After the Cold War ended, both the United States and Russia sharply reduced their stockpile of short-range nuclear weapons, thereby bringing the average range of tactical nuclear weapons closer to the average range of strategic nuclear weapons. See Amy Woolf, "Nonstrategic nuclear weapons," *Congressional Research Service*, September 6, 2019, https://fas.org/sgp/crs/nuke/RL32572.pdf.

13. From Stephen J. Cimbala and Roger N. McDermott, "A new cold war? Missile defenses, nuclear arms reductions, and cyber war," *Comparative Strategy*, 34, No. 1 (2015), 99, "official Russian defense ministry definition of these weapons in Voyennyy Entsiklopedicheskiy Slovar' Military Encyclopedic Dictionary states: Strategic NW [nuclear weapons] have nuclear warheads with a capacity of up to several megatons and capability to reach every continent. . . . Non-strategic NW have nuclear ammunitions with a capacity of up to several hundred kilotons, and are intended to engage targets at operational and tactical depth of the location of the enemy's troops (forces)."

14. Data from Stephen Schwartz (ed.), *Atomic Audit* (Washington, DC: Brookings, 1998), Table 1–3.

15. For a discussion of effective explosion estimation, see CNS Staff, "North Korea's nuclear test and its aftermath: Coping with the fallout," *NTI*, June 24, 2009, https://www.nti.org/analysis/articles/north-koreas-nuclear-test-aftermath/.

16. As suggested by Amy F. Woolf, "Nonstrategic nuclear weapons," but China, not covered by New START, may have its own ideas.

17. See, for instance, Mukherjee, "Climbing."

18. http://www.dtic.mil/doctrine/jel/doddict/index.html.

19. Olga Oliker, "U.S. and Russian nuclear strategies: Lowering thresholds, intentionally and otherwise," in Dorminey, "America's nuclear crossroads," 45.

20. Kofman and Loukianova, "Escalation management."

21. James Mattis, testimony before the House Armed Services Committee; from Aaron Mehta, "Mattis: No such thing as a 'tactical' nuclear weapon, but new cruise missile needed,"

Defense News, February 6, 2018, https://www.defensenews.com/space/2018/02/06/mattis-no-such-thing-as-a-tactical-nuclear-weapon-but-new-cruise-missile-needed/.

22. See Lawrence Freedman, *The Evolution of Nuclear Strategy* (Second Edition) (New York: St. Martin's Press, 1989), 234–44. Thomas Schelling, who developed the original idea, ("Arms and influence," 284) countered that despite their initial reaction Soviet leaders were still thinking about McNamara's proposal as late as 1966. Barry Watts ("Nuclear-conventional firebreaks and the nuclear taboo," *Center for Strategic and Budgetary Alternatives*, 2013, https://csbaonline.org/uploads/documents/Nuclear-Conventional-Firebreaks-Report1.pdf, 26–27) argued, "Instead of embracing LNOs [limited nuclear options], Soviet officials denounced them on the grounds that any nuclear use would, inevitably, lead to uncontrolled escalation and the destruction of both the American and Soviet homelands." Even after exploring LNOs circa 1979 the Soviet "General Staff remained pessimistic about escalation control.... As a result, if U.S. decision makers had actually chosen to execute an LNO in a crisis or conflict with the USSR in order to avoid an all-out exchange, the likely Soviet response would have revealed that, for the Russians, there was virtually no firebreak between a few nuclear weapons and massive retaliation."

23. Thomas Schelling, *The Strategy of Conflict* (Cambridge, MA: Harvard University Press, 1960), 42.

24. James S. Johnson, "Chinese evolving approaches to nuclear 'war-fighting': An emerging intense US–China security dilemma and threats to crisis stability in the Asia Pacific," *Asian Security*, 15, No. 3 (2019), 215–32.

25. Michael Quinlan, *Thinking about Nuclear Weapons* (Oxford, UK: Oxford University Press, 2009), 36.

26. By way of example: "A decision by Washington to send noncombat advisers 19 months into the war is consistent with the U.S. policy of gradually increasing aid, which some argue has effectively managed escalation thus far. (Sending combat troops would be a sharp escalation that breaks with this pattern.)" From Alexandra Chinchilla and Sam Rosenberg, "Why America should send military advisers to Ukraine," *Foreign Affairs*, September 22, 2023; https://www.foreignaffairs.com/united-states/why-america-should-send-military-advisers-ukraine. "Russian incentives to escalate may also have been diminished because support to Ukraine has increased gradually." From Bryan Frederick, Mark Cozad, and Alexandra Stark, "Understanding the risk of escalation in the war in Ukraine," *RAND*, September 21, 2023, https://www.rand.org/pubs/research_briefs/RBA2807-1.html.

27. The classic treatment being Robert Jervis, *Perception and Misperception in International Politics* (Princeton, NJ: Princeton University Press, 1976).

28. Matthew Goldstein, Nicole Perlroth, and David Sanger, "Hackers' attack cracked 10 financial firms in major assault," *New York Times*, October 3, 2014, http://dealbook.nytimes.com/2014/10/03/hackers-attack-cracked-10-banks-in-major-assault/.

29. Schelling, "Arms and influence," 238 and then 114 after the ellipsis.

30. Quinlan, "Thinking," 66.

31. Sarah Starkey, "Putin reminds everyone that Ukraine joining NATO could lead to nuclear war," *Bulletin of the Atomic Scientists*, February 11, 2022, https://thebulletin.org/2022/02/putin-says-ukraine-membership-in-nato-would-make-nuclear-war-more-likely/. This was said during a press conference with French President Macron.

7

Will Thresholds Emerge on Their Own?

Escalation in this [China/Taiwan war] game did not adhere to the traditional model of a symmetric ladder that each side climbed deliberately and could stop at any point. Instead, both sides had their own escalation ladder with different rungs, reflecting their different approaches, perceptions, and capabilities. But what was most striking was that their actions quickly led to consequences beyond the intentions of both teams.[1]

Problems with asymmetry (discussed previously) and misapprehension (discussed subsequently) darken the prospects for thresholds. Although thresholds are unlikely to spontaneously emerge on their own, they might result from efforts made, notably by one or another superpower, to advocate for them. To be sure, advocates will look for thresholds that work to their advantage. But their advocacy could be the beginning of a give-and-take process that yields results useful to both.

We pursue this prospect in several steps. First, we examine how mismatched and missing rungs complicate the emerging of thresholds, especially when escalation has lattice-like characteristics. We also examine how thresholds may be imperiled if defined when measures sit below the threshold and countermeasures sit above it. Second, we examine and find wanting two ways to manage escalation in the absence of thresholds: escalation dominance and tacit maneuvering (as in the Russo-Ukrainian war). Third, we discuss how advocacy and negotiations for thresholds could work.

MISMATCHED AND MISSING RUNGS

A threshold marks a boundary line within the continuum of warfare. One state may define a particular rung in the belief that something significant distinguishes conflict below it and above it. Another state may see a significant distinction somewhere else. To one side the other side's movement crossed a line; but to the other side its actions were within the real line.

To show why mutual recognition matters for thresholds, consider Figure 7.1, depicting a hypothetical Chinese invasion of Taiwan.

The image on the left depicts a world in which the United States and China agree on what distinguishes the many levels of conflict. An escalation sequence that goes from the invasion of Taiwan to the use of nuclear weapons on civilians must consciously cross four mutually agreed thresholds.

On the right-hand side, though, the United States and China recognize *different* thresholds.[2] Here when China invades Taiwan, the United States thinks China breached the threshold between war and peace. But to China, Taiwan is an internal affair, and operations against it are not interstate war, which is

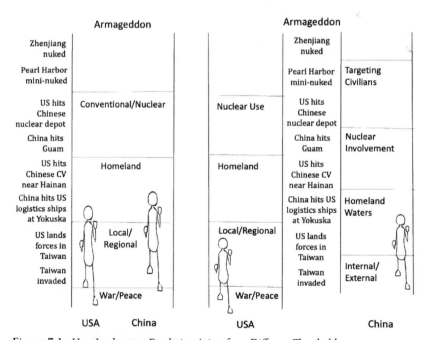

Figure 7.1. How Inadvertent Escalation Arises from Different Thresholds

external. Chinese draw the peace–war line *above* internal Chinese affairs. When the United States lands forces to defend Taiwan against Chinese invaders, the Chinese deem the United States to have crossed the line into interstate war. During the conflict (as per the figure) China strikes US Navy ships leaving Yokosuka, Japan, escalating, in US eyes, a local conflict to a regional conflict. The Chinese however do not see it as escalation because they do not recognize any threshold separating local conflict from regional conflict. The United States in turn sees Chinese actions as giving it license to strike a Chinese aircraft carrier in international waters off Hainan Island. The Chinese react as if they hold a broader conception of territorial waters than the United States does (note the 2001 EP-3 incident 50 miles from Hainan Island and China's claim to all the waters within its nine-dash line). To them, it is a homeland waters attack. China hits Guam, which it considers no less a legitimate target than its own coastal waters. The United States sees Guam as equivalent to the US homeland. This opens the field for conventional operations against the Chinese homeland, which includes a US strike on Chinese nuclear weapons facilities. The Chinese hold that the United States has crossed the nuclear threshold by jeopardizing deterrence forces, a threshold the United States does not recognize. China, then feels free to hit ships sitting at Pearl Harbor with tactical nuclear weapons. In US eyes, that act makes all nuclear use acceptable, and it returns the favor to the Zhenjiang Naval Base. The Chinese conclude that the United States has violated the last standing restraint, one against killing civilians in large numbers. This opens up the prospect of unrestrained nuclear war.

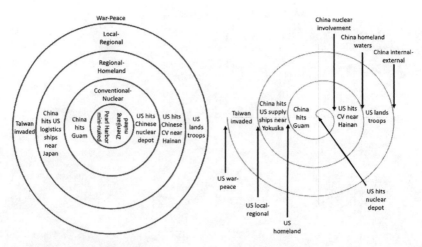

Figure 7.2. An Escalation Spiral

From what starts as a local conflict, divergent threshold perceptions allow each to escalate with neither believing it has crossed a threshold—merely responding to the other side's having done so.

To say the same thing in two dimensions, consider Figure 7.2.[3] On the left escalation is mapped to a set of concentric circles. Each act of escalation requires breaking into a circle. On the right is a spiral (US thresholds are denoted by the arrows below the spiral; China's by arrows above) where both sides slide into escalation—but neither crosses a line. Here an escalation spiral implies more than just going down the drain (note that by grabbing a spiral in the middle, pulling it to make a slinky, and then looking at it from the side, one sees a zig-zag ladder of Figure 7.1).

There already are differences between China and the United States on escalation and nuclear weapons. As the *Economist* argued, "Chinese officials are overconfident about their ability to prevent a conventional war from turning nuclear, they argue, while American ones are overconfident about their subsequent ability to keep a nuclear war limited in scope."[4] Accordingly, China's escalation decisions would underplay the odds of Armageddon because its leaders believe they can control events to prevent excessive escalation.[5] Some conversely believe that sensitized US policymakers can manage the problem of Chinese escalation "through the careful design of military campaigns"[6] or by geographically circumscribing "the range of its operations on Chinese territory or conduct[ing] most of its attacks with stand-off weapons that would reduce the need to suppress Chinese air defenses."[7] But, adds CSIS's Ralph Cossa, "Beijing may have excessive confidence in the United States' clear understanding of its escalation limits."[8] Neither side by this argument takes due regard of the other's perspectives: not China by underestimating the US propensity (as claimed) to escalate from conventional war to the tactical nuclear level, and not the United States by underestimating China's indifference to any threshold between the tactical and the strategic nuclear level.

Common words may obscure differences in thresholds. The term "weapons of mass destruction (WMDs)" suggests that one side's use of any WMD would cross a threshold that would then free the other side to use WMDs as well. But WMDs include not only nuclear weapons but biological, chemical, and radiological weapons (aka "dirty bombs"). Does one side's use of chemical weapons, heinous as they are, give the other side license to use nuclear weapons because they are both WMDs? If WMD use is mutually acknowledged as a keep-away zone, why not recognize, say, swarms of armed drones as WMDs?[9]

The problem of threshold definition if anything is worse when defined over a lattice, not a ladder. As Michael Fitzsimmons argued, "Rapidly improving and proliferating capabilities in long-range precision strike, and cyber and space operations have complicated the concept of an escalation 'ladder.' ... Where in the hierarchy of escalation does a disabling but reversible Chinese attack on U.S. military satellites belong? Is a Russian cyber-attack on the U.S. electrical grid more or is it less escalatory than missile strikes on European bases?"[10]

So take the nuclear threshold. It would operate as expected if everyone understood it to be about the *use* of nuclear weapons. One could imagine a circle within which nuclear operations would be inaccessible from the world of conventional operations without one side first crossing an escalation threshold. But would countries with stated NFU postures (e.g., China) stick to them if their sovereignty were in jeopardy, their nuclear deterrent imperiled, or even if the integrity of their borders were in play? In other words, would a nuclear threshold also include all the bad things that a state's possession of nuclear weapons was meant to prevent? To be consistent, a forbidden circle that included nuclear weapons would have to include serious threats against a superpower's sovereignty, borders, or nuclear deterrent. But then no operation could threaten a nuclear state's sovereignty, borders, or nuclear deterrence without crossing into nuclear territory. This would be a huge ask on China's part, and one that creates ambiguities (do militarized border disputes count?) and exposes asymmetries that a nuclear–conventional threshold does not. If countries unilaterally decide to protect additional interests (e.g., the integrity of their critical infrastructures or satellites) with a nuclear threat, the circle would expand even further. There may be no new and agreed-on circles once the original circle is redefined.

Incompatible views on the nature of thresholds (not merely their definition) also create instabilities. For the West escalation—and not just escalation to the nuclear level—largely works like a ratchet. Once a threshold has been violated, then, like a taboo, it cannot be unviolated. Reportedly the Chinese (and to a lesser extent the Russians) tend to view escalation as a rheostat that can be set warmer or colder; the level it reaches matters less than the level[11] it can be set back to. The rheostat metaphor raises questions, though. The Soviet Union's 1948–49 blockade of Berlin was reversible—but had a confrontation between US and Soviet forces become a conflict, disengagement would have been more difficult, not only psychologically but also from a military perspective (retreating gives up land and unless controlled raises the vulnerability of land forces). Would China's reported attitude suggest it prefers escalating by using stand-off rather than close-contact operations because the former can be more easily dialed back? Regarding thresholds as taboos provides more deterrence but less freedom to hold back if thresholds are broken since conflict has reached a new level it cannot easily go back from.

Seeing escalation as a rheostat also raises the question: how can the other side tell when it has been set back? Declarations help, but countries do not always trust the words of their foes. A physical withdrawal that prevents carrying out certain operations could be indicative. But otherwise for one side to believe that the other side deescalated would require a lengthy cessation of an activity, coupled perhaps with a conspicuous failure to exploit opportunities to act anew. Unforeseen consequences may follow when China deems a reversible escalation to be low risk because it can walk it back down, and carries it out only to find that the US believes that it cannot be walked back down. Each side sees different rules. Or consider the role played by accident and inadvertence. "Chinese strategists believe that the era of unlimited war is over . . . [so that] there is no *ipso facto* reason that warfare cannot be controlled."[12] As per Nicholas Wright,[13] "Chinese thinking on escalation management . . . places much less emphasis on inadvertent or accidental escalation. That is, escalation is seen a more deliberate and controllable process." Thus Chinese leaders would likely dismiss an excuse that an attack on them was unintentional. That noted, China had no problem declaring that the violation of US sovereignty from its spy balloon was accidental. Zhou Enlai, China's Cold War–era foreign minister, worried that there was "a common pattern in warfare: accidents and miscalculations rather than deliberate planning often led to war between reluctant opponents."[14]

Escalation rungs can go missing when one side has little or no effective capability or willingness to act (e.g., by responding to a chemical attack with a chemical attack) at one level or the other side has little vulnerability there (e.g., North Korea, despite employing hackers, is not itself very dependent on computers). Economic sanctions, for instance, are a US advantage that no other country can match; its use forces other countries to accede or escalate. As one Chinese interlocutor asserted at a Track II meeting on cybersecurity: the United States is the only country that cannot be sanctioned.[15] To date, no US sanctions have engendered violent retaliation (or even cyber retaliation as far as known), but for how long?

Missing rungs create serious asymmetries in developing thresholds: the side that can compete at one level would want the serious threshold to be above or beyond that capability; the other side would want it below or before that capability. By way of example, if one side could disable electronic equipment without breaking it (e.g., by forcing a lengthy system reset) and the other side lacked the ability to do likewise, it could only answer nondestructive disruption through destruction. It would not want a threshold distinguishing destructive and nondestructive actions—although it may accept a distinction between destructive and lethal actions. If the two nevertheless disagree, then missing rungs can, like mismatched rungs, drive escalation.

Consider how the missing US rung of tactical nuclear weapons (vis-a-vis Russia) might play out. In an oft-bruited scenario, war in Europe starts. NATO does well. Russia worries that NATO will not stop taking territory (whether it was its own or Russia's is secondary). Escalating to deescalate, Russia drops a tactical nuclear weapon on Europe. This is consistent with Russian exercises such as Zapad-1999[16] or Vostok-2010[17], which did terminate with the Russian use of tactical nuclear weapons (cruise missiles and SS-21 missiles, respectively). The Vice-Chairman of the Joint Staff General Paul Selva[18] has argued, "There is compelling evidence that at least one of our potential competitors... [Russia] believes they can get away with striking us with a low-yield weapon." At that point United States then[19] must either cede the initiative or escalate to the strategic level.[20] If the latter, Russia's gambit could therefore backfire, and badly. Because a strong threshold between tactical and strategic nuclear use lowers the risk of escalation and thus lowers the risks from tactical nuclear weapons use, it makes Russia's tactical use less risky—hence more likely. The alternative to NATO's acquiring more tactical nuclear weapons[21] in this scenario may be to weaken that threshold.

Another example may be a nuclear-generated EMP (electro-magnetic pulse) that could fry the electronics of all satellites within line of sight of the explosion. By increasing radiation, it would damage satellites in similar orbits (as well as domestic electronics over a wide area). Although known since 1962, it returned to concern in February 2024 when Congress disclosed[22] that Russia would be launching a nuclear satellite allowing them to take out multiple satellites at once (Russia denied as much[23]). Russia may well have been motivated by Ukraine's use of Starlink, a privately owned satellite system whose highly distributed nature makes it very hard to turn off by taking down one satellite at a time. Because Russia itself has no such constellation (China lacks one, so far[24]), placing EMP below the nuclear threshold could work to its military advantage.[25] Putting EMP above the nuclear threshold may inhibit such use, but would EMP use really be followed by lethal nuclear use when the latter would clearly raise the odds of Armageddon? Or might it may make more sense to group nuclear EMP with tactical nuclear use, as distinct from strategic nuclear use—if a workable tactical/strategic threshold exists?

So, difficult choices for the side that lacks a specific rung on the escalation ladder may not necessarily help the side that does. The more capable (or less vulnerable) side may hope that the other side, having been passed the onus and forced to escalate or do nothing, would blanche at the former. Caitlin Talmadge has argued,

> the United States has embraced more escalatory and expansive concepts for conventional warfare despite the availability of alternative concepts that might stand a better chance of keeping conflict limited.... [and] despite a recent force reorganization that afforded opportunities to better separate its nuclear and conventional missile forces, China continues to intertwine them, including developing a new missile that likely can carry both conventional and nuclear warheads. Likewise, Russia continues to station air defense assets in Kaliningrad. All three states seem to be making efforts, both technological and otherwise, to convince opponents that there is no "safe" way to fight a conventional war against a state with nuclear weapons.[26]

Despite Schelling's argument that eliminating options can strengthen one's hand in the game of chicken, countries usually want to fill out their rungs. Two authors have recently speculated that China is using its Strategic Support Force, established in late 2015, to create escalation "options for coercion and incremental escalation" previously missing in the region between conventional war and nuclear war.[27] These options supposedly allow China to exercise "calibrated escalation" instead of brinkmanship.

Yet those thinking that rungs are missing because the other side has no good immediate escalation options may be painfully surprised when the other side reveals options the one side did not anticipate (perhaps for not knowing what was being developed in secret). Indeed, many of the more decisive acts of war are surprises, something that others did not imagine could be done or would be done. Being hard to imagine or at least take seriously, there may be no red line or threshold their use would cross.

Strategists complain that having more options means less stability. For instance, "Stephen Lovegrove, Britain's national-security adviser, [has argued] during the cold war the risk of nuclear escalation involved just two blocs and was largely predictable, he argued; now there are more paths to escalation, not least through cyber-attacks."[28] But having a multiplicity of escalation paths may also make it easier to steer away from Armageddon. A standard model of escalation where A, B, and C represent states of successively more intense conflict is that A leads to B and reaching B makes C more attainable. But what if A (e.g., cyberattacks with fatal consequences) leads to B1 (e.g., retaliatory air strikes), and it was not B1 but B2 (e.g., seizing outlying territory) that led to C (e.g., full-scale conventional war)? Here B1 and B2 represent comparable states of intensity, but only one of them (B1) is a plausible result of reaching A, and only one of them (B2) is a plausible precursor for C. This leaves no clear path from A through B to C. Level C would have to be reached from other paths. Analogously although the road from, say, cyberespionage to Armageddon looks like a continuous path with waypoints, a closer look suggests that it can be piecewise continuous. Every step creates the conditions for the next but in no smooth, much less certain, fashion.

Any escalation process can be seen as an information-gathering exercise: what happens if one side does something new in a conflict? The more paths, the more information is gathered. To the extent that wars—and by extension escalation—arise from misinformation[29] about each side's military strength and resolve, more information is likely to mean fewer wars—and by extension less escalation. Moving across the lattice fills the same role that moving up the ladder would have—but with less overall risk.

THRESHOLDS THAT SEPARATE MEASURE AND COUNTERMEASURE

The introduction of a measure is likely to weaken a threshold's stability when potential countermeasures sit on the far side of a threshold. Here, countermeasures are limited to those motivated largely by the threat or deployment of the measure.[30] By way of historical example, Germany's adhering to the norm of giving commercial ships notice before attacking them was frustrated when Britain's exploitation of that norm led to their arming merchant vessels, which persuaded German to break that norm, tantamount to crossing a threshold.[31]

Examining thin national missile defenses and China's actions in the South China Sea (SCS) can illustrate how measures and countermeasures can affect thresholds. An NMD system with low inventories but high accuracy, for instance, might frustrate the other side's strategy of firing a few nuclear weapons to show resolve but without creating mass effects. The dilemma requires both NMD attributes. If the NMD has capacious inventories, then the other side's escalating to cross a threshold from demonstration to warfighting use could also be defeated. If the NMD is inaccurate a few shots will get through and make the point; conversely seeing nuclear shots intercepted may not signal enough to those who measure a signal in terms of effect (maybe a failure means one was not trying too hard) rather than effort. Such an NMD may frustrate the other side's nuclear signaling strategy (one escalation level) without frustrating its nuclear war strategy of firing for effect (a higher escalation level). The other side may be tempted to forget the signaling and just start at the higher level.

In recent decades China built up several surficial features in the South China Sea (SCS) into islands—and then placed military and intelligence assets atop them.[32] This improved China's ability to monitor nearby seas—on, below, or above the waterline—and helped China sustain air and naval vessels used to enforce its claims over other geographic features (e.g., those associated with the *Sierra Madre*, a sunken Philippines ship). These newly built advantages raise its odds of prevailing in any gray-zone confrontation below the serious use of force.[33] Because only China recognizes these "islands" as part of its sovereign territory[34] (and a "core interest"), a military attack on such assets might be seen by everyone else as less serious than if they sat in China proper (e.g., Hainan Island). Therein lies potential escalation instability. Posit a confrontation short of war in which China's island assets could be decisive. The other side sees a need to neutralize these islands, but would doing so constitute an escalation of the conflict? A lot depends on how. Cyberattacks, not violent by nature, might be able to hinder Chinese activities long enough for the other side to prevail in a confrontation, but are hit or miss (especially against military targets). Electronic warfare may help reduce China's intelligence gathering/communications activities, but fixed facilities have advantages over mobile emitters when it comes to generating power for electronic warfare. Perhaps the only effective countermeasure would be physical force made attractive by the fact that, fixed facilities located on known small islands can be sitting ducks. Here China's measure (building up "islands" to prevail in gray zone confrontations) may tempt others to do countermeasures (using force to neutralize these islands) and thereby cross thresholds.

China has also vigorously used its Coast Guard vessels and fishing boat militias to intimidate fishermen, oil drillers, and other commercial sea-goers. Its Coast Guard is much larger than those of its neighbors combined. Although adding the power of the US Coast Guard to those of China's neighbors (notably the Philippines) could even things up a bit,[35] it is hard to sustain so large a share of its Coast Guard halfway around the world. The US Navy, however, is both more powerful and easier to redeploy. Erasing any threshold between Coast Guard and Navy use would facilitate escalation. The strengthening of China's Coast Guard in the direction of sea control may therefore backfire by drawing the US Navy into waters abutting China. Indeed, in early 2019, the US Navy warned that it would respond to provocations by Chinese coast guard and maritime militia vessels no differently than if they were part of the Chinese Navy.[36]

The prospect for certain thresholds can also be imperiled when one side fears that potential technological measures adopted by the other side can leave the one side unable to come up with countermeasures for having agreed to the threshold. Not all potential measures merit concern. Those that do would have to: (1) provide a military edge sufficient to warrant the possessor crossing a threshold, (2) be difficult to acquire *and* difficult defend against (otherwise the other side could acquire them or countermeasures to them in short order),[37] and (3) be acquired in secrecy or at least in obscurity lest the other side react prematurely. Given secrecy the other side must guess the likelihood that it will need such investments. But a state's exploration of countermeasures can suggest that it is ready to violate the relevant threshold.

ESCALATION DOMINANCE PRESUMES COMMON THRESHOLDS

Herman Kahn's concept of escalation dominance states that prevailing at the current level of confrontation and demonstrating that one can do so at all higher levels will suppress the other side's desire to escalate.[38] The policy prescription, not surprisingly, is for countries to ensure that their rivals see no higher level at which they would rather fight. This would inhibit them from trying to win by raising the stakes. Strict threshold adherence would therefore appear secondary or irrelevant beside the reality of relative power.

Escalation dominance requires that the other side, dissatisfied at outcomes at one escalation level, believe that its prospects will not improve at the next. This in turn assumes that both sides see fighting at the same escalation level. But thresholds may not be mutually understood. For example, the United States may think it has escalation dominance in a fight over Taiwan because its next move up is going after the other side's nuclear weapons with conventional strikes. But maybe the Chinese believe that going after nuclear weapons is nuclear war, which is a level where no one prevails. If no distinctions can be relied upon, can escalation dominance mean any more than the ability to prevail by doing what the other side has not *yet* done? Missing rungs do not help, since the side with the gap is apt to define escalation levels to its advantage, playing down the relevance of levels where it lacks capabilities.[39]

Establishing or determining escalation dominance is clearly harder if and when there are multiple escalation pathways of lattices rather than ladders. Saying "no farther" is easier in a unidimensional world than in a multidimensional world. The more paths upward, the more bets must be covered. If one side escalates along one dimension (e.g., going from less to more sensitive targets), the other side may believe that abandoning restraint in another direction (e.g., increasing intensity) breaks no promise save those that the other side already broke. Then add novel actions[40] and dominance is that much harder to ensure. And novelty may arise more frequently these days because it lies at the heart of what makes cyber operations succeed, the counterintuitive nature of many AI-aided strategies, and because techniques of hiding and hunting require tricks the other side does now know. One side may think it enjoys escalation dominance when the other side knows it has a trick up its sleeve (even if not yet validated in combat). As with deterrence, emphasizing escalation dominance favors revealing capabilities to influence the other side's thinking rather than hiding capabilities so that their use can surprise and disorient the other side.

Despite the allure of achieving escalation dominance by *adding* rungs,[41] the likelihood that doing so would backfire is greater than if capability were added to an existing rung. Calling a capability a higher rung admits that one has escalated. But it is to the other side's advantage to claim that additional capabilities are a new rung because it allows it to argue: they escalated, and therefore so shall I.

HAVE THRESHOLDS INFLUENCED RUSSIAN ESCALATION BEHAVIOR?

Another alternative to working on defining thresholds is believing that countries will find a way to work out a set of restraints by trial and error. Each side will thereby learn what the other side's red lines are. Inadvertent escalation through miscalculation would thus be unlikely; deliberate escalation would be inhibited.

A good place to explore this hypothesis is the Russo-Ukrainian war, admittedly an asymmetric conflict. Although Russia has the attributes of a superpower, Ukraine does not. NATO is essentially a superpower but not a direct participant. NATO countries, however, support Ukraine with materiel and, it is believed, intelligence.

When it comes to escalation NATO has enormous unused scope. It could ship more weapons to Ukraine or ship weapons to Ukraine that were previously off limits.[42] It could also free Ukraine to use such weapons against targets on Russian soil. And all that is before sending in its own troops—which would be deemed a new level of war even if doing so introduces no new weapons and no new Russian targets into the war. Russia has unused escalatory potential, largely[43] but not entirely in the form of nuclear weapons. Ukraine has minimal unused escalatory potential except insofar as it conforms with NATO's wishes not to use certain NATO-supplied weapons for operations inside Russia.[44] Each naturally would see different thresholds operating.

Until Ukraine recaptured its Kharkiv oblast (September 21, 2022), Russia's military behavior was consistent with limits it had observed after the invasion. Russia mobilized 200,000 fighters but, initially, sent only a third of these into Ukraine. Then it ran into problems and ultimately sent in the rest. Based on its destruction of Grozny in 2000 and Aleppo in 2016, wanton attacks on Ukrainian cities were something Russia was always prepared to do, even if it would have preferred to win without them (captured cities are more valuable when intact). The profligate use of artillery itself is consistent with its comparatively large role in the Russian table of organization and equipment. Nothing that Russia had done at that point was an escalated response to Ukraine's crossing some Russian red line (notably, if asymmetrically, Ukraine's attack on fuel depots inside Russia). Nor had Russia responded to anything NATO had done that Russia had earlier deemed objectionable.

Russia had, indeed, made many threats—to go nuclear if interfered with, to attack supply lines from NATO, and to regard economic war as tantamount to a general war. But its retaliation for economic war by the West was limited to responding in kind: for instance, forcing debtholders and energy buyers to pay in rubles and throttling Ukraine's food exports. Similarly, the Russian response to the growing shipment of arms from NATO was to attack a Ukrainian warehouse—albeit within hailing distance of Poland. Little of this was escalation.

After Ukraine recovered the Kharkiv oblast, Putin declared he would mobilize 300,000 Russians with prior military service. Russia formally annexed four Ukrainian oblasts, placing them, in principle, under the nuclear umbrella: "In the event of a threat to the territorial integrity of our country . . . we will certainly make use of all weapon systems available to us. This is not a bluff."[45]

Until that point Putin probably expected to win without mobilization or nuclear weapons. Using either could have been seen as an admission of error. Thus escalation may have been avoided, in part, for psychological reasons. The same psychology may explain why Russia had downplayed some Ukrainian operations—notably attacks on Crimea, the earlier sinking of the *Moskva*, operations that forced the withdrawal of naval forces from Crimea, and the Ukrainian incursion into the Kursk oblast. Admitting that Ukraine could do serious damage to Russia would put it in a bad light, even though Russia could have argued, however implausibly, that these operations indicated Ukrainian escalation.

The United States and NATO have tried to understand what would induce Putin to escalate[46] to nuclear weapons use. Putin's original formulation hinted at a nuclear response to any attempts to "hinder" Russia's campaign against

Ukraine. A later demarche[47] warned that shipments of "most sensitive" weapons systems could bring "unpredictable consequences." Putin also threatened "nuclear" escalation if the UK supplied depleted-uranium shells to Ukraine.[48] Early in the war, "the White House authorized an initial shipment of only 100 [lightweight UAVs] to Ukraine—a small batch that could be intended to see how Mr. Putin reacts to their deployment on the Ukrainian front lines."[49] As the war continued (and the slaughter of civilian Ukrainians, notably at Bucha, came to light), light weapons were supplemented by heavier ones such as air defense missiles, armored vehicles, and mobile rocket artillery (HIMARS). Similarly, "the United States . . . increased the volume and speed of the intelligence it [was] providing."[50] Only in the summer of 2023 did the United States allow the export of long-range artillery (ATACMS); as of this writing, the United States hesitated to provide Ukraine its own F-16 aircraft. By the end of 2022 Ukraine demonstrated it could strike deep inside Russia using UAVs, and the United States was no longer insisting that Ukraine refrain from such strikes—so long as Ukraine used its own weapons to do so. Perhaps US officials concluded that short of using nuclear weapons, Russia had run out of escalation options *against Ukraine*.[51]

It is also unclear whether, *pace* President Biden's remark, Russian tactical nuclear use would result in an ever-increasing nuclear tit-for-tat. The United States sent the CIA's director to warn his Russian counterpart against nuclear use,[52] but it is unknown what the United States threatened if nuclear weapons went off. Many would have the United States and NATO respond to Russian nuclear use only by using NATO's conventional capabilities, which could seriously degrade Russia's forces in Ukraine (and especially on the Black Sea).[53] If so it would suggest that having an abundance of precision weapons can not only spur escalation (by putting nuclear systems at risk) but stall it (by creating warfighting options that do not necessarily keep the conflict over the nuclear level). But would Russia stop using nuclear weapons if it sees no nuclear retaliation? And if NATO responds by also enforcing a no-fly zone, is that de-escalation (a conventional response to a nuclear event) or escalation (direct intervention from a force that had earlier supplied only materiel and information)? Thresholds associated with intervention into other countries' wars have even more horizontal elements than those of direct conflicts.

Perhaps NATO and Russia stumbled into a *modus vivendi* over Ukraine based on linked red lines. NATO does not intervene directly into the conflict, and the Russians do not use nuclear weapons. But is that the deal— or is it that NATO not supply Ukraine with any weapons that could strike Russian territory[54] or at least not too deeply[55] and the Russians do not use nuclear weapons? Or maybe the deal is that the West not increase aid too quickly: for instance, if sending too many HIMARS at one time would cross a line. Or is the deal that Russia will not use nuclear weapons if NATO does not do anything that leads to Russia's humiliation—which could variously be Ukraine's recovering Crimea or even Ukraine's recovering territory lost in the 2022 invasion? Avril D. Haines, the director of national intelligence, said that officials believed Putin would reach for his arsenal only if "he perceives that he is losing the war in Ukraine, and that NATO in effect is either intervening or about to intervene."[56] If so then Russia's forbearance has little to do with what NATO members are doing—and more to do with how unsatisfied its leaders are with outcomes on the ground.

Inferring tacit thresholds from what one side has yet to do can be misleading. What looks like the willingness to respect a threshold may be a disclination arising from the other side's belief that doing so under current circumstances and with current assets is not cost-effective, not merited by the risks that must be run, or otherwise frowned upon. But if circumstances change, the option is still there. Sometimes not doing something means not doing so successfully, which reflects quiet failure—which later with luck and skill may yield success. Thresholds associated with combat in the air or in space can only be inferred from episodic operations, not patterns of deployment. Finally, not striking certain types of targets may reflect only a failure to find them.

Israel's campaign to squelch Iran's post–Arab Spring activities in Syria offers a parallel mechanism, albeit one where tacit escalation management worked at least until the October 7 massacres. It launched several hundred air strikes against Iran's efforts to establish a capability to shoot missiles into Israel from Syria.[57] Before such air strikes Israel's planners exploited their fine-grained intelligence on Iranians to gauge what would cause Iran to escalate. Even though Iran lacks nuclear weapons, Israel does not want to see Iran locking itself into a full-scale war against it,[58] and so it needed to figure out the odds of war—as distinct from the tit-for-tat that it engaged with Iran (it helps that Israel did not challenge Iran's primary goal: supporting Assad's continued rule).[59] Like NATO Israel felt its way forward to determine what it can do without provoking an overreaction. Likewise, because the conflict is asymmetric (e.g., Iran is not bombing Israel's assets in Syria and Israel is not placing missiles near Iran), few mutually observed thresholds can be called on to limit conflict.

DECLARING THRESHOLDS

If thresholds are unlikely to emerge on their own to curb or at least channel superpower conflict, perhaps countries should declare, assert, offer, or nominate thresholds. One side may offer that its idea of threshold-compliant targets (or actions) includes this (e.g., air bases in Guam) but not that (e.g., air bases on the Chinese mainland) and the other side makes corresponding assertions. Discussions then ensue. In this section we examine the choices that countries should make in declaring or offering thresholds; in the next section, we examine additional issues associated with negotiations as such.

Threshold declarations would differ from red lines by being crafted as universal or at least bilateral rules: for instance X is within and Y is beyond a declared threshold regardless of who does X or Y (in contrast to asserting rules but not playing by them[60]). They can also be built around similar if not necessarily identical restraints. A sovereignty-based trade—such as not interfering with China's Great Firewall if China leaves other countries' elections alone—exemplifies a threshold regime where the forbidden actions are different but follow the same underlying principles. Conversely, geographical-based rules (e.g., the Monroe Doctrine) often make for difficult thresholds (but not always, e.g., violating a known DMZ).

Those declaring or nominating thresholds would, in effect, draw a circle to allow what they want within any one threshold and disallow what they do not want. A target may be fenced off to where attacking it would be deemed an escalation even if the other side did not feel that way. Declarations need not be explicit. If one side worried out loud that providing long-range missiles to its friend would tempt the other side to use tactical nuclear weapons, this creates an implicit equivalence: if tactical nuclear weapons are used, the reason to withhold long-range missiles disappears.

States can also declare against particular thresholds. During the Cold War, NATO threatened nuclear use in response to a serious Soviet invasion; it integrated nuclear weapons into NATO force postures and doctrines. In effect NATO was saying that general war was general war: it sat in a circle that contained nuclear war with no obvious exclusion of any one type of nuclear war (e.g., tactical versus strategic). But as parity settled in between Soviet and US nuclear inventories, sentiment grew that NATO should *not* use nuclear weapons until it had given its conventional defense a chance to repel the invasion. After the Soviet Union ended, archives indicated that the Soviet Union never anticipated a conventional-only invasion of Europe but only one using nuclear weapons from the start. This may have reflected a military attitude that did not see a nuclear threshold—or a conclusion that NATO itself did not see a nuclear threshold, and therefore its observing one was pointless.

Similarly, a US readiness to blockade China if it invades Taiwan conveys an immediate predisposition to raise a local conflict (in which the United States is not an immediate party) to a global one, obviating attempts to establish a local–global threshold for such a conflict. Yet making any threshold declaration about blockades themselves, if not caveated, could create an equivalence between a Chinese blockade of Taiwan (which they foreshadowed in their 2022 protest of former Speaker Pelosi's visit[61]) and a US-led blockade of China. The Chinese may resist such an equivalence. It is less clear whether they would then deem a blockade more severe (thus justifying, say, China's attacks on Guam if a blockade is imposed) or less severe (perhaps indicating that a blockade of Taiwan may sit at a lower intensity level than an invasion of Taiwan). Such a choice reflects the lattice-like nature of escalation.

Declarations may be not only threats but assurances. Robert D. Blackwill and Philip Zelikow[62] argue that, in a crisis, the United States should "attempt to limit the fight to a local conflict over and around Taiwan. Taiwan may not end up winning that battle, in the short run, but its resistance could force China to face a much wider and lasting conflict. Instead of escalating to general war, this plan would prepare, in advance, the political and economic breaks and reactions that would likely accompany a local war with China, although the possibility of a wider war would still exist." Similarly, advocating a threshold that sits below homeland attacks suggests that ends such as forceable regime change are off the table. A threshold declaration that embodies a red line also concedes a red line for the other side. It legitimizes some concerns that the other side may have.

Where appropriate countries can use international law to justify a threshold. For instance,

> When America and other NATO countries rule out putting boots on the ground in Ukraine, they emphasise such a step would make them parties to the conflict. This, Mr Haque [author of *Law and Morality at War*] thinks, is a useful way to draw red lines between nuclear powers. America is using these rules of international law to signal to Russia that we will come up to a clear red line but not cross it. I think Russia understands that signalling," he says. "But they will try to contest the American interpretation of those rules and invent their own red lines—not based on law—to serve their aims.[63]

As discussed in Appendix A, however, thresholds need no *a priori* basis in LOAC.

Tradeoffs are involved in declaring or offering thresholds. Just as banning some exports from a country to support a minor goal leaves little to take away to enforce a major one—stuffing too much into the circle of subthreshold operations erodes the ability to make other important distinctions. China's declaring, as discussed previously, that US warships transiting the Qiongzhou strait (which separates Hainan Island from the Chinese mainland)[64] would be taken more seriously than transiting the Strait of Taiwan would erode the argument that Taiwan is just another part of China. A US avowal that Japan's homeland is equivalent to the US homeland would leave little scope for a US homeland sanctuary if Japan is nevertheless attacked. If Russia insinuates that attacks on a SAM site located just inside its border are an attack on a country's sovereignty and thereby merit a vigorous response *and* the SAM site is hit anyway, what credibility does Russia have left to, for instance, protect assets located deeper in Russia or that are part of its critical infrastructure? If Russia annexes four Ukrainian oblasts and declares that it will defend them as it would defend Mother Russia, they are attacked anyway, and no escalation follows, can sanctuary be assigned to Crimea—or the Russian oblast of Kursk for that matter?[65]

Henry Kissinger recognized as much in arguing for a threshold between tactical and nuclear weapons should the Soviet Union attack NATO. But he deprecated both NATO's staying below the nuclear threshold as leaving it with options too weak to deter such aggression and any threshold between counterforce and countervalue nuclear use because the loser at one level would escalate anyway.[66]

As another example, a spectrum of contention from friendly peace to cyberespionage to cyberwar to nonlethal operations to lethal operations can admit of four potential thresholds. Where should it lie: between peace and cyberespionage, between cyberespionage and cyberwar, between cyberwar and nonlethal (destructive) operations, or between nonlethal and lethal operations? A threshold that separates peace from cyberespionage war may discourage cyberespionage but leaves a smaller barrier between cyberespionage and cyberwar. One that distinguishes between cyberespionage and cyberwar makes it difficult to call out a cyber operation in progress as above or below the threshold. A threshold that separates cyberwar from nonlethal operations makes the world "safe" for cyberwar but creates no incentives for ensuring that operations meant to take out, say, infrastructure do not hurt people. A threshold that lumps together peace, cyberespionage, cyberwar, and nonlethal operations makes the world "safe" for such operations even if it forces those who break things to limit their actions to those where no one is hurt.

States could treat all five actions as separate, threatening to increase the intensity of their operations in lockstep with what the other side does. But if there are more thresholds, then the consequences of blowing through any one of them are smaller. That being so, would each be so carefully considered?

Having just one or two clearly defined and agreed-on thresholds raises the odds that none is crossed casually. Inasmuch as each threshold is a tacit promise of mutual restraint, every threshold that is crossed is tantamount to a broken promise. After too many broken promises, who would believe that mutual forbearance, having failed at a lower level, would succeed at a higher one? Multiple thresholds also create more scope for disagreement about who crossed what. The closer one side operates to a fuzzy threshold, the greater the odds the other side will judge or at least declare that the threshold has been crossed. Having multiple thresholds is like having no serious ones.

With what details should thresholds be described when many actions are hypothetical and others are untested in warfare (and thus may not contribute much to outcomes)? A threshold is simple to the extent that it is readily conveyed, easily understood, and contains few exceptions or clarifications. Thresholds make certain distinctions at the expense of others and if the history of information technology standards—also where some distinctions get priority over others—suggests that the simpler the standard the more readily it will be adopted: note the triumph of TCP/IP over OSI's data communications suite. Simpler arrangements are also easier to keep and monitor against. Added elements create more things to disagree over, both in negotiation and in monitoring.

A simpler threshold also sounds more like one based on principles. In 2015, Presidents Xi and Obama could have agreed that neither should conduct cyberespionage on private businesses.[67] But the United States reportedly spied on telecommunications companies (service providers and equipment manufacturers) to more efficiently go after targets (e.g., terrorists) that used such services. So, what China agreed to was to not conduct cyberespionage for commercial purposes (e.g., stealing trade secrets or business strategies): two criteria rather than one. This allowed the United States to continue its practices, while China was not allowed to do things the United States took exception to. By early 2017, China was no longer abiding by the deal.

Complexity, on the other hand, may be necessary to distinguish the acceptable from the unacceptable fairly, in part to accommodate differences—geostrategic, technological, doctrinal—between each side. Consider, for instance, how the United States (which has overseas territories) and China (with its controversial nine-dash line claim) might define their respective homelands.

There should also be some common understanding whether a clear but unsuccessful attempt to cross a threshold merits the same response as a successful crossing. Failed operations can be hard to characterize (e.g., would that errant missile launch have landed in a proscribed area if it had worked) and attribute (e.g., a failed cyberspace operation leaves fewer artifacts to analyze). But even a failed attempt signals the other side's intent to ignore the threshold. Giving it a pass inclines it toward high-risk actions that with little downside for failure and a chance to change the war with success. Current practice is mixed. Israel retaliated to a failed Iranian attempt to poison local water supplies, but the United States did not respond to a failed North Korean missile launch[68] or an attempted assassination of President Bush in 1993.

Should the United States declare or offer thresholds? Because the United States takes law seriously, it may be wary of declaring or offering thresholds without understanding their full implications. Maintaining the credibility of its threats and promises, which is core to implementation thresholds, is also more important to the United States because its national security strategy relies on allies, and keeping those allies on board rests on its honoring commitments. Conversely Russia or China—governed not by laws but nevertheless having many of them—may use law-like standards to create and justify equivalences that are transparently self-serving. They also may feel free to breach them (and maybe even deny as much) as security considerations require. Alliances play a far smaller role in their national security strategy.

The choice to declare rather than negotiate thresholds is the easier one, but will a professed magnanimity in choosing thresholds over red lines ("see, these rules apply to us, too") suffice to legitimize rules made without the other side's consent? The other side *could* say: if the simultaneous threat-promise pair to stay on one side of the threshold really governs your choices, our decisions will take it into account. Yet, not having an input into the definition of the threshold, we are under no obligation to follow suit; if we breach *your* threshold, it is not a broken promise on our part and says nothing about our willingness to keep our own promises. At least if such declarations are phrased as mutual thresholds, they need a category-based rationale that justifies equivalence.

NEGOTIATING THRESHOLDS

But negotiations, as distinct from declarations, raise several issues.

First, how formal should an accord be? Where should it sit on a spectrum ranging from a mutual tacit understanding, to oral arrangements (such as the 1962 deal that swapped US missiles in Turkey for Soviet missiles in Cuba) to Presidential-level agreements (such as the 2015 Xi-Obama agreement on cyberespionage or the agreement on Iranian nuclear weapons) to a formal treaty (even if formal treaties that limit violence are rare[69])? Secret agreements are usually easier to make (the side-deals that persuaded so many countries to enter WWI were not publicized at the time)—but also easier to break since there are no audience costs for doing so if there is no audience.[70]

Threshold discussions could start at unofficial (Track II) levels if doing so at official levels might prematurely imply a national commitment. But asymmetries will remain. Presumably, US participants can raise ideas more easily than Russian or Chinese participants can without others assuming that they represent official positions (which might contradict the US threat posture). Yet, having seen himself quoted by Chinese back to American Track II participants on cyberspace talks as if having discovered US Government hypocrisy, the author suspects that the Chinese see no such distinction. And discussing a threshold at all may legitimize a form of warfare that countries say they would abjure. Until China stood up its Strategic Support Force (December 2015), it disavowed any interest in offensive cyber operations and thus any interest in discussing thresholds that might modulate cyberattacks.

But ambiguity of the sort that can occur when agreements are informal can backfire if each side has a different notion of what has been agreed upon. Consider what can happen when one side thinks the thresholds are set at one level of conflict intensity but fears that the other side misunderstands what that level is (each, of course, believes that its own understanding of the threshold is correct). If one side perceives that the other underestimates the level of the threshold, it will be confident that the other side's expected behavior will not force it to respond, but may worry that its own actions may set the other side off. Conversely, if it thinks that the other side overestimates the level of threshold it may fear that the other side will cross it, but worry less that it will react if it crosses the threshold itself. The more explicit the threshold, the greater the confidence that each has in the other's understanding of where it lies.

Second, what exactly is being negotiated?

Both sides could promise not to do something specific (to each other), like a cease-fire deal but one implemented during rather than after conflict. Reciprocity is implied, if not stated; violations strain a reputation for honesty. The problem here is that both sides may have also promised not to wage war on one another; a threshold to govern war assumes little faith in the first promise, thereby leaving open whether both sides believe in a newer one.

Or both sides could mutually recognize that certain thresholds, so defined, are actions significant enough to allow the other side to reciprocate if the one side carries them out.[71] This is a definition that, as circumstances warrant, can be invoked as a threshold: we will not cross it and expect you to do likewise. Invocation then converts a contingent promise into a standing one. A variant on a precise definition is some recognition that two different actions (such as election and censorship interference) are comparable. If China does one, the United States is entitled to do the other, and vice versa.

If the purpose of negotiations is to define thresholds for later invocation, then presumably, multiplying thresholds provides additional choices. But if the two sides would invoke different thresholds, having a tractable threshold requires coming to one more understanding (which threshold do we choose?) later and under more difficult circumstances.

Third, how comprehensive should the result corpus of thresholds be? Anything sufficiently comprehensive to govern actions across a lattice of options would be long and complicated. It must make assumptions about technology-enabled conflict that could become obsolete as technologies evolve. Having many potential thresholds may assuage fears that breaching one threshold would leave both sides few pegs to hang a mutual understanding at higher conflict intensity levels to forestall yet further escalation. And, if one can get to negotiations at all, why waste the opportunity to gain mutual understanding across all levels of potential conflict?

Conversely, multiplying thresholds lengthens negotiations (already trying to resolve issues of definition, legitimacy, fairness, and tractability) and lengthens the odds that disagreement at one level would stymie some overall agreement. If the thresholds are regarded as extant and in force (rather than options to be invoked after conflict has started), then crossing one threshold can compromise the credibility of those higher up, notably the conventional/nuclear threshold. And why have higher-level thresholds if the lower-level ones are credible?

In a one-dimensional conflict spectrum, a well-observed threshold should also block every escalation path to higher levels. But multi-dimensionality creates multiple escalation paths: for example, from tactical conventional combat to strategic nuclear use via tactical nuclear use, attacks on nuclear C2/EW satellites, or strategic conventional attack. Should agreement extend to cover all pathways or just those deemed most likely at the time?

Fourth, what does entering into negotiations signal? At very least, two countries, each professing peaceful intentions, would find war likely enough to require some provisions for its mutual management. For the United States to offer such talks with China would suggest a non-trivial likelihood that the latter may try to seize Taiwan—and that the United States could well join the fight (different thresholds would be called for if the United States wanted to avoid being drawn into a conflict). Almost conversely, expressing an interest in limiting the costs and risks associated with such conflict can be an expensive signal if it weakens deterrence, replacing *do not do X or there is no limit to how I may respond* with *do not do X or I may also do X*. But the latter warning may be considered more credible by dint of appearing to have been thought through, as a request to negotiate may imply.

Context matters. The aggressor's signaling that it might start a fight carries different echoes than the defender's worrying that it would have a fight imposed on it. The former's asking for thresholds indicates that the decision is close to having been made; what's left is a small matter of modulating the risks of going ahead. The latter says: I cannot stop you, but maybe I can ask you to limit yourself.

The United States, itself, has to be sensitive to what allies infer. As noted, entertaining thresholds that would distinguish the US homeland from the homeland of formal Allies (or likewise, between tactical and strategic nuclear weapons) can cast doubt on the promise that an attack on one is an attack on all. If the United States abjures an NFU policy so as to signal to Allies that the United States is willing to take nuclear risks to defend them against losing their country to *conventional* attack, it either cannot also formalize a conventional/nuclear threshold or has to put conditions on such a threshold, such as to allow its use to protect an Ally's sovereignty or national capital (this is consistent with Russia's state nuclear posture, but not China's).

Of course, *not* negotiating at all also sends signals, but their clarity should not be overestimated. Maybe the other side thinks that no threshold would leave it better off. Maybe it lacks confidence it can understand what it may be asked to sign up for. Maybe, leadership is ready but is still trying to get its bureaucracies (e.g., the military) aboard. Maybe, it is conscious of its own inferiority or the asymmetric circumstances it faces (e.g., a continental power facing a naval power). Or maybe it is a matter of basic mistrust: if you want them, then I should not want them. Or maybe, such deals are just not in their culture.

NOTES

1. Stacie Pettyjohn, Becca Wasser, and Chris Dougherty, "Dangerous straits: Wargaming a future conflict over Taiwan," *Center for a New American Security*, June 2020, https://www.cnas.org/publications/reports/dangerous-straits-wargaming-a-future-conflict-over-taiwans.
2. A similar portrait of escalation driven by unmatched thresholds, but limited to cyberspace, can be found in Martin Libicki, *Crisis and Escalation in Cyberspace* (Santa Monica, CA: RAND, 2011), 94.
3. Two nuclear use events were removed from the spiral for lack of space.
4. *Economist*, "China's nuclear arsenal was strikingly modest, but that is changing," November 21, 2019, https://www.economist.com/china/2019/11/21/chinas-nuclear

-arsenal-was-strikingly-modest-but-that-is-changing; they were drawing conclusions from Cunningham, "Assuring assured." Similarly, Al Mauroni ("Would Russia use a tactical nuclear weapon in Ukraine?" *Modern War Institute*, March 16, 2022, https://mwi.usma.edu/would-russia-use-a-tactical-nuclear-weapon-in-ukraine/) argues that it is "folly to discuss military conflict with China and Russia that remains at the conventional level" at the same time as he castigates analysts "who are fixated on a number of hypotheses that are based in Cold War thought. Notable among them: that there is no such thing as a tactical nuclear weapon because all nuclear weapons are strategic; that any use of a nonstrategic nuclear weapon would inevitably lead to a full-scale nuclear war." In other words, the nuclear taboo is no threshold, but the tactical–strategic distinction is. From Stålhane, "Dynamics," Chinese experts believe that the United States seeks to lower the threshold for nuclear use, especially by emphasizing lower-yield weapons.

5. From Johnson, "Chinese evolving," 216: "Chinese overconfidence in the ability to control escalation could prompt Beijing to countenance the use of conventional missiles (including ASMs) as 'firebreaks' between conventional and nuclear warfare domains, which it would not expect an adversary to breach. Assumptions of this kind may cause China to underestimate the escalation risks inherent in use of conventional weapons during a conflict."
6. Elbridge Colby, "Don't sweat airsea battle," *National Interest*, July 31, 2013, http://nationalinterest.org/commentary/dont-sweat-airsea-battle-8804.
7. Vincent Manzo, "After the first shots: Managing escalation in northeast Asia," *Joint Forces Quarterly*, 2nd Quarter 2015, especially pp. 96–97.
8. Ralph Cossa, Brad Glosserman, and David Santoro, "US-China strategic nuclear relations: Time to move to track-1 dialogue," *Pacific Forum*, February 2015, https://pacforum.org/publication/issues-and-insights-vol-15-no-7-us-china-strategic-nuclear-relations-time-to-move-to-track-1-dialogue.
9. "Some experts have called for classifying swarms of autonomous, armed drones—such as the Foji swarming drones that the Iranian army claims it successfully used during the January exercise—as weapons of mass destruction." From Evan Omeed Lisman, "Iran's bet on autonomous weapons," *War on the Rocks*, August 30, 2021, https://warontherocks.com/2021/08/irans-bet-on-autonomous-weapons/.
10. Michael Fitzsimmons, "The false allure of escalation dominance," *War on the Rocks*, November 18, 2017, https://warontherocks.com/2017/11/false-allure-escalation-dominance.
11. This observation arises from discussions. This is consistent with a statement in Alexander George and Richard Smoke, *Deterrence in American Foreign Policy: Theory and Practice* (New York: Columbia University Press, 1974), 402: "In Soviet doctrine, risks are acceptable not necessarily when they are low, but when they are controllable—that is, when they can be unilaterally reduced at any time they may seem to grow too large."
12. Morgan, "Dangerous thresholds," 52–53.
13. Wright, "China and escalation," 11. This corroborates personal observation by the author.
14. Qiang Zhai, *China and the Vietnam Wars, 1950–1975* (Chapel Hill: University of North Carolina Press, 2000), 144, as cited in Carson, "Secret wars."
15. China's withholding of gallium (and later carbon graphite exports) to the United States suggests that China may nevertheless try. See Annabelle Liang and Nick Marsh,

"Gallium and germanium: What China's new move in microchip war means for world," *BBC*, August 2, 2023, https://www.bbc.com/news/business-66118831.
16. Arms Control Association, "Russia adopts new security concept," January 2000, https://www.armscontrol.org/act/2000-01/press-releases/russia-adopts-new-security-concept.
17. The Jamestown Foundation, "Reflections on Vostok 2010: Selling an image," July 13, 2010, https://jamestown.org/program/reflections-on-vostok-2010-selling-an-image/.
18. From Lisa Ferdinando, "Vice chairman highlights importance of nuclear deterrence," *DoD News*, March 6, 2018, https://www.defense.gov/News/Article/Article/1459640/vice-chairmanhighlights-importance-of-nuclear-deterrence/.
19. For a good treatment of NATO's current nuclear strategy, see Hans Binnendijk and David Gompert, "Decisive response: A new nuclear strategy for NATO," *Survival*, 61, No. 5 (October–November 2019), 113–28.
20. Keir A. Lieber and Daryl G. Press ("The nukes we need," *Foreign Affairs* [November/December 2009], 39–51) argued that if the only retaliatory option entailed killing millions of civilians, any such US deterrent would lack credibility. But that assumes that our foes think that the United States is sufficiently nice to avoid wanting to kill civilians—while they themselves have little qualms about killing civilians in large numbers, even their own civilians.
21. Assuming these tactical nuclear weapons are *not* fired from platforms built to fire strategic nuclear weapons. If so Russia may preempt as if under strategic attack. See for instance Paul Sonne, "U.S. military arms its submarines with new 'low-yield' nuclear warheads," *Washington Post*, February 4, 2020, https://www.washingtonpost.com/national-security/us-military-arms-its-submarines-with-new-low-yield-nuclear-warheads/2020/02/04/b43e0244-4766-11ea-8949-a9ca94a90b4c_story.html; and Fred Kaplan, "The senseless danger of the military's new 'low-yield' nuclear warhead," *Slate*, February 18, 2020, https://slate.com/news-and-politics/2020/02/low-yield-warhead-nuclear-weapons-navy-trident-submarines.html.
22. Julian E. Barnes et al., "Russia's advances on space-based nuclear weapon draw U.S. concerns," *New York Times*, February 14, 2024, https://www.nytimes.com/2024/02/14/us/politics/intelligence-russia-nuclear.html.
23. Guy Faulconbridge, "Russia denies US reports Moscow plans to put nuclear weapons in space," *Reuters*, February 20, 2024, https://www.reuters.com/world/europe/russia-denies-us-claims-that-moscow-plans-deploy-nuclear-weapons-space-2024-02-20/.
24. Clarence Leong, "China seeks to counter Musk's Starlink with own satellite network," *Wall Street Journal*, May 21, 2023, https://www.wsj.com/articles/china-seeks-to-counter-musks-starlink-with-own-satellite-network-ca94aa52.
25. Tim Fernholz, "How the US is preparing to fight—and win—a war in space," *Vox.com*, February 15, 2014, https://www.vox.com/the-highlight/2024/1/16/24034692/national-security-threat-russia-space-weapons-true-anamoly-china-united-states-space-war: "nuclear weapons are banned in space according to the 1967 Outer Space Treaty, to which both the US and Russia are a party. Although there are no signs a weapon has been deployed, it does raise questions about whether Russia might be preparing to abandon the treaty. The bottom line is that, at the moment, the US would have no real way to counter such a threat."
26. Caitlin Talmadge, "Emerging technology and intra-war escalation risks: Evidence from the Cold War, implications for today," *Journal of Strategic Studies*, 42, No. 6 (2019), 864–87.

27. Elsa B. Kania and John Costello, "Seizing the commanding heights: The PLA Strategic Support Force in Chinese military power," *Journal of Strategic Studies*, 44, No. 2 (2021), 218–64, and Cunningham, "The maritime rung."
28. *Economist*, "Will the Ukraine war ring the knell for nuclear arms control?" July 31, 2022, https://www.economist.com/united-states/2022/07/31/will-the-ukraine-war-ring-the-knell-for-nuclear-arms-control. See also Timothy R. Heath, Kristen Gunness, and Tristan Finazzo, *The Return of Great Power War* (Santa Monica, CA: RAND, 2022), 7: "The dangers of a global confrontation could be amplified by the advent of new, poorly understood civilian and military technologies and unprecedented historical developments. As one example, the ability of cybertechnologies to inflict massive damage and dislocation raises problematic new escalation risks."
29. James D. Fearon, "Rationalist explanations for war," *International Organization*, 49, No. 3 (Summer 1995), 379–414.
30. Todd S. Sechser, Neil Narang, and Caitlin Talmadge, "Emerging technologies and strategic stability in peacetime, crisis, and war," *Journal of Strategic Studies*, 42, No. 6 (2019), 727–35; and Caitlin Talmadge, "Emerging technology and intra-war escalation risks: Evidence from the Cold War, implications for today," *Journal of Strategic Studies*, 42, No. 6 (2019), 864–87. The introduction of more powerful nuclear weapons, for instance, did not intensify NATO's nuclear threat against a Russian invasion. The US development of laser-guided bombs (1972) did not lead the United States to escalate its air war against North Vietnam.
31. Unrestricted submarine warfare stopped after the *Lusitania* sinking when Germany feared that it might draw the United States into a war—a decision that was reversed when Germany felt more desperate. Matthew Stibbe, "Germany's 'last card,': Wilhelm II and the decision in favour of unrestricted submarine warfare in January 1917," in Annika Mombauer and Wilhelm Deist (eds.), *The Kaiser: New Research on Wilhelm II's Role in Imperial Germany* (Cambridge, UK: Cambridge University Press), 2003.
32. See https://amti.csis.org/island-tracker/china/ for a detailed description of what facilities are on these islands. See also Associated Press, "China has fully militarized three islands in South China Sea, US admiral John C. Aquilino says Beijing is flexing its military muscle by arming isles with fighter jets, anti-ship systems and other military facilities," March 20, 2022, https://www.theguardian.com/world/2022/mar/21/china-has-fully-militarized-three-islands-in-south-china-sea-us-admiral-says.
33. As for where gray-zone operations end and armed attacks begin (thus triggering the US-Philippines mutual defense pact), the US Secretary of State, visiting Manila, "gave no indication that recent Chinese provocations—which include ramming Philippine vessels and blasting them with water cannons—crossed the threshold of 'armed' attacks." From Michael Crowley, "Blinken warns China against armed attack on Philippines," *New York Times*, March 19, 2024, https://www.nytimes.com/2024/03/19/us/politics/blinken-china-philippines.html.
34. Oriana Skylar Mastro, "How China is bending the rules in the South China Sea," February 17, 2021, *Lowy Institute*, https://www.lowyinstitute.org/the-interpreter/how-china-bending-rules-south-china-sea. See also Lisa Curtis and Nilanthi Samaranayake, "Countering coercion managing Chinese gray zone activity in the South China Sea and Indian Ocean region," Center for a New American Security, March 2024, https://www.cnas.org/publications/reports/countering-coercion.

35. Eric Cooper, "The era of coast guards," RAND_PEA3044-1, February 24, 2024, https://www.rand.org/content/dam/rand/pubs/perspectives/PEA3000/PEA3044-1/RAND_PEA3044-1.pdf.
36. See Demetri Sevastopulo and Kathrin Hille, "US warns China on aggressive acts by fishing boats and coast guard; Navy chief says washington will use military rules of engagement to curb provocative behavior," *Financial Times*, April 28, 2019.
37. Cathal Nolan, *The Allure of War* (Oxford, UK: Oxford University Press, 2019), can be read as a long disquisition on wars foolishly started because the aggressor thought it had a persistent advantage only to have its adversaries catch up.
38. Consider how escalation dominance permeates the analysis in Paul Davis et al., *Exploring the Role Nuclear Weapons Could Play in Deterring Russian Threats to the Baltic States* (Santa Monica, CA: RAND, 2009).
39. Colin Gray, "What Rand hath wrought," *Foreign Policy*, 4 (1971): 111–29: "Because one can conceive of thresholds for thought, it does not follow that those thresholds will in fact exist. An escalation ladder, in the mind of a harassed policymaker, may offer an illusion of control or of a margin of safety that is likely to be negated by the systemic nature of conflict. In the mind of the adversary, some of the rungs may be missing."
40. The use of water cannons by China's Coast Guard against Philippine naval forces creates a dilemma: concede, invest in similar capabilities (which may work until China comes up with a new trick), or deem water cannons the use of force and escalate correspondingly (see Camille Elemia, "What it feels like to be the target of China's water cannons," *New York Times*, December 11, 2023, https://www.nytimes.com/2023/12/11/world/asia/china-water-cannon-philippines.html).
41. See for instance Aaron Bateman, "Why Russia might put a nuclear weapon in space," *Foreign Affairs*, March 7, 2024, https://www.foreignaffairs.com/russian-federation/why-russia-might-put-nuclear-weapon-space: "But even if Moscow never detonates a nuclear weapon in space . . . threatening to field such a weapon provides the Kremlin with another rung on its escalation ladder, which it could use to try to deter the United States from taking any actions it opposes." Or from Christian Ruhl et al., "Policy roundtable: The future of trans-Atlantic nuclear deterrence," *Texas National Security Review*, August 23, 2021, https://tnsr.org/roundtable/policy-roundtable-the-future-of-trans-atlantic-nuclear-deterrence/ (from Ambassador Alexander Vershbow, "Reflections on NATO deterrence in the 21st century"): "By adding additional rungs to the escalation ladder, the United States was conveying the message to Moscow (and to its allies in Europe and Asia) that it could retaliate [for tac nuke strikes] without escalating to the strategic level." Or from Benjamin Jensen ("Bringing the swarm"): "In an era of great-power competition between nuclear adversaries, drone swarms offer a new rung on the escalation ladder that buys time and space for political leaders to form prudent crisis response strategies."
42. Megan Specia and Ben Hubbard, "Britain says it will give Ukraine tanks, breaching a Western taboo: Western countries have balked at giving Ukraine tanks and other powerful weapons. As increased spring fighting looms, that seems to be changing," *New York Times*, January 14, 2023, https://www.nytimes.com/2023/01/14/world/middleeast/britain-ukraine-tanks-leopards.html.
43. Austin Carson ("The missing escalation in Ukraine: In defense of the West's go-slow approach," *Foreign Affairs* [September 14, 2023], https://www.foreignaffairs.com/eastern-europe-caucasus/missing-escalation-ukraine) argues that Russia's decision

not to use nuclear weapons was just one element of forbearance. Others include Russia's not carrying out cyberattacks on Western targets (as if they were so effective against Ukrainian targets) and not overtly attacking civilian grain shipments (which were anyway throttled by Russian threats to do so).

44. Janice Kai Chen and Mary Ilyushina, "Drone strikes, sabotage, shelling: Russia's war on Ukraine comes to Russia," *Washington Post*, March 20, 2023, https://www.washingtonpost.com/world/2023/03/21/ukraine-war-russian-soil/.
45. Translated speech from *Washington Post*, "Read Putin's national address on a partial military mobilization," September 21, 2022, https://www.washingtonpost.com/world/2022/09/21/putin-speech-russia-ukraine-war-mobilization/.
46. Worries about escalation from Moscow have precedents. "Many officials were initially reluctant to provide vigorous support for the Afghans, fearing that it might unrealistically raise their hopes for a military victory or provoke Soviet reprisals against Pakistan, the main conduit for aid to the guerrillas." From Robert Pear, "Arming Afghan guerrillas: A huge effort led by U.S.," *New York Times*, April 18, 1988, https://www.nytimes.com/1988/04/18/world/arming-afghan-guerrillas-a-huge-effort-led-by-us.html.)
47. Karen DeYoung, "Russia warns U.S. to stop arming Ukraine," *Washington Post*, April 14, 2022, https://www.washingtonpost.com/national-security/2022/04/14/russia-warns-us-stop-arming-ukraine/.
48. *The Guardian*, "Putin says Russia 'will respond' if UK supplies depleted uranium shells to Ukraine," March 21, 2023, https://www.theguardian.com/world/2023/mar/21/putin-says-russia-will-respond-if-uk-supplies-depleted-uranium-shells-to-ukraine.
49. Mark Mazzetti, Helene Cooper, Julian E. Barnes, and David E. Sanger, "For the U.S., a tenuous balance in confronting Russia," *New York Times*, March 22, 2022, https://www.nytimes.com/2022/03/19/us/politics/us-ukraine-russia-escalation.html
50. Harris, "U.S. provided intelligence."
51. Institute for the Study of War, "Russian offensive campaign assessment," December 10, 2022, https://www.understandingwar.org/backgrounder/russian-offensive-campaign-assessment-december-10.
52. Jim Tankersley and Edward Wong, "The C.I.A. director meets with his Russian counterpart to warn against the use of nuclear weapons in Ukraine," *New York Times*, November 14, 2022, https://www.nytimes.com/2022/11/14/world/europe/cia-burns-ukraine-russia-nuclear.html.
53. Eric Schlosser ("What if Russia uses nuclear weapons in Ukraine?" *The Atlantic*, June 20, 2022, https://www.theatlantic.com/ideas/archive/2022/06/russia-ukraine-nuclear-weapon-us-response/661315/): "Sam Nunn, former chair of the Senate Armed Services Committee (as paraphrased by Rose Gottemoeller) argued, 'if Russia uses a nuclear weapon in Ukraine, the United States should not respond with a nuclear attack. He favors some sort of horizontal escalation instead, doing everything possible to avoid a nuclear exchange between Russia and the United States. For example, if Russia hits Ukraine with a nuclear cruise missile launched from a ship,' that ship should be immediately sunk; indeed, Russia's Black Sea fleet might be sunk in retaliation, and a no-fly zone could be imposed over Ukraine." See also (1) Fred Kaplan, "Why the U.S. might not use a nuke, even if Russia does," *Slate*, October 7, 2022, https://slate.com/news-and-politics/2022/10/why-the-us-might-not-use-a-nuke-even-if-russia-does.html; (2) James Stavridis, "What the West should do if Putin uses a nuclear weapon," *Time*, October 26, 2022, https://time.com/6225138/putin-nuclear-weapons-what-the-west

-should-do/; and (3) *The Guardian*, "Petraeus: US would destroy Russia's troops if Putin uses nuclear weapons in Ukraine," October 2, 2022, https://www.theguardian.com/world/2022/oct/02/us-russia-putin-ukraine-war-david-petraeus.
54. See Radio Free Europe, "Retired General James L. Jones: West 'too cautious about giving Ukraine weapons that could strike into Russia,'" November 26, 2023; https://www.rferl.org/a/ukraine-russia-general-jones-interview-long-range-weapons/32700251.html. But also note Vladimir Putin's essentially saying that supplying F-16s to Ukraine will not lead to escalation but merely justify his shooting them down: *Reuters*, "Putin says Russia will not attack NATO, but F-16s will be shot down in Ukraine," March 28, 2024; https://www.reuters.com/world/europe/putin-tells-pilots-f16s-can-carry-nuclear-weapons-they-wont-change-things-2024-03-27/.
55. Edward Wong, "Zelensky says Western Allies must allow Ukrainian strikes deep into Russia," September 24, 2024; https://www.nytimes.com/2024/09/24/us/politics/zelensky-ukraine-russia-strikes.html.
56. Cited in David E. Sanger and William J. Broad, "Putin's threats highlight the dangers of a new, riskier nuclear era: After generations of stability in nuclear arms control, a warning to Russia from President Biden shows how old norms are eroding," *New York Times*, June 1, 2022, https://www.nytimes.com/2022/06/01/us/politics/nuclear-arms-treaties.html.
57. See Ilan Goldenberg, Nicholas A. Heras, Kaleigh Thomas, and Jennie Matuschak, "Countering Iran in the gray zone: What the United States should learn from Israel's operations in Syria," *Center for a New American Security*, April 14, 2020, https://www.cnas.org/publications/reports/countering-iran-gray-zone.
58. Whether a major war could emerge from an Israeli strike that crosses the line is undetermined. As for hostile interactions between United States and Iran, Michael Eisenstadt ("Deterring Iran in the gray zone," *Washington Institute*, April 14, 2021, https://www.washingtoninstitute.org/policy-analysis/deterring-iran-gray-zone-insights-four-decades-conflict) argues: "For forty years now ... the United States and Iran have more or less successfully managed conflict, limited escalation, and avoided all-out war—and are likely to continue to do so. In the unlikely event that a major war occurs between the United States and Iran, it will be because one of the parties opts for it, and the other side obliges by joining battle."
59. Itamar Lifshitz and Erez Seri-Levy, "Israel's inter-war campaigns doctrine: From opportunism to principle," *Journal of Strategic Studies*, 46, No. 2 (2023), 293–318: "Israel took a tremendous risk when it first struck Hezbollah arms in Syria, and once again when it initiated the campaign against Iranian entrenchment. It had no prior experience of how they would react to such aggression. Nevertheless, Israel's risks were well calculated, taking into consideration the balance of power, geopolitical conditions, and the alternative consequences of not competing. Indeed, Hezbollah and Iran continued their efforts and retaliated by threatening the Israeli home front and harming Israeli soldiers along the border on several occasions. These interactions consolidated the rules of agreed battle."

It helped that Iran's primary ally in Syria declared a principle of strict equivalent in the tit for tat; "they killed us in broad daylight, we killed them in broad daylight; they killed us around 11:30 A.M., we killed them at 11:30 A.M.; they targeted two cars, we targeted two cars; they had killed and wounded, we too had martyrs," quoted in Nour Samaha, "Nasrallah: Hezbollah to respond to Israeli attacks," *Al Jazeera*, January 30,

2015, https://www.aljazeera.com/news/2015/1/30/nasrallah-hezbollah-to-respond-to-israeli-attacks.
60. Isaac Kardon, *China's Law of the Sea* (New Haven, CT: Yale University Press, 2023), 180: "the PRC rule [for navigation rights] as practiced does not promote a rule that others can adopt."
61. See for instance Paul Haenle and Nathaniel Sher, "How Pelosi's Taiwan visit has set a new status quo for U.S-China tensions," *Carnegie Endowment*, August 17, 2022, https://carnegieendowment.org/2022/08/17/how-pelosi-s-taiwan-visit-has-set-new-status-quo-for-u.s-china-tensions-pub-87696.
62. Robert D. Blackwill and Philip Zelikow, "The United States, China, and Taiwan: A strategy to prevent war," *Council on Foreign Relations*, February 2021, https://www.cfr.org/report/united-states-china-and-taiwan-strategy-prevent-war, 45. See also Andrew Bacevich et al., "A restraint approach to U.S.–China relations," *Quincy Institute*, April 2023, https://quincyinst.org/report/u-s-relations-with-china-a-strategy-based-on-restraint/, who argues against the United States developing capabilities useful for "striking logistics points and C4ISR locations deep within the Chinese mainland [and] thereby limiting escalation."
63. *Economist*, "Giving Ukraine heavy weapons does not mean NATO is at war with Russia," April 17, 2022, https://www.economist.com/europe/giving-ukraine-heavy-weapons-does-not-mean-nato-is-at-war-with-russia/21808835.
64. Indeed, in 1964 the Chinese declared the Qiongzhou Strait (but not the Taiwan Strait) as an inland waterway through which no military vessels were allowed to pass. See Kardon, "China's law," 176.
65. "Moscow's other big red line was that there must be no attacks on Russian territory, even though it was acting with impunity against Ukrainian territory. This was a line blurred by the Russians once they insisted that they had transferred chunks of Ukrainian territory to the Russian Federation." From Lawrence Freedman, "Salami slicing, boiled frogs, and Russian red lines," June 4, 2023, https://samf.substack.com/p/salami-slicing-boiled-frogs-and-russian.
66. "In Paul Nitze's hypothetical general war confined to airfields and SAC installations, the bombing of cities would be unwise in the early stages of the war and unnecessary in the later ones after air superiority has been achieved. . . . But for the side which stands to lose the air battle and which seeks to exact a maximum price for its own defeat, the most rational strategy may well be to inflict maximum destruction. From Henry Kissinger, "Force and diplomacy in the nuclear age," *Foreign Affairs*, 34, No. 3 (April 1956), https://www.foreignaffairs.com/print/node/1112979.
67. White House Office of the Press Secretary, "Remarks by President Obama and President Xi of the People's Republic of China in joint press conference," September 25, 2015, https://obamawhitehouse.archives.gov/the-press-office/2015/09/25/remarks-president-obama-and-president-xi-peoples-republic-china-joint.
68. Anna Fifield, "N. Korea didn't test a nuclear weapon, but it did try to launch another missile," *Washington Post*, April 16, 2017, https://www.washingtonpost.com/world/asia_pacific/n-korea-didnt-test-a-nuclear-weapon-but-its-display-of-military-hardware-wasnt-exactly-good-news/2017/04/15/49944da8-221c-11e7-bcd6-6d1286bc177d_story.html.
69. The Chinese and Indians agreed that confrontations along their common border could use sticks and rocks but not guns. See the UN document "Agreement between

India and China 1996.doc," https://peacemaker.un.org/sites/peacemaker.un.org/files/CN%20IN_961129_Agreement%20between%20China%20and%20India.pdf.
70. When the Bolsheviks came to power in Moscow, they revealed many of these secret agreements. There may be an audience tomorrow even if there is none today.
71. The difference between an absolute promise and a conditional promise may be seen in the difference between the current New START agreement on strategic nuclear arms (this but no more) and the following potential successor, "For example, for each interceptor fielded by one side, the other side could have the right to raise its ceiling by a specified number of warheads." From Samuel Charap, Christian Curriden, "U.S. Options for Post–New START Arms Control with Russia," July 2024 (RAND, Santa Monica); https://www.rand.org/content/dam/rand/pubs/perspectives/PEA700/PEA739-1/RAND_PEA739-1.pdf, p.10.

Conclusions

Conflict escalation reflects each side's urge to fight and both sides' appreciation of war's consequences. But thresholds can alter the odds and timing of escalation. They create opportunities to stop, or at least pause, escalation or turn it towards less risky directions. Thresholds can force leaders to consciously weigh the benefits, costs, and risks associated with their breaching this or that limit. If thresholds are mutual, the inhibition to escalation is that it would be a tacit promise broken and the other side would also escalate. We have argued the advantages of a threshold that is easy to measure and monitor so that one side cannot escalate unknowingly or undetectably. If two sides are inclined to escalate and lack a plausible excuse in the other side's behavior, then clarity matters more. But if the two sides are disinclined to escalate, they are apt to be more forgiving if some veneer of plausibility allows them to be deem the other side's behavior as roughly compliant.

Alas, even as existing thresholds between war and peace, and between conventional and nuclear war, erode, the prospects for additional or alternative thresholds are not encouraging, at many levels of conflict.

One problem with establishing thresholds within cyberspace, for instance, is that escalation itself is hard to define absent requisite norms. Gauging escalation beyond cyberspace, for instance, rests in part on whether states consider it like (kinetic) war or unlike war: agreement either way fosters stability, but disagreement can lead to inadvertent escalation. Similar questions can be asked of the relationship between cyberattack and economic sanctions; both occupy incomparable points on the lattice of conflict.

In principle a threshold between lethal and nonlethal conflict may supplement or even complement the one between peace and war. But doing that could place satellites and other unmanned infrastructure at risk—making such distinctions difficult to maintain if damage becomes great enough. Furthermore, such a threshold (that, for instance, allows attacks on UAVs) defined in domains where manned platforms (e.g., jets) also operate can easily be breached by accident.

Distinguishing between a local and a global conflict among superpowers for threshold purposes is similarly hard, especially when the logistics and intelligence support to ostensibly local battles are globally supplied. Unless both sides are willing to forgive small transgressions by the other, other differences in the definition of local—nearby waters, offshore islands, overseas territories (e.g., Guam)—can lead to disagreement about who is operating at what scale. And the relative vulnerability of Chinese and Russian homelands compared to the inviolability of the US homeland—complicated in turn by the promises built into US alliances—dampen the prospect of any homeland threshold.

The conventional–nuclear threshold has been well defined for decades. But whereas in the Cold War one could not destroy most nuclear weapons without starting a nuclear war, cyberspace plus advanced precision-guided conventional weapons now mean they can be consequentially targeted with conventional means alone. So is nuclear war war *using* nuclear weapons or war *against* nuclear weapons? Disagreement in conflict can be destabilizing.

Once nuclear weapons are used, the last question is whether Armageddon can still be avoided. Potential thresholds—between tactical and strategic nuclear use, between counterforce and countervalue operations, between exemplary and instrumental use—have been chewed on since the 1950s. But none are firmly established because different states look at these matters differently.

Asymmetries among even otherwise peer powers—some arising from fixed parameters such as geography and persistent ones such as geopolitics—can easily frustrate consensus on where to put thresholds. Many thresholds—such as between tactical and strategic nuclear weapons—have no one clear definition, obscuring when a threshold has been crossed even when the facts are not in dispute. Even when definitions are clear, measurement may be contested. Since recognized thresholds are promises ("if you don't, then I won't") as well as threats ("if you do, then I will"), it hardly helps that the capacity of adversaries—because they are adversaries—to believe in each other's promises is weak to begin with.

The lattice-like nature of escalation in the current era adds complications. Lateral movement (e.g., from attacks on satellites to counterattacks on ground stations in the other side's homelands) makes it difficult to conclude that escalation has or has not taken place. Many of the cyberspace-related forces that erode thresholds—such as the use of precision conventional munitions against nuclear assets, or the grey-zone application of nonkinetic warfare—could also take conflict in new directions. The broader the option space, the less one can know whether one action is escalation vis-à-vis another. To properly inhibit escalation, thresholds may be forced to encompass actions that are different in form if arguably similar in intensity. Such thresholds lack obviousness, hence credibility.

Thresholds are therefore unlikely to arise through the mutual recognition of some obvious Schellingesque focal point, inferences drawn from what the other side is *not* doing, or any other form of immaculate conception. That being so, superpowers may have to restrain themselves unilaterally. They may calculate that they would be worse off escalating if they believe the other side will do likewise as a result. They may declare red lines girded by threats and hope that the other side, even if seeing them as unfair, nevertheless respects them.

Or leaders could try harder to develop thresholds. If we want them—and they can be a useful tool—we are thousands of conversations away from getting them. Even so success is not guaranteed. If new thresholds are just not forthcoming, perhaps the traditional ones—between peace and war, and the nuclear taboo—need to be reinforced against the temptations afforded from cyberspace or at least the blithe exploitation of its grey areas. Doing so will require Western leadership because neither China nor Russia is likely to make any attempts to discuss thresholds seriously.

APPENDIX A

Deterrence, Thresholds, and Norms

The concepts of deterrence, thresholds, and norms seem parallel, perhaps even interchangeable. All of them are exercises in behavior modification. All create inhibitions to action by promising consequences: deterrence through threats, thresholds through threats and promises, and norms through pressure, notably from third parties. Escalation management itself has been described as intrawar deterrence (classic deterrence is interwar deterrence). Nevertheless, there are fundamental differences among the three. To begin with, deterrence is essentially unilateral, thresholds are bilateral (although they often have multilateral roots), and norms are usually multilateral. In laying out these differences—many already noted—the focus is first on deterrence and then on norms, contrasting first one and then the other to thresholds.

DETERRENCE AND THRESHOLDS

The essence of deterrence is the threat that if you do this, then I will do that. The threat need not be two-sided: a country with nuclear weapons can threaten non-nuclear countries (as the United States did to China in 1954 and 1958). This threat also need not be coupled with its converse promise—if you do not do this, then I will not do that—although the converse reinforces the power of the threat (otherwise it's damned if you do and damned if you don't). Thresholds by contrast tend to be bilateral—a set of linked barriers. As noted, because a threshold has as much or more the character of a promise than a threat, it explicitly invokes its own converse. For thresholds the assurance component merits the same emphasis as the threat component.

A threshold can be inferred from both sides' deterrence postures, but that requires some assumptions. For thresholds "this" and "that" are equal (e.g., if you attack my homeland, I will attack yours) or at least can be deemed equivalent (e.g., two operations at roughly the same level on the lattice).

During the Cold War, the interaction of each side's nuclear deterrence looked as if it had established a *de facto* threshold for conflict, but as noted, the United States never limited its nuclear threats to retaliation for Soviet nuclear attacks. A large conventional attack on NATO could also meet a nuclear response. Although the 1980s Soviet Union officially had an NFU policy, Washington did not take its promises seriously. There was little attempt to ensure that the United States and the Soviet Union were using nuclear threats in the same way. There was little haggling about whether US triggers (which were never completely spelled out) matched Soviet triggers (which also were never spelled out).

Fairness and legitimacy do influence whether any specific deterrence or threshold posture works—but with nuclear deterrence the threat of an apocalypse received far more attention. With sub-apocalyptic deterrence, it may matter whether a state is being coerced into refraining from what it thinks it has the right to do. States may ask whether threats are legitimate, downplaying those that are not and respecting those that are. With nuclear deterrence, the cost of guessing wrong is prohibitive; with non-catastrophic threats, less so.

Another distinction in practice, if not necessarily in theory, is that deterrence tends to be a single-level restraint while any single threshold would exist in the context of other thresholds. When deterrence at one level fails, there is rarely a back-up position articulated. Doing so tends to erode the credibility of the original threat. But having multiple thresholds is entirely consistent with the metaphor of the escalation ladder or lattice. When a threshold fails, there are likely to be fallback thresholds. The back-up does not lose all credibility; the side that crossed the threshold may have done so to move to the next one, where it feels at less of a disadvantage. There are escalation issues that can only be associated with multiple threshold levels—as noted, one side matching the other side's crossing a threshold could itself cross a higher threshold and start a new round of escalation. But as argued, trying to maintain too many thresholds weakens the protection that any one threshold offers.

Deterrence and thresholds also have different narratives. The narrative of deterrence is harsh: one country telling another what not to do—as if the former sat in judgement on the latter. The narrative of thresholds is more akin to rule-setting, a signaling of mutual restraint and "agreed competition." It tends to concede that both sides enter conflicts as moral peers, at least notionally. Defying threats of the sort that come with deterrence is not considered immoral (even if perhaps foolish). Violating mutually agreed-on thresholds is to admit to cynicism; it suggests that rules are rules only so long as they are convenient.

NORMS AND THRESHOLDS

Arguably thresholds could be candidates for formalization as norms, analogous to LOAC. A case for formalizing thresholds is that crossing one could add third-party disapproval as one more reason not to do so. It could also provide a basis for third-party sanctions if such thresholds are written in to a country's laws: for instance, sanctions are imposed on parties that cross this threshold. Formalization provides a standard vocabulary for talking about the conflict. The term *escalation*, as noted, is often thrown around casually and inappropriately. Some standardization of escalation (at least of type *vice* degree) in terms of crossed thresholds could clear out combustible brush from the narrative landscape.

Nevertheless, formalization of thresholds into a LOAC-like status can be problematic.

As hard as it is to define thresholds for a specific two-party conflict, doing so for future conflicts among undetermined countries is harder. Even as norms persist, changes in technology can erode their relevance: Chapters 2 and 3 of this work could not have been written forty years ago. Who can say that forthcoming advances in autonomous weapons or artificial intelligence will not create meaningful differences in the conduct of war that should become thresholds? More broadly, thresholds need to be meaningful and what is meaningful in one context may be meaningless in another. Geography, alliance structures, governance structures, and the relative technological level of the combatants lend force to context-specific thresholds. Thresholds relevant to a naval conflict off China, a land conflict in Ukraine, a subcontinental clash between India and Pakistan, or war between Israel and Iran are potentially all very different. A threshold whose crossing makes a difference for one side in one conflict may make little difference to sides in another conflict.

Another problem with setting a threshold as a norm is that anything that says "but no farther" implicitly justifies the preceding "only so far" as somehow being acceptable. Laws are written with thresholds, such as those that distinguish manslaughter from first-degree murder, without making the former acceptable—but such distinctions are rarely applied to sequential events (e.g., murder as an escalation from manslaughter). Will international norms tolerate nuances and differences of degree?

Similarly, many norms that exist cannot be converted into symmetric thresholds. It requires considerable moral gymnastics for a country to argue that the use of, say, chemical weapons is heinous—and then threaten to do likewise if the other side goes ahead and uses chemical weapons. At most, such thresholds would have to be asymmetric—the victim does something else it had not done before if attacked by chemical weapons—to create a sufficiently credible threat.

There is also value in having opposing sides work out or discover the relevant thresholds, even if they must do so using give and take—rather than having thresholds, however well-designed and stable, imposed on them. Workable thresholds require buy-in from both sides, and people are more likely to abide by rules that they have explicitly agreed to. Insofar as thresholds are implicit promises, they must be made by those who would keep them. The shame associated with breaking a promise implied by a threshold disappears if the threshold is not a promise but a standard. Even if formalization allows one side to refer to something universally recognized as a limit on their activities, there are other ways to improve definitions.

The conversations required to generate working thresholds among two sides are thus benefits, not costs. In developing norms dialogue takes place mostly among third parties and applies to a general context. Norms negotiators may not truly represent their country's national security establishment (as noted, deterrence policies that threaten unlimited consequences are at odds with limits implied by thresholds). Signing up to limits promotes a country's peaceable narrative—something of primary interest only to those factions who find it useful and necessary. Finally, thresholds only merit serious attention as they are approached; until then they may not be given much attention, hence careful thought, by potential combatants—much less bystanders. Conversely *general* discussions on thresholds may be the only ones possible among two states, neither of whom can publicly envision a conflict between them that may require thresholds to modulate.

Once combat looms or starts, though, both sides will be talking from a national security perspective. Discussions are likely to be more fit for a specific purpose even if clouded by lies, bluster, and threats. They may elicit what the other side's true red lines are, the better to limit inadvertent escalation of the sort that comes from mismatched expectations.

As noted, Track II discussions on thresholds for cyberspace have gone nowhere: Russia and China initially denied wanting to violate the sanctuary of cyberspace and were loath to discuss intermediate limits on activities in a domain in which they foreswore activity altogether. Both now admit to having and having had offensive cyber forces. The problems of getting, say, China to discuss nuclear thresholds (or even anything nuclear) or getting Russia to discuss similar topics outside of treaty obligations suggests that cyberspace may not be all that unique in that regard.

APPENDIX B

With Nuclear Threats, Might Makes Won't

States can threaten nuclear use to manipulate the other side's calculations of how much its actions (or inactions) would alter the odds of Armageddon. A threat from a country that can and wants to escalate is credible. But carrying out a nuclear threat against those with nuclear weapons or nuclear allies usually makes one much worse off. Because making a solemn vow and doing nothing hurts credibility, many countries talk not of what they *would* but what they *might* do (e.g., the United States might respond to devastating cyberattacks with nuclear weapons[1]).

Threats that one can wiggle out of[2] or that are phrased obliquely (e.g., "unpredictable consequences"[3]) are worth little, though. To see why, ask: how much credibility is lost from backing away from a threat? If retaliation were said to be certain, backing away would clearly reduce credibility. But if retaliation was said to be possible, less credibility is lost: a tossed coin that lands on tails does not mean the coin is biased. The less credibility is lost, the weaker the case for risking Armageddon by fulfilling threats—and thus the less often it pays to keep them, and thus the less the other side would believe that the threat would be carried out. If the side making threats understands that the other side makes such calculations ("we never expected them to carry out the threat"), it will realize that there is even less credibility to be lost by not carrying through. And the side being threatened will conclude that the odds of carrying out the threat are therefore even lower. And so on to zero.

This does not mean that nuclear weapons would never get used in such cases—but such use would reflect the case for using nuclear weapons rather than the need to maintain credibility. An early 1950 presentation by the US secretary of state put South Korea outside of America's defined western Pacific defense perimeter,[4] implying that the United States would not defend it. Thus, US credibility would not be dented if it did nothing after South Korea was invaded. When several months later North Korea did exactly that, the United States intervened, not to make some prior threat credible but because the cost of an unanswered invasion (e.g., a larger and more emboldened communist bloc) was seen as greater than the cost of opposing it. Intervention made sense on its own.

NOTES

1. When directly questioned, Patrick Shanahan, the deputy secretary of defense, did not deny that link. US Department of Defense, "News briefing on the 2018 nuclear posture review," February 2, 2018, https://www.defense.gov/News/Transcripts/Transcript-View/Article/1431945/.
2. Try to define "interfere" in Vladimir Putin's war-opening statement, "Whoever tries to interfere with us, and even more so to create threats to our country, to our people, should know that Russia's response will be immediate and will lead you to such consequences as you have never experienced in your history," cited in Nathan Hodge, Tim Lister, Ivana Kottasová, and Helen Regan, "Russia launches military attack on Ukraine with reports of explosions and troops crossing border," *Cable News Network*, February 24, 2022, https://www.cnn.com/2022/02/23/europe/russia-ukraine-putin-military-operation-donbas-intl-hnk/index.html.
3. "Stung by war losses and massing troops for a new battle in eastern Ukraine, Russia has warned the Biden administration to stop supplying advanced weapons to Ukrainian forces or face 'unpredictable consequences,' American officials said Friday." From David E. Sanger, Helene Cooper, and Anton Troianovski, "Girding for new battle, Russia warns U.S. on advanced weapons for Ukraine," *New York Times*, April 15, 2022, https://www.nytimes.com/2022/04/15/world/europe/ukraine-russia-us-weapons-warning.html.
4. He was not an outlier. General Douglas MacArthur had also spoken of an American "line of defense" that excluded South Korea. The United States had also just withdrawn two divisions from the peninsula. From Robert Osgood, *Limited War: The Challenge to American Security* (Chicago, IL: University of Chicago Press, 1957), 164.

BIBLIOGRAPHY

VIDEOS

Joyce, Rob, at the USENIX Enigma 2016 conference: https://www.youtube.com/watch?v=bDJb8WOJYdA.

Miller, James, (former undersecretary of defense for policy, Obama administration) at the Lawrence Livermore Lab's Center for Global Security Research. https://www.youtube.com/watch?v=LKzp-WX4p_s, 17:18 to 17:27.

Panetta, Leon, on March 15, 2022. https://www.youtube.com/watch?v=-rECMn-J50WA: 2:00 to 2:07 and 2:38 to 2:42.

ARTICLES, BOOKS, AND REPORTS

Acton, James. "Cyber warfare & inadvertent escalation," *Daedalus*, 149, No. 2 (Spring 2020), 133–49.

Acton, James. "Escalation through entanglement: How the vulnerability of command-and-control systems raises the risks of an inadvertent nuclear war," *International Security* 43, No. 1 (2018), 56–99.

Acton, James. "Managing vulnerability," *Foreign Affairs* 89, No. 2 (2010), 146–8.

Adamsky, Dmitry. "The 1983 nuclear crisis—Lessons for deterrence theory and practice," *Journal of Strategic Studies*, 36, No. 1 (2013), 4–41.

Aerospace Corporation. "A brief history of space debris," November 2, 2022. https://aerospace.org/article/brief-history-space-debris.

AFP. "US launched cyber attacks on Iran after drone shootdown: Reports," June 22, 2019. https://news.yahoo.com/us-launched-cyber-attacks-iran-drone-shootdown-reports-232123877.html.

Albon, Courtney. "US Navy, Air Force running 'capstone test' of new high-power microwave missile," *C4ISRNet*, July 1, 2022. https://www.c4isrnet.com/battlefield-tech/2022/07/01/us-navy-air-force-running-capstone-test-of-new-high-power-microwave-missile/.

Ali, Indris, and Phil Stewart. "Exclusive: U.S. carried out secret cyber strike on Iran in wake of Saudi oil attack: Officials," *Reuters*, October 16, 2019. https://www.reuters.com/article/us-usa-iran-military-cyber-exclusive/exclusive-u-s-carried-out-secret-cyber-strike-on-iran-in-wake-of-saudi-oil-attack-officials-idUSKBN1WV0EK.

Allen, George W. *None So Blind: A Personal Account of the Intelligence Failure in Vietnam* (Chicago: Ivan R. Dee, 2001, p. 46).

Alperovitch, Dmitri. "The dangers of Putin's paranoia," *Foreign Affairs*, March 18, 2022, https://www.foreignaffairs.com/articles/russia-fsu/2022-03-18/dangers-putins-paranoia.

Alperovitch, Dmitri, and Ian Ward. "How should the U.S. respond to the SolarWinds and Microsoft Exchange hacks?" *Lawfare*, March 12, 2021. https://www.lawfareblog.com/how-should-us-respond-solarwinds-and-microsoft-exchange-hacks.

Al-Monitor, "Exclusive: Hezbollah suspicions forced Israel to expedite Lebanon pager attack," September 18, 2024. https://www.al-monitor.com/originals/2024/09/exclusive-hezbollah-suspicions-forced-israel-expedite-lebanon-pager-attack.

Ambinder, Mark. "How Obama made it easier for Trump to launch a nuke: Maybe we should talk about this?," *Politico*, September 14, 2018. https://www.politico.com/magazine/story/2018/09/14/barack-obama-nukes-donald-trump-219912.

Anderson, Ross. *Security Engineering: A Guide to Building Dependable Distributed Systems*, 2nd ed. Hoboken, NJ: Wiley, 2008.

Arbatov, Alexei. "Challenges of the new nuclear era: The Russian perspective," In *Meeting the Challenges of the New Nuclear Age: U.S. and Russian Nuclear Concepts, Past and Present*, edited by Linton Brooks, Francis J. Gavin, and Alexei Arbatov, 21–46. Cambridge, MA: American Academy of Arts and Sciences, 2018.

Arbatov, Alexei, Vladimir Dvorkin, and Petr Topychkanov. "Entanglement as a new security threat: A Russian perspective," *Carnegie Moscow Center*, November 8, 2017. https://carnegie.ru/2017/11/08/entanglement-as-new-security-threat-russian-perspective-pub-73163.

Arms Control Association. "Russia adopts new security concept," January 2000. https://www.armscontrol.org/act/2000-01/press-releases/russia-adopts-new-security-concept.

Asia Maritime Transparency Initiative. "China island tracker." https://amti.csis.org/island-tracker/china/.

Associated Press. "China has fully militarized three islands in South China Sea, US Admiral John C Aquilino says Beijing is flexing its military muscle by arming isles with fighter jets, anti-ship systems and other military facilities," March 20, 2022. https://www.theguardian.com/world/2022/mar/21/china-has-fully-militarized-three-islands-in-south-china-sea-us-admiral-says.

Avey, Paul C. "Just like yesterday? New critiques of the nuclear revolution," *Texas National Security Review*, 6, No. 2 (Spring 2023), 9–31.

BIBLIOGRAPHY

Azizi, Hamidreza. "How Iran and its allies hope to save Hamas," *War on the Rocks*, November 16, 2023. https://warontherocks.com/2023/11/how-iran-and-its-allies-hope-to-save-hamas/.

Bahney, Benjamin W., Jonathan Pearl, and Michael Markey. "Antisatellite weapons and the growing instability of deterrence," In *Cross-Domain Deterrence*, edited by Jon R. Lindsay and Erik Gartzke, 121–43. Oxford, UK: Oxford University Press, 2019.

Baker, Peter, Eric Schmitt, and Michael Crowley. "An abrupt move that stunned aides: Inside Trump's aborted attack on Iran," *New York Times*, September 21, 2019. https://www.nytimes.com/2019/09/21/us/politics/trump-iran-decision.html.

Barnes, Julian, Helene Cooper, and Eric Schmitt. "U.S. intelligence is helping Ukraine kill Russian generals, officials say," *New York Times*, May 5, 2022. https://www.nytimes.com/2022/05/04/us/politics/russia-generals-killed-ukraine.html.

Barnes, Julian E., Karoun Demirjian, Eric Schmitt, and David E. Sanger. "Russia's advances on space-based nuclear weapon draw U.S. concerns," *New York Times*, February 14, 2024. https://www.nytimes.com/2024/02/14/us/politics/intelligence-russia-nuclear.html.

Barrett, Brian. "The Air Force will let hackers try to hijack an orbiting satellite," *Wired*, September 17, 2019. https://www.wired.com/story/air-force-defcon-satellite-hacking/.

Barry, Ben. "Pakistan's tactical nuclear weapons: Practical drawbacks and opportunity costs." *Survival* 60, no. 1 (2018): 75–81.

Bateman, Aaron. "America can protect its satellites without kinetic space weapons," *War on the Rocks*, July 30, 2020. https://warontherocks.com/2020/07/america-can-protect-its-satellites-without-kinetic-space-weapons/.

Bateman, Aaron. "Why Russia might put a nuclear weapon in space," *Foreign Affairs*, March 7, 2024. https://www.foreignaffairs.com/russian-federation/why-russia-might-put-nuclear-weapon-space.

Bateman, Jon. "Russia's wartime cyber operations in Ukraine: Military impacts, influences, and implications," *Carnegie Endowment*, December 2022. https://carnegieendowment.org/2022/12/16/russia-s-wartime-cyber-operations-in-ukraine-military-impacts-influences-and-implications-pub-88657.

Beaufre, Andre. *Deterrence and Strategy*. New York: Praeger, 1965.

Beebe, George. "We're more at risk of nuclear war with Russia than we think," *Politico*, October 7, 2019. https://www.politico.com/magazine/story/2019/10/07/were-more-at-risk-of-nuclear-war-with-russia-than-we-think-229436.

Berger, Eric. "Russia threatens a retaliatory strike against US commercial satellites," *Arstechnica*, October 27, 2022. https://arstechnica.com/science/2022/10/russia-threatens-a-retaliatory-strike-against-us-commercial-satellites/.

Berger, Eric. "The US military just proved it can get satellites into space super fast: Alpha becomes the first of the US 1-ton rockets to reach its target orbit," *Arstechnica*,

September 15, 2023. https://arstechnica.com/space/2023/09/firefly-and-space-force-demonstrate-ability-to-rapidly-launch-a-satellite/.

Bergman, Ronen, and David M. Halbfinger. "Israel hack of Iran port is latest salvo in exchange of cyberattacks," *New York Times*, May 20, 2020. https://www.nytimes.com/2020/05/19/world/middleeast/israel-iran-cyberattacks.html.

Biddle, Stephen. *Military Power: Explaining Victory and Defeat in Modern Battle*. Princeton, NJ: Princeton University Press, 2006.

Biddle, Stephen, and John Severini. "Military effectiveness and naval warfare," *Security Studies*, 33, 3 (published online: 08 Aug 2024), 325–347.

Binnendijk, Hans, and David Gompert. "Decisive response: A new nuclear strategy for NATO," *Survival*, 61, No. 5 (October–November 2019), 113–128.

Bird, Kai. *The Color of Truth* (New York: Simon and Schuster, 2000), 48.

Birnbaum, Michael, David L. Stern, and Emily Rauhala. "Russia's methodical attacks exploit frailty of Ukrainian power system," *Washington Post*, October 25, 2022. https://www.washingtonpost.com/world/2022/10/25/russias-methodical-attacks-exploit-frailty-ukrainian-power-system/.

Blackwill, Robert D., and Philip Zelikow. "The United States, China, and Taiwan: A strategy to prevent war," *Council on Foreign Relations*, February 2021. https://www.cfr.org/report/united-states-china-and-taiwan-strategy-prevent-war.

Blair, Bruce. *Global Zero Commission on Nuclear Risk Reduction, De-Alerting and Stabilizing the World's Nuclear Force Postures*. April 2015. https://www.globalzero.org/wp-content/uploads/2018/09/global_zero_commission_on_nuclear_risk_reduction_report_0.pdf.

Blair, Bruce. "Why our nuclear weapons can be hacked," *New York Times*, March 14, 2017. https://www.nytimes.com/2017/03/14/opinion/why-our-nuclear-weapons-can-be-hacked.html.

Blair, Dennis. Letter to the editor, *Foreign Affairs* 98, No. 1 (January–February 2019), 218–19.

Blank, Stephen. "Can information warfare be deterred?" *Defense* Analysis 17, No. 2 (2001), 121–38.

Blume, Susanna, and Molly Parrish. "Investing in great-power competition," *Center for Naval Analyses*, July 9, 2020. https://www.cnas.org/publications/reports/investing-in-great-power-competition.

Borghard, Erica, and Jacquelyn Schneider. "Israel responded to a Hamas cyberattack with an airstrike. That's not such a big deal," *Washington Post*, May 9, 2018. https://www.washingtonpost.com/politics/2019/05/09/israel-responded-hamas-cyberattack-with-an-airstrike-thats-big-deal/.

Bowen, Tyler Bowen. "The logic of escalation and the benefits of conventional power preponderance in the nuclear age," PhD diss., Yale Graduate School of Arts and Sciences, August 19, 2021. https://elischolar.library.yale.edu/gsas_dissertations/.

Bowers, Ian, and Henrik Stålhane Hiim. "Conventional counterforce dilemmas: South Korea's deterrence strategy and stability on the Korean peninsula," *International Security*, 45, No. 3 (Winter 2020/2021), 7–39.

Bracken, Paul. "The cyber threat to nuclear stability," *Orbis*, 60, No. 2 (February 12, 2016).

Brands, Hal. "Getting ready for a long war with China," *American Enterprise Institute*, July 2022. https://www.aei.org/research-products/report/getting-ready-for-a-long-war-with-china-dynamics-of-protracted-conflict-in-the-western-pacific/.

Broad, William, and David Sanger. "A 2nd new nuclear missile base for China, and many questions about strategy," *New York Times*, July 26, 2021. https://www.nytimes.com/2021/07/26/us/politics/china-nuclear-weapons.html.

Brodie, Bernard. "Implications for military policy," in *The Absolute Weapon: Atomic Power and World Order*, edited by Bernard Brodie, 70–107. New York: Harcourt, 1946.

Brodie, Bernard. *Strategy in the Missile Age*. Princeton, NJ: Princeton, 1967.

Browlie, Ian. *International Law and the Use of Force by States*. Oxford, UK: Clarendon Press, 1963.

Brown, Harold. Statement before a joint meeting of the House and Senate Budget Committees on January 31, 1979 (regarding the fiscal 1980 budget).

Buchanan, Ben. *The Cybersecurity Dilemma: Hacking, Trust and Fear between Nations*. Oxford, UK: Oxford University Press, 2017.

Buchanan, Ben, and Fiona Cunningham. "Preparing the cyber battlefield: Assessing a novel escalation risk in a Sino-American crisis," *Texas National Security Review*, 3, No. 4 (Fall 2020), 54–81.

Budiansky, Stephen. *Air Power*. New York: Penguin, 2004.

Burgess, Matt. "A mysterious satellite hack has victims far beyond Ukraine," *Wired*, March 23, 2022. https://www.wired.com/story/viasat-internet-hack-ukraine-russia/.

Burgess, Matt. "North Korea's elite hackers are funding nukes with crypto raids," *Wired*, April 3, 2019. https://www.wired.co.uk/article/north-korea-hackers-apt38-cryptocurrency.

Burgess, Matt. "To protect Putin, Russia is spoofing GPS signals on a massive scale," *Wired*, March 27, 2019. https://www.wired.co.uk/article/russia-gps-spoofing.

Cameron, James. "China's silos: New intelligence, old problems," *War on the Rocks*, August 12, 2021. https://warontherocks.com/2021/08/beijings-silos-new-intelligence-old-problems/.

Campbell, Matthew. "'Logic bomb' arms race panics Russians," *The Sunday Times*, November 29, 1998.

Carson, Austin. "Facing off and saving face: Covert intervention and escalation management in the Korean War." *International Organization* 70, No. 1, (Winter 2016), 103–131.

Carson, Austin. "The missing escalation in Ukraine: In defense of the West's go-slow approach," *Foreign Affairs*, September 14, 2023. https://www.foreignaffairs.com/eastern-europe-caucasus/missing-escalation-ukraine.

Carson, Austin. *Secret Wars*. Princeton, NJ: Princeton University Press, 2018.

Cave, Damien. "China creates a coast guard like no other, seeking supremacy in Asian seas," *New York Times*, June 12, 2023. https://www.nytimes.com/2023/06/12/world/asia/china-coast-guard.html.

Charap, Samuel, and Christian Curriden. "U.S. options for post–new START arms control with Russia," July 2024 (RAND, Santa Monica). https://www.rand.org/content/dam/rand/pubs/perspectives/PEA700/PEA739-1/RAND_PEA739-1.pdf, p.10.

Charap, Samuel, and Jeremy Shapiro. "The U.S. and Russia need to start talking before it's too late," *New York Times*, July 27, 2022. www.nytimes.com/2022/07/27/opinion/ukraine-russia-us-diplomacy.html.

Charney, Scott, Erin English, Aaron Kleiner, Nemanja Malisevic, Angela McKay, Jan Neutze, and Paul Nicholas, "From articulation to implementation: Enabling progress on cybersecurity norms," *Microsoft*, June 2016. https://query.prod.cms.rt.microsoft.com/cms/api/am/binary/REVmc8.

Chen, Janice Kai, and Mary Ilyushina. "Drone strikes, sabotage, shelling: Russia's war on Ukraine comes to Russia," *Washington Post*, March 20, 2023. https://www.washingtonpost.com/world/2023/03/21/ukraine-war-russian-soil/.

Chinchilla, Alexandra, and Sam Rosenberg. "Why America should send military advisers to Ukraine," *Foreign Affairs*, September 22, 2023. https://www.foreignaffairs.com/united-states/why-america-should-send-military-advisers-ukraine.

Cho, Hyun-Binn. "Nuclear coercion, crisis bargaining, and the Sino-Soviet border conflict of 1969," *Security Studies*, 30, No. 4 (2020), 550–77.

Chow, Brian. "Stalkers in space: Defeating the threat," *Strategic Studies Quarterly*, 11, No. 2 (Summer 2017), 82–116.

Christensen, Thomas J. "The meaning of the nuclear evolution: China's strategic modernization and US-China security relations," *Journal of Strategic Studies*, 35, No. 4 (2012), 447–87.

Churchill, Winston. *National Churchill Museum*, "Do Your Worst; We'll Do Our Best," (speech of July 14, 1941). https://www.nationalchurchillmuseum.org/do-your-worst-well-do-our-best.html.

Cimbala, Stephen J., and Roger N. McDermott. "A new cold war? Missile defenses, nuclear arms reductions, and cyber war," *Comparative Strategy*, 34, No. 1 (2015), 95–111.

Clark, Bryan, Mark Gunzinger, and Jesse Sloman. "Winning in the gray zone: Using electromagnetic warfare to regain escalation dominance," *Center for Strategic and Budgetary Assessments*, 2017. https://csbaonline.org/research/publications/winning-in-the-gray-zone-using-electromagnetic-warfare-to-regain-escalation.

Clark, Christopher. *The Sleepwalkers: How Europe Went to War in 1914*. New York: Harper, 2013.

Clem, Ralph. "Risky encounters with Russia: Time to talk about real deconfliction," *War on the Rocks*, February 18, 2021. https://warontherocks.com/2021/02/risky-encounters-with-russia-time-to-talk-about-real-deconfliction/.

Clement, Peter. "Putin's risk spiral: The logic of escalation in an unraveling war," *Foreign Affairs*, October 26, 2022. https://www.foreignaffairs.com/ukraine/putin-risk-spiral-logic-of-escalation-in-war.

CNS Staff. "North Korea's nuclear test and its aftermath: Coping with the fallout." *NTI*, June 24, 2009. https://www.nti.org/analysis/articles/north-koreas-nuclear-test-aftermath/.

Coalson, Robert. "Top Russian general lays bare Putin's plan for Ukraine," *Huffpost*, September 2, 2014. https://www.huffpost.com/entry/valery-gerasimov-putin-ukraine_b_5748480.

Cody, Poplin. "Cyber sections of the latest G20 leaders' communiqué," *Lawfare*, November 17, 2015. https://www.lawfareblog.com/cyber-sections-latest-g20-leaders-communiqué.

Colby, Eldridge. "Against the great powers: Reflections on balancing nuclear and conventional power," *Texas National Security Review*, 2, No. 1 (November 2018), 144–152.

Colby, Elbridge. "Don't sweat airsea battle," *National Interest*, July 31, 2013. http://nationalinterest.org/commentary/dont-sweat-airsea-battle-8804.

Colby, Elbridge. "If you want peace prepare for nuclear war," *Foreign Affairs*, 97, No. 6 (November–December 2018), 25–32.

Colchester, Nico. "Crunchiness," *Financial Times*, October 24, 2006.

Commission on Integrated Long-Term Strategy (Fred Iklé and Albert Wohlstetter, co-chairs). *Discriminate Deterrence*, January 1988. https://www.airforcemag.com/PDF/DocumentFile/Documents/2008/DiscriminateDeterrence_010188.pdf.

Cooper, Eric. "The era of coast guards," RAND_PEA3044-1, February 24, 2024. https://www.rand.org/content/dam/rand/pubs/perspectives/PEA3000/PEA3044-1/RAND_PEA3044-1.pdf.

Cooper, Helene, and Julian E. Barnes. "U.S. considers warning Ukraine of a Russian invasion in real-time," *New York Times*, December 23, 2021. https://www.nytimes.com/2021/12/23/us/politics/russia-ukraine-military-biden.html.

Cooper, Jim. "Updating space doctrine: How to avoid World War III." *War on the Rocks*, July 23, 2021. https://warontherocks.com/2021/07/updating-space-doctrine-how-to-avoid-world-war-iii/.

Corkery, Michael, Jessica Silver-Greenberg, and David Sanger. "Obama had security fears on JPMorgan data breach," *New York Times*, October 8, 2014. http://dealbook.nytimes.com/2014/10/08/cyberattack-on-jpmorgan-raises-alarms-at-white-house-and-on-wall-street/.

Cossa, Ralph, Brad Glosserman, and David Santoro. "US-China strategic nuclear relations: Time to move to track-1 dialogue," *Pacific Forum*, February 2015. https://pacforum.org/publication/issues-and-insights-vol-15-no-7-us-china-strategic-nuclear-relations-time-to-move-to-track-1-dialogue.

Craig, Campbell, and Sergey Radchenko. "MAD, not Marx: Khrushchev and the nuclear revolution," *Journal of Strategic Studies*, 41, No. 1–2 (2018), 219.

Crowley, Michael. "Blinken warns China against armed attack on Philippines," *New York Times*, March 19, 2024. https://www.nytimes.com/2024/03/19/us/politics/blinken-china-philippines.html.

Cunningham, Fiona. "The maritime rung on the escalation ladder: Naval blockades in a US-China conflict." *Security Studies*, 29, No. 4 (2020), 730–68.

Cunningham, Fiona, and M. Taylor Fravel. "Assuring assured retaliation: China's nuclear posture and US-China strategic stability," *International Security*, 40, No. 2 (Fall 2015), 7–50.

Curtis, Lisa, and Nilanthi Samaranayake. "Countering coercion managing Chinese gray zone activity in the South China Sea and Indian Ocean region," *Center for a New American Security*, March 2024. https://www.cnas.org/publications/reports/countering-coercion.

Damiani, Jesse. "A voice deepfake was used to scam a CEO out of $243,000," *Forbes*, September 3, 2019. https://www.forbes.com/sites/jessedamiani/2019/09/03/a-voice-deepfake-was-used-to-scam-a-ceo-out-of-243000/#61b8d9002241.

Davenport, Brandon, and Rich Ganske. "'Recalculating route': A realistic risk assessment for GPS," *War on the Rocks*, March 11, 2019. https://warontherocks.com/2019/03/recalculating-route-a-realistic-risk-assessment-for-gps/.

Davis, Paul K., J. Michael Gilmore, Dave Frelinger, Edward Geist, Christopher K. Gilmore, Jenny Oberholtzer, and Danielle C. Tarraf. *Exploring the Role Nuclear Weapons Could Play in Deterring Russian Threats to the Baltic States*. Santa Monica, CA: RAND, 2009.

Debre, Isabel, and Jon Gambrell. "Iran's hard-line president-elect says he won't meet Biden," *Associated Press*, June 21, 2021. https://apnews.com/article/iran-president-elect-ebrahim-raisi-biden-63db1fbbdb1ff9fe40aca40f3f8046a2.

Defense Science Board. *Task Force Report: Resilient Military Systems and the Advanced Cyber Threat*, 2013. http://www.acq.osd.mil/dsb/reports/ResilientMilitarySystems.CyberThreat.pdf.

Demchak, Chris, and Yuval Shavitt. "China's maxim—Leave no access point unexploited: The hidden story of China telecom's BGP hijacking," *Military Cyber Affairs*, 3, No. 1 (2018).

Deveraux, Brennan. "Why intermediate-range missiles are a focal point in the Ukraine Crisis," *War on the Rocks*, January 28, 2022. https://warontherocks.com/2022/01/why-intermediate-range-missiles-are-a-focal-point-in-the-ukraine-crisis/.

DeYoung, Karen. "Russia warns U.S. to stop arming Ukraine," *Washington Post*, April 14, 2022. https://www.washingtonpost.com/national-security/2022/04/14/russia-warns-us-stop-arming-ukraine/.

Dixon, Robyn, Miriam Berger, and David L. Stern. "Russia accuses Ukraine of helicopter strike on Belgorod fuel depot," *Washington Post*, April 1, 2022. https://www.washingtonpost.com/world/2022/04/01/russia-belgorod-fire-helicopter-ukraine/.

Dougherty, Chris. "Confronting chaos: A new concept for information advantage," *War on the Rocks*, September 9, 2021. https://warontherocks.com/2021/09/confronting-chaos-a-new-concept-for-information-advantage/.

Dougherty, Chris. "More than half the battle: Information and command in a new American way of war," *Center for Naval Analyses*, May 2021. https://www.cnas.org/publications/reports/more-than-half-the-battle.

Downing, Taylor. *1983: Reagan, Andropov, and a World on the Brink*. New York: Hachette, 2018.*

Economist. "A new era of high tech war has begun," July 6, 2013. https://www.economist.com/leaders/2023/07/06/a-new-era-of-high-tech-war-has-begun.

Economist. "The siege," July 12, 2014. https://www.economist.com/leaders/2014/07/12/the-siege.

Economist. "Obituary: Stanislav Petrov was declared to have died on September 18th," September 30, 2017. https://www.economist.com/obituary/2017/09/30/obituary-stanislav-petrov-was-declared-to-have-died-on-september-18th.

Economist. "Why nuclear stability is under threat," January 25, 2018. https://www.economist.com/special-report/2018/01/25/why-nuclear-stability-is-under-threat.

Economist. "Mutually assured detection," March 8, 2018. https://www.economist.com/technology-quarterly/2018/03/08/mutually-assured-detection.

Economist. "It will soon be possible to send a satellite to repair another," November 24, 2018. https://www.economist.com/science-and-technology/2018/11/24/it-will-soon-be-possible-to-send-a-satellite-to-repair-another.

Economist. "Skirmishing between India and Pakistan could escalate," February 28, 2019. https://www.economist.com/briefing/2019/02/28/skirmishing-between-india-and-pakistan-could-escalate.

Economist. "China's nuclear arsenal was strikingly modest, but that is changing," November 21, 2019. https://www.economist.com/china/2019/11/21/chinas-nuclear-arsenal-was-strikingly-modest-but-that-is-changing.

Economist. "Democracies need to relearn the art of deception," December 16, 2020. https://www.economist.com/christmas-specials/2020/12/16/democracies-need-to-re-learn-the-art-of-deception.

Economist. "China is rapidly building new nuclear-missile silos," July 31, 2021. https://www.economist.com/china/2021/07/31/china-is-rapidly-building-new-nuclear-missile-silos.

Economist. "Why space is about to enter its nuclear age," February 5, 2022. https://www.economist.com/science-and-technology/why-space-is-about-to-enter-its-nuclear-age/21807486.

Economist. "What America has been shooting down in the sky," February 15, 2023. https://www.economist.com/united-states/2023/02/15/what-america-has-been-shooting-down-in-the-sky.

Economist. "Dmitri Alperovitch on the risks of escalation," February 24, 2022. https://www.economist.com/by-invitation/2022/02/23/dmitri-alperovitch-on-the-risks-of-escalation.

Economist. "History will judge Vladimir Putin harshly for his war," February 26, 2022. https://www.economist.com/leaders/2022/02/26/history-will-judge-vladimir-putin-harshly-for-his-war.

Economist. "Giving Ukraine heavy weapons does not mean NATO is at war with Russia," April 17, 2022. https://www.economist.com/europe/giving-ukraine-heavy-weapons-does-not-mean-nato-is-at-war-with-russia/21808835.

Economist. "Artillery is playing a vital role in Ukraine," May 2, 2022. https://www.economist.com/europe/2022/05/02/artillery-is-playing-a-vital-role-in-ukraine.

Economist. "Will the Ukraine war ring the knell for nuclear arms control?" July 31, 2022. https://www.economist.com/united-states/2022/07/31/will-the-ukraine-war-ring-the-knell-for-nuclear-arms-control.

Economist. "An interview with the head of Ukraine's defence intelligence," September 17, 2023. https://www.economist.com/europe/2023/09/17/an-interview-with-the-head-of-ukraines-defence-intelligence.

Eddy, Melissa, and Nicole Perlroth. "Cyber attack suspected in German woman's death," *New York Times*, September 18, 2020. https://www.nytimes.com/2020/09/18/world/europe/cyber-attack-germany-ransomeware-death.html.

Eisenstadt, Michael. "Deterring Iran in the gray zone," *Washington Institute*, April 14, 2021. https://www.washingtoninstitute.org/policy-analysis/deterring-iran-gray-zone-insights-four-decades-conflict.

Eisenstadt, Michael. "Iran's gray zone strategy," *PRISM*, 9, No. 2 (2021), 76–97.

The Electricity Consumers Resource Council, "The economic impacts of the August 2003 blackout" (2004), http://www.elcon.org/Documents/Profiles%20and%20Publications/Economic%20Impacts%20of%20August%202003%20Blackout.pdf.

Elemia, Camille. "What it feels like to be the target of China's water cannons," *New York Times*, December 11, 2023. https://www.nytimes.com/2023/12/11/world/asia/china-water-cannon-philippines.html.

Engstrom, Jeffrey. *Systems Confrontation and System Destruction Warfare*. Santa Monica, CA: RAND, 2018.

Erwin, Sandra. "STRATCOM chief Hyten: 'I will not support buying big satellites that make juicy targets.'" *Space News*, November 29, 2017. https://spacenews.com/stratcom-chief-hyten-i-will-not-support-buying-big-satellites-that-make-juicy-targets/.

Estes, Madison. "Prevailing under the nuclear shadow: A new framework for US escalation management," *Center for Naval Analyses*, September 2020. https://www.cna.org/CNA_files/PDF/DRM-2020-U-027973-Final%20(003).pdf.

Fahim, Kareem, and Sarah Dadouch. "Missile strike on U.S. targets 'did not intend to kill,' says Iranian commander," *Washington Post*, January 9, 2020. https://www.washingtonpost.com/world/middle_east/missile-strike-on-us-bases-did-not-intend-to-kill-says-iranian-commander/2020/01/09/c5c2295c-3260-11ea-971b-43bec3ff9860_story.html.

BIBLIOGRAPHY 203

Falcone, Johnathan, Jonathan Rodriguez Cefalu, Michael Kneeshaw, and Maarten Bos. "Prove it before you use it: Nuclear retaliation under uncertainty," *War on the Rocks*, June 1, 2023. https://warontherocks.com/2023/06/prove-it-before-you-use-it-nuclear-retaliation-under-uncertainty/.

Farkas, Evelyn. (deputy assistant secretary of defense for Russia/Ukraine/Eurasia from 2012 to 2015). "We can do more to help Ukraine without provoking World War III: In aiding Ukraine, why are missiles fine but fighter jets unthinkable?" *Washington Post*, March 11, 2022. https://www.washingtonpost.com/outlook/2022/03/11/ukraine-no-fly-escalation-humanitarian/.

Faulconbridge, Guy. "Russia denies US reports Moscow plans to put nuclear weapons in space," *Reuters*, February 20, 2024. https://www.reuters.com/world/europe/russia-denies-us-claims-that-moscow-plans-deploy-nuclear-weapons-space-2024-02-20/.

Fearon, James. "Rationalist explanations for war," *International Organization*, 49, No. 3 (Summer 1995), 379–414.

Fearon, James. "Selection effects and deterrence," *International Interactions*, 28, No. 1 (2002), 5–29.

Ferdinando, Lisa. "Vice chairman highlights importance of nuclear deterrence," *DoD News*, March 6, 2018. https://www.defense.gov/News/Article/Article/1459640/vice-chairmanhighlights-importance-of-nuclear-deterrence/.

Fernholz, Tim. "How the US is preparing to fight—and win—a war in space," *Vox.com*, February 15, 2014. https://www.vox.com/the-highlight/2024/1/16/24034692/national-security-threat-russia-space-weapons-true-anamoly-china-united-states-space-war.

Fifield, Anna. "N. Korea didn't test a nuclear weapon, but it did try to launch another missile," *Washington Post*, April 16, 2017. https://www.washingtonpost.com/world/asia_pacific/n-korea-didnt-test-a-nuclear-weapon-but-its-display-of-military-hardware-wasnt-exactly-good-news/2017/04/15/49944da8-221c-11e7-bcd6-6d1286bc177d_story.html.

Fischerkeller, Michael P., and Richard J. Harknett. "Persistent engagement, agreed competition, cyberspace interaction dynamics, and escalation (IDA NS D-9076)," *Institute for Defense Analysis*, May 2018. https://www.ida.org/-/media/feature/publications/p/pe/persistent-engagement-agreed-competition-cyberspace-interaction-dynamics-and-escalation/d-9076.ashx.

Fitzpatrick, Mark. "The world after: Proliferation, deterrence and disarmament if the nuclear taboo is broken," *Proliferation Papers*, IFRI (Spring 2009). https://www.ifri.org/en/publications/etudes-de-lifri/proliferation-papers/world-after-proliferation-deterrence-and.

Fitzsimmons, Michael. "The false allure of escalation dominance," November 16, 2017. *War on the Rocks*. https://warontherocks.com/2017/11/false-allure-escalation-dominance/.

Fix, Liana, and Michael Kimmage. "What if the war in Ukraine spins out of control? How to prepare for unintended escalation," *Foreign Affairs*, July 19, 2022. https://www

.foreignaffairs.com/articles/ukraine/2022-07-18/what-if-war-in-ukraine-spins-out-control.

Flaherty, Mary Pat, Jason Samenow, and Lisa Rein. "Chinese hack U.S. weather systems, satellite network," *Washington Post*, November 12, 2014. https://www.washingtonpost.com/local/chinese-hack-us-weather-systems-satellite-network/2014/11/12/bef1206a-68e9-11e4-b053-65cea7903f2e_story.html.

Flanagan, Stephen, Nicholas Martin, Alexis A. Blanc, and Nathan Beauchamp-Mustafaga. *A Framework of Deterrence in Space Operations*. Santa Monica, CA: RAND, 2023.

Flournoy, Michèle A. "How to prevent a war in Asia: The erosion of American deterrence raises the risk of Chinese miscalculation," *Foreign Affairs*, June 18, 2020. https://www.foreignaffairs.com/articles/united-states/2020-06-18/how-prevent-war-asia.

Fravel, M. Taylor. *Active Defense: China's Military Strategy since 1949*. Princeton, NJ: Princeton University Press, 2019.

Frederick, Bryan, Mark Cozad, and Alexandra Stark. "Understanding the risk of escalation in the war in Ukraine," *RAND*, September 21, 2023. https://www.rand.org/pubs/research_briefs/RBA2807-1.html.

Fredrick, Bryan, Samuel Charap, Scott Boston, Stephen J. Flanagan, Michael J. Mazarr, Jennifer D. P. Moroney, and Karl P. Mueller. "Pathways to Russian escalation against NATO from the Ukraine war," *RAND*, July 2022. https://www.rand.org/pubs/perspectives/PEA1971-1.html.

Freedman, Lawrence. *The Evolution of Nuclear Strategy*, 2nd ed. New York: St. Martin's Press, 1989.

Freedman, Lawrence. "General deterrence and the balance of power," *Review of International Studies*, 15, No. 2 (April 1989), 199–210.

Freedman, Lawrence. "Salami slicing, boiled frogs, and Russian red lines," June 4, 2023. https://samf.substack.com/p/salami-slicing-boiled-frogs-and-russian.

Friedberg, Aaron. *Beyond Air-Sea Battle: The Debate over U.S. Military Strategy in Asia*. Adelphi Paper No. 444. London, UK: International Institute of Strategic Studies, April 2014.

Futter, Andrew. *Hacking the Bomb: Cyber Threats and Nuclear Weapons*. Washington, DC: Georgetown University Press, 2018.

Ganguly, Simit, and Devin Hagerty. *Fearful Symmetry: India-Pakistan Crises in the Shadow of Nuclear Weapons*. Seattle: University of Washington Press, 2015.

Garanich, Gleb, and Sergiy Karazy. "Kyiv says it shoots down volley of Russian hypersonic missiles," *Reuters*, May 16, 2023. https://www.reuters.com/world/europe/air-defence-systems-repelling-attacks-ukraine-early-tuesday-officials-2023-05-16/.

Gartzke, Erik, and Jon R. Lindsay. "Thermonuclear cyberwar," *Journal of Cybersecurity*, 3, No. 1 (2017), 37–48.

Gebrekidan, Selam. "Electronic warfare confounds civilian pilots, far from any battlefield," *New York Times*, November 21, 2023. https://www.nytimes.com/2023/11/21/world/europe/ukraine-israel-gps-jamming-spoofing.html.

Gelb, Leslie, and Richard Betts. *The Irony of Vietnam: The System Worked*. Washington, DC: Brookings, 1979.

George, Alexander, and Smoke Richard. *Deterrence in American Foreign Policy: Theory and Practice*. New York: Columbia University Press, 1974.

Gershgorn, Dave. "Your computer thinks this turtle is a rifle," *Quartz*, November 2, 2017. https://qz.com/1117494/theres-a-glaring-mistake-in-the-way-ai-looks-at-the-world/.

Gibbons, Rebecca Davis, and Keir Lieber. "How durable is the nuclear weapons taboo?" *Journal of Strategic Studies*, 42, No. 1 (2019), 29–54.

Gibbons-Neff, Thomas. "How a 4-hour battle between Russian mercenaries and U.S. commandos unfolded in Syria," *New York Times*, May 24, 2018. https://www.nytimes.com/2018/05/24/world/middleeast/american-commandos-russian-mercenaries-syria.html.

Glaser, Bonnie S., and Zack Cooper. "Nancy Pelosi's trip to Taiwan is too dangerous," *New York Times*, July 28, 2022. https://www.nytimes.com/2022/07/28/opinion/china-us-taiwan-pelosi.html.

Godwin Paul H. B., and Alice L. Miller. *China's Forbearance Has Limits: Chinese Threat and Retaliation Signaling and Its Implications for a Sino-American Military Confrontation*. Washington, DC: NDU Press, 2013.

Goldenberg, Ilan, Nicholas A. Heras, Kaleigh Thomas, and Jennie Matuschak. "Countering Iran in the gray zone: What the United States should learn from Israel's operations in Syria," *Center for a New American Security*, April 14, 2020. https://www.cnas.org/publications/reports/countering-iran-gray-zone.

Goldstein, Avery. "First things first: The pressing danger of crisis instability in U.S.-China relations," *International Security*, 37, No. 4 (Spring 2013), 49–89.

Goldstein, Matthew, Nicole Perlroth, and David Sanger. "Hackers' attack cracked 10 financial firms in major assault," *New York Times*, October 3, 2014. http://dealbook.nytimes.com/2014/10/03/hackers-attack-cracked-10-banks-in-major-assault/.

Gomez, Eric. "The future of extended deterrence: Are new U.S. nuclear weapons necessary?" In *America's Nuclear Crossroads*, edited by Caroline Dorminey and Eric Gomez, 57–68. Washington, DC: CATO Institute, 2019.

Gompert, David, Astrid Stuth Cevallos, and Cristina L. Garafola. *War with China: Thinking Through the Unthinkable*. Santa Monica, CA: RAND, 2016.

Gompert, David, and Martin Libicki. "Cyber war and nuclear peace," *Survival*, 61, No. 4 (August–September 2019), 45–62.

Gompert, David, Stuart Johnson, Martin C. Libicki, David R. Frelinger, John Gordon IV, Raymond Smith, and Camille A. Sawak. *Underkill*. Santa Monica, CA: RAND, 2009. https://www.rand.org/pubs/monographs/MG848.html.

Gorman, Siobhan, and Julian E. Barnes. "Cyber combat: Act of war," *Wall Street Journal*, May 31, 2011.

Gray, Colin. "What Rand hath wrought." *Foreign Policy*, No. 4 (1971), 111–29.

Green, Brendan, and Caitlin Talmadge. "Then what? Assessing the military implications of Chinese control of Taiwan," *International Security*, 47, No. 1 (Summer 2022), 7–45.

Green, Brendan Rittenhouse. *The Revolution that Failed: Nuclear Competition, Arms Control, and the Cold War*. Cambridge, UK: Cambridge University Press, 2020.

Greenberg, Andy. "The highly dangerous 'Triton' hackers have probed the US grid," *Wired*, June 14, 2019. https://www.wired.com/story/triton-hackers-scan-us-power-grid/.

Greenberg, Andy. "The untold story of the 2018 Olympics cyberattack, the most deceptive hack in history: How digital detectives unraveled the mystery of Olympic Destroyer—and why the next big attack will be even harder to crack," *Wired*, October 17, 2019. https://www.wired.com/story/untold-story-2018-olympics-destroyer-cyberattack/.

Grigsby, Alex. "The United Nations doubles its workload on cyber norms, and not everyone is pleased," *Council on Foreign Relations*, November 15, 2018. https://www.cfr.org/blog/united-nations-doubles-its-workload-cyber-norms-and-not-everyone-pleased.

Grynaviski, Eric. *Constructive Illusions: Misperceiving the Origins of International Cooperation* Ithaca, NY: Cornell University Press, 2014.

The Guardian. "Petraeus: US would destroy Russia's troops if Putin uses nuclear weapons in Ukraine," October 2, 2022. https://www.theguardian.com/world/2022/oct/02/us-russia-putin-ukraine-war-david-petraeus.

The Guardian. "Putin says Russia 'will respond' if UK supplies depleted uranium shells to Ukraine," March 21, 2023.

The Guardian. "Russia reasserts right to use nuclear weapons in Ukraine," March 26, 2022. https://www.theguardian.com/world/2022/mar/26/russia-reasserts-right-to-use-nuclear-weapons-in-ukraine-putin.

Guest, Edward. "Qualities precede quantities: Deciding how much is enough for U.S. Nuclear forces," *RAND*, September 2023. https://www.rand.org/pubs/perspectives/PEA2555-2.html.

Guyer, Jonathan. "What US weapons tell us about the Russia-Ukraine war: The debate around which weapons to send to Ukraine, explained," *Vox*, March 29, 2023. https://www.vox.com/world-politics/2023/3/29/23652435/debate-weapons-ukraine-abrams-leopard-tanks-biden-zelenskyy.

Haenle, Paul, and Nathaniel Sher. "How Pelosi's Taiwan visit has set a new status quo for U.S-China tensions." *Carnegie Endowment*, August 17, 2022. https://carnegieendowment.org/2022/08/17/how-pelosi-s-taiwan-visit-has-set-new-status-quo-for-u.s-china-tensions-pub-87696.

Halberstam, David. *The Best and the Brightest* (NY: Random House, 1972).

Hammes, T. X. "A military strategy to deter China," *Real Clear Defense*, December 1, 2013. http://www.realcleardefense.com/articles/2013/12/01/a_military_strategy_to_deter_china_106987.html.

Harris, Mark. "Ghost ships, crop circles, and soft gold: A GPS mystery in Shanghai," *Technology Review*, November 15, 2019. https://www.technologyreview.com/2019/11/15/131940/ghost-ships-crop-circles-and-soft-gold-a-gps-mystery-in-shanghai/.

Harris, Shane, and Dan Lamothe. "Intelligence-sharing with Ukraine designed to prevent wider war," *Washington Post*, May 11, 2022. https://www.washingtonpost.com/national-security/2022/05/11/ukraine-us-intelligence-sharing-war/.

Harris, Shane, Paul Sonne, Dan Lamothe, and Michael Birnbaum. "U.S. provided intelligence that helped Ukraine sink Russian warship," *Washington Post*, May 6, 2022. https://www.washingtonpost.com/national-security/2022/05/05/us-intelligence-ukraine-moskva-sinking/.

Harrison Todd, Kaitlyn Johnson, Joe Moye, and Makena Young. "Space threat assessment 2020," *Center for Strategic and International Studies*, March 2020. https://www.csis.org/analysis/space-threat-assessment-2020.

Harrison, Todd, Zack Cooper, Kaitlyn Johnson, and Thomas G. Roberts. "Escalation and deterrence in the second space age," *Center for Strategic and International Studies*, October 3, 2017. https://www.csis.org/analysis/escalation-and-deterrence-second-space-age, 11.

Hartnett, Kevin. "Machine learning confronts the elephant in the room," *Quanta Magazine*, September 20, 2018. https://www.quantamagazine.org/machine-learning-confronts-the-elephant-in-the-room-20180920/.

Hauer, Neil. "Russia's favorite mercenaries," *The Atlantic*, August 27, 2018. https://www.theatlantic.com/international/archive/2018/08/russian-mercenaries-wagner-africa/568435/.

Heath, Timothy R., Kristen Gunness, and Tristan Finazzo. *The Return of Great Power War*. Santa Monica, CA: RAND, 2022.

Hennigan, W. J. "Exclusive: Strange Russian spacecraft shadowing U.S. spy satellite, general says," *Time*, February 10, 2010. https://time.com/5779315/russian-spacecraft-spy-satellite-space-force/.

Herken, Greg, Avner Cohen, and George M. Moore. "3 scenarios for how Putin could actually use nukes," *Politico*, May 16, 2022. https://www.politico.com/news/magazine/2022/05/16/scenarios-putin-nukes-00032505.

Hern, Alex. "North Korean 'cyberwarfare' said to have cost South Korea £500m," *The Guardian*, October 16, 2013. https://www.theguardian.com/world/2013/oct/16/north-korean-cyber-warfare-south-korea.

Hersman, Rebecca. "Wormhole escalation in the new nuclear age." *Texas National Security Review*, 3, No. 3 (2020), 90–109.

Hersman, Rebecca, Reja Younis, Bryce Farabaugh, Bethany Goldblum, and Andrew Reddie. *Under the Nuclear Shadow: Situational Awareness Technology and Crisis Decisionmaking*. Center for Strategic and International Studies, March 2020. https://www.csis.org/analysis/under-nuclear-shadow-situational-awareness-technology-and-crisis-decisionmaking.

Higgins, Andrew. "Maybe private Russian hackers meddled in election, Putin says," *New York Times*, June 1, 2017. https://www.nytimes.com/2017/06/01/world/europe/vladimir-putin-donald-trump-hacking.html.

Hiim, Henrik Stålhane, M. Taylor Fravel, and Magnus Langset Trøan. "The dynamics of an entangled security dilemma: China's changing nuclear posture," *International Security*, 47, No. 4 (Spring 2023), 147–87.

Hitchens, Theresa. "No US missile defense system proven capable against 'realistic' ICBM threats," *Breaking Defense*, February 22, 2022. https://breakingdefense.com/2022/02/no-us-missile-defense-system-proven-capable-against-realistic-icbm-threats-study/.

Hodge, Nathan, Tim Lister, Ivana Kottasová, and Helen Regan. "Russia launches military attack on Ukraine with reports of explosions and troops crossing border," *Cable News Network*, February 24, 2022. https://www.cnn.com/2022/02/23/europe/russia-ukraine-putin-military-operation-donbas-intl-hnk/index.html.

Hoffman, Stanley. *Janus and Minerva: Essays in the Theory and Practice of International Politics*. London: Westview Press, 1987.

Hogeveen, Bart. "The UN norms of responsible state behaviour in cyberspace," *UNODA*, March 2022. https://documents.unoda.org/wp-content/uploads/2022/03/The-UN-norms-of-responsible-state-behaviour-in-cyberspace.pdf.

Hooker, Richard D. "Climbing the ladder: How the West can manage escalation in Ukraine and beyond," *Atlantic Council*, April 21, 2022. https://www.atlanticcouncil.org/in-depth-research-reports/report/managing-escalation-in-ukraine/.

Hopfield, J. J. "Neural networks and physical systems with emergent collective computational abilities," *Proceedings of the National Academy of Sciences*, 79, No. 8 (April 1, 1982): 2554–2558.

Horowitz, Michael. "When speed kills: Lethal autonomous weapon systems, deterrence and stability." *Journal of Strategic Studies*, 42, No. 6 (2019), 764–88.

Hunzeker, Michael A. "Taiwan's defense plans are going off the rails." *War on the Rocks*, November 18, 2021. https://warontherocks.com/2021/11/taiwans-defense-plans-are-going-off-the-rails/.

Ignatius, David. "As Ukraine braces for a second round, the West has a duty to stand up," *Washington Post*, April 7, 2022. https://www.washingtonpost.com/opinions/2022/04/07/ignatius-russia-ukraine-heavy-weapons/.

Ignatius, David. "The U.S.-Russia conflict is heating up—in cyberspace," *Washington Post*, June 7, 2022. https://www.washingtonpost.com/opinions/2022/06/07/us-russia-conflict-is-heating-up-cyberspace/.

Infosecurity Magazine. "Cyber-terrorism shut down Israel's Carmel Tunnel," *Info Security*, October 28, 2013. http://www.infosecurity-magazine.com/news/cyber-terrorism-shut-down-israels-carmel-tunnel/.

Institute for the Study of War. "Russian offensive campaign assessment," December 10, 2022. https://www.understandingwar.org/backgrounder/russian-offensive-campaign-assessment-december-10.

Irshad, Muhammad. "Crisis of nuclear neighbors," *Defense Journal*, 6, No. 2 (2002), 120–25.

Jamestown Foundation. "Reflections on Vostok 2010: Selling an image," July 13, 2010. https://jamestown.org/program/reflections-on-vostok-2010-selling-an-image/.

Jenkins, Cameron. "Kremlin official says West has declared 'total war' on Russia," *The Hill*, March 25, 2022. https://thehill.com/policy/international/russia/599722-lavrov-says-west-has-declared-total-war-on-russia/.

Jensen, Benjamin. "Bringing the swarm to life: Roles, missions, and campaigns for the Replicator initiative," *War on the Rocks*, February 13, 2024. https://warontherocks.com/2024/02/bringing-the-swarm-to-life-roles-missions-and-campaigns-for-the-replicator-initiative.

Jensen, Benjamin, and Brandon Valeriano. "What do we know about cyber escalation? Observations from simulations and surveys," *Atlantic Council*, November 2019. https://www.atlanticcouncil.org/wp-content/uploads/2019/11/What_do_we_know_about_cyber_escalation_.pdf.

Jervis, Robert. "Cooperation under the security dilemma," *World Politics*, 30, No. 2 (January 1978), 167–214.

Jervis, Robert. *Perception and Misperception in International Politics*. Princeton, NJ: Princeton University Press, 1976.

Jervis, Robert. "Why nuclear superiority doesn't matter," *Political Science Quarterly*, 94, No. 4 (Winter 1979/1980), 617–33.

Johnson, Dave. *Russia's Conventional Precision Strike Capabilities, Regional Crises, and Nuclear Thresholds*. Livermore Papers on Global Security, No. 3, February 2018. https://cgsr.llnl.gov/content/assets/docs/Precision-Strike-Capabilities-report-v3-7.pdf.

Johnson, James S. "China's 'Guam Express' and 'carrier killers': The anti-ship asymmetric challenge to the U.S. in the western Pacific." *Comparative Strategy*, 36, No. 4, 319–33.

Johnson, James S. "Chinese evolving approaches to nuclear "war-fighting": An emerging intense US–China security dilemma and threats to crisis stability in the Asia Pacific," *Asian Security*, 15, No. 3 (2019), 215–32.

Johnson, Loch K. "On drawing a bright line for covert operations." *American Journal of International Law*, 86, No. 2 (April 1992), 284–309.

Johnson, Mark. "Russia issues travel warning about US, citing threat of 'kidnapping.'" *IB Times*, September 3, 2013. http://www.ibtimes.com/russia-issues-travel-warning-about-us-citing-threat-kidnapping-1402265.

Jones, Harry. "The recent large reduction in space launch cost," 48th International Conference on Environmental Systems, July 2018. https://ttu-ir.tdl.org/bitstream/handle/2346/74082/ICES_2018_81.pdf.

Kahn, Herman. *On Escalation: Scenarios and Metaphors*. New York: Praeger, 1965.

Kania, Elsa B., and John Costello. "Seizing the commanding heights: The PLA Strategic Support Force in Chinese military power," *Journal of Strategic Studies*, 44, No. 2 (2021), 218–64.

Kaplan, Fred. "The senseless danger of the military's new "low-yield" nuclear warhead," *Slate*, February 18, 2020. https://slate.com/news-and-politics/2020/02/low-yield-warhead-nuclear-weapons-navy-trident-submarines.html.

Kaplan, Fred. "What Ukraine's drone strike deep in Russian territory means," *Slate*, December 6, 2022. https://slate.com/news-and-politics/2022/12/ukraine-drone-strike-putin-russia.html.

Kaplan, Fred. "Why the U.S. might not use a nuke, even if Russia does," *Slate*, October 7, 2022. https://slate.com/news-and-politics/2022/10/why-the-us-might-not-use-a-nuke-even-if-russia-does.html.

Kaplan, Fred. "The senseless danger of the military's new 'low-yield' nuclear warhead," *Slate*, February 18, 2020. https://slate.com/news-and-politics/2020/02/low-yield-warhead-nuclear-weapons-navy-trident-submarines.html.

Kapur, Paul. *Dangerous Deterrent*. Palo Alto, CA: Stanford, 2007.

Kapur, Paul. "India and Pakistan's unstable peace: Why nuclear South Asia is not like Cold War Europe." *International Security*, 30, No. 2 (Fall 2005), 127–52.

Kardon, Isaac. *China's Law of the Sea*. New Haven, CT: Yale University Press, 2023.

Katz, Amron. *Hiders and Finders: An Approach to Inspection and Evasion Technology*. Santa Monica, CA: RAND, 1961.

Kendall-Taylor, Andrea, and Michael Kofman. "Russia is down. but it's not out." *New York Times*, June 2, 2022. https://www.nytimes.com/2022/06/02/opinion/russia-ukraine-war-nato.html.

Kissinger, Henry. "Force and diplomacy in the nuclear age," *Foreign Affairs*, 34, No. 3 (April 1956), 349–66.

Kissinger, Henry. *Nuclear Weapons and Foreign Policy*. New York: Harper and Brothers, 1957.

Klein, Ezra. "Transcript: Ezra Klein interviews Emma Ashford." *New York Times*, March 18, 2022. https://www.nytimes.com/2022/03/18/podcasts/transcript-ezra-klein-interviews-emma-ashford.html//.

Klein, John J., "Space warfare: Deterrence, dissuasion, and the law of armed conflict," *War on the Rocks*, August 26, 2016. https://warontherocks.com/2016/08/space-warfare-deterrence-dissuasion-and-the-law-of-armed-conflict/.

Kofman, Michael, Anya Fink, and Jeffrey Edmonds. "Russian strategy for escalation management: Evolution of key concepts." *Center for Naval Analyses*, April 13, 2020. https://www.cna.org/CNA_files/PDF/DIM-2020-U-026101-Final.pdf.

Kofman, Michael, and Anya Loukianova Fink. "Escalation management and nuclear employment in Russian military strategy," *War on the Rocks*, June 23, 2020. https://warontherocks.com/2020/06/escalation-management-and-nuclear-employment-in-russian-military-strategy/.

Kostyuk, Nadiya, and Yuri M. Zhukov. "Invisible digital front: Can cyber attacks shape battlefield events?" *Journal of Conflict Resolution*, 63, No. 2 (2017), 1–31.

Kozłowski, Andrzej. "Polish cyber defenses and the Russia-Ukraine war," *Council on Foreign Relations*, January 18, 2023. https://www.cfr.org/blog/polish-cyber-defenses-and-russia-ukraine-war.

Kramer, Andrew. "Russian troop movements and talk of intervention cause jitters in Ukraine," *New York Times*, April 9, 2021. https://www.nytimes.com/2021/04/09/world/europe/russia-ukraine-war-troops-intervention.html.

Krebs, Brian. "At least 30,000 U.S. organizations newly hacked via holes in Microsoft's email software," *Krebs on Security*, March 5, 2021. https://krebsonsecurity.com/2021/03/at-least-30000-u-s-organizations-newly-hacked-via-holes-in-microsofts-email-software/.

Kreps, Sarah, and Jacquelyn Schneider. "Escalation firebreaks in the cyber, conventional, and nuclear domains: Moving beyond effects-based logics," 2019. https://ssrn.com/abstract=3104014.

Kristensen, Hans M., and Matt Korda. "Chinese nuclear forces," *Bulletin of the Atomic Scientists*, 75, No. 4 (2019), 171–78.

Kroenig, Matthew. *The Logic of American Nuclear Strategy*. Oxford, UK: Oxford University Press, 2018.

Kroenig, Matthew. "Deterring Chinese strategic attack: Grappling with the implications of China's strategic forces buildup," *Atlantic Council*, November 2021. https://www.atlanticcouncil.org/in-depth-research-reports/report/deterring-chinese-strategic-attack-grappling-with-the-implications-of-chinas-strategic-forces-buildup/.

Kroenig, Matthew, and Mark Massa. "Are dual-capable weapon systems destabilizing? Questioning nuclear-conventional entanglement and inadvertent escalation." *Atlantic Council*, June 2021. https://www.atlanticcouncil.org/in-depth-research-reports/issue-brief/are-dual-capable-weapon-systems-destabilizing/.

Kube, Courtney, Dan De Luce, and Corky Siemaszko. "Moscow's claim about firing hypersonic missiles could be more hype, experts say," *NBC News*, March 21, 2022. https://www.nbcnews.com/news/world/moscows-claim-firing-hypersonic-missiles-hype-experts-say-rcna20925.

Kuo, Raymond. "The counter-intuitive sensibility of Taiwan's new defense strategy," *War on the Rocks*, December 6, 2021. https://warontherocks.com/2021/12/the-counter-intuitive-sensibility-of-taiwans-new-defense-strategy/.

Laird, Burgess. "War control: Chinese writings on the control of escalation in crisis and conflict," *Center for New American Studies*, April 2017. https://s3.amazonaws.com/files.cnas.org/documents/CNASReport-ChineseDescalation-Final.pdf, 18.

Lambeth, Benjamin S. *NATO's Air War for Kosovo: A Strategic and Operational Assessment*. Santa Monica, CA: RAND, 2001.

Lau, Stuart. "China's Xi warns Putin not to use nuclear arms in Ukraine," *Politico*, November 4, 2022. https://www.politico.eu/article/china-xi-jinping-warns-vladimir-putin-not-to-use-nuclear-arms-in-ukraine-olaf-scholz-germany-peace-talks/.

Leavitt, Lydia. "NASA confirms satellite hacks in congressional advisory panel," *Engadget*, November 2, 2011. https://www.engadget.com/2011/11/02/nasa-confirms-satellite-hacks-in-congressional-advisory-panel/.

Leicester, John, and Hanna Arhirova. "Russia claims advances in Ukraine amid barrages, troop boost," *Associated Press*, June 7, 2022. https://apnews.com/article/russia-ukraine-kyiv-moscow-411ca8f38524e0d2b120479acef4ad56.

Leong, Clarence. "China seeks to counter Musk's Starlink with own satellite network," *Wall Street Journal*, May 21, 2023. https://www.wsj.com/articles/china-seeks-to-counter-musks-starlink-with-own-satellite-network-ca94aa52.

Lewis, Jeffrey. *The 2020 Commission Report on the North Korean Nuclear Attacks against the United States: A Speculative Novel*. Boston, MA: Mariner Books, 2018.

Liang, Annabelle, and Nick Marsh. "Gallium and germanium: What China's new move in microchip war means for world," *BBC*, August 2, 2023. https://www.bbc.com/news/business-66118831.

Liang, Qiao, and Wang Xiangsui. *Unrestricted Warfare*. 1999. https://www.c4i.org/unrestricted.pdf.

Libicki, Martin. *Crisis and Escalation in Cyberspace*. Santa Monica, CA: RAND, 2011.

Libicki, Martin. *Cyberspace in Peace and War*. Annapolis, MD: Naval Institute Press, 2021.

Libicki, Martin. *Quest for the Common Byte*. Boston, MA: Digital Press, 1994 and 2016.

Lieber, Keir A., and Daryl G. Press. *Coercive Nuclear Campaigns in the 21st Century: Understanding Adversary Incentives and Options for Nuclear Escalation*. US Naval Postgraduate School, March 2013. http://www.dtic.mil/dtic/tr/fulltext/u2/a585975.pdf.

Lieber, Keir A., and Daryl G. Press. "The end of MAD? The nuclear dimension of U.S. primacy," *International Security*, 30, No. 4 (Spring 2006), 7–44.

Lieber, Keir A., and Daryl G. Press. "The new era of nuclear weapons, deterrence, and conflict," *Strategic Studies Quarterly*, 10, No. 5 (USSTRATCOM 2016 issue), 31–42.

Lieber, Keir A., and Daryl G. Press. "The nukes we need," *Foreign Affairs*, 98, No. 6 (November–December 2009), 39–51.

Lieber, Keir A., and Daryl Press. "The new era of counterforce: Technological change and the future of nuclear deterrence," *International Security*, 41, No. 4 (Spring 2017), 9–49.

Lifshitz, Itamar, and Erez Seri-Levy. "Israel's inter-war campaigns doctrine: From opportunism to principle," *Journal of Strategic Studies*, 46, No. 2 (2023), 293–318.

Lin, Herbert. *Cyber Threats and Nuclear Weapons*. Palo Alto, CA: Stanford University Press, 2021.

Lin, Herbert. "Escalation dynamics and conflict termination in cyberspace," *Strategic Studies Quarterly*, 7, No. 3 (Fall 2012), 46–70.

Lindsay, Jon. *Cyber Operations and Nuclear Weapons, Nautilus Institute: NAPSNet Special Reports*, June 20, 2019. https://nautilus.org/napsnet/napsnet-special-reports/cyber-operations-and-nuclear-weapons/.

Lindsay, Jon. "Stuxnet and the limits of cyber warfare," *Security Studies*, 22, No. 3 (2013), 365–404.

Lin-Greenberg, Erik. "Wargame of drones: Remotely piloted aircraft and crisis escalation," *Journal of Conflict Resolution*, 66, No. 10 (June 6, 2022), 1737–66.

Lisman, Evan Omeed. "Iran's bet on autonomous weapons," *War on the Rocks*, August 30, 2021. https://warontherocks.com/2021/08/irans-bet-on-autonomous-weapons/.

Logan, David C. "Are they reading Schelling in Beijing? The dimensions, drivers, and risks of nuclear-conventional entanglement in China," *Journal of Strategic Studies*, 46, No. 1 (2023), 5–55.

Logevall, Fredick. *Embers of War*, (New York: Random House, 2012), 443.

Lonergan, Erica, and Shawn Lonergan. *Escalation Dynamics in Cyberspace*. Oxford, UK: Oxford University Press, 2023.

Long, Austin, and Brendan Green. "Stalking the secure second strike: Intelligence, counterforce, and nuclear strategy," *Journal of Strategic Studies*, 38, Nos. 1–2 (2015), 38–73.

Lowther, Adam. "The big and urgent task of revitalizing nuclear command, control, and communications," *War on the Rocks*, October 4, 2019. https://warontherocks.com/2019/10/the-big-and-urgent-task-of-revitalizing-nuclear-command-control-and-communications/.

MacDonald, Bruce W., Adm. Dennis Blair (Ret.), Dean Cheng, Karl Mueller, Victoria Samson, and Brian Weeden. *Crisis Stability in Space: China and Other Challenges* (Washington, D.C.: Foreign Policy Institute, 2016).

Majumdar, David. "How Russia and China would wage war against America: Kill the satellites," *National Interest*, May 14, 2017. https://nationalinterest.org/blog/the-buzz/how-russia-china-would-wage-war-against-america-kill-the-20658.

Manzo, Vincent. "Managing escalation in northeast Asia," *Joint Forces Quarterly*, 77 (2015), 91–100.

Markoff, John. "Threats and responses: Intelligence; Pentagon plans a computer system that would peek at personal data of Americans," *New York Times*, November 9, 2002. https://www.nytimes.com/2002/11/09/us/threats-responses-intelligence-pentagon-plans-computer-system-that-would-peek.html.

Martin, Alexander. "US military hackers conducting offensive operations in support of Ukraine, says head of Cyber Command," *Sky News*, June 1, 2022. https://news.sky.com/story/us-military-hackers-conducting-offensive-operations-in-support-of-ukraine-says-head-of-cyber-command-12625139.

Mauroni, Al. "Tearing down the nuclear firewall," *War on the Rocks*, October 15, 2019. https://warontherocks.com/2019/10/tearing-down-the-nuclear-firewall/.

Mauroni, Al. "Would Russia use a tactical nuclear weapon in Ukraine?" *Modern War Institute*, March 16, 2022, https://mwi.usma.edu/would-russia-use-a-tactical-nuclear-weapon-in-ukraine/.

Mazzetti, Mark, Helene Cooper, Julian E. Barnes, and David E. Sanger. "For the U.S., a tenuous balance in confronting Russia," *New York Times*, March 19, 2022. https://www.nytimes.com/2022/03/19/us/politics/us-ukraine-russia-escalation.html.

McDonald, Andrew, and Hans von der Burchard. "UK to Germany: Sending Taurus missiles won't escalate Ukraine war," *Politico*, March 7, 2024. https://www.politico.eu/article/sending-taurus-missiles-to-ukraine-wont-escalate-war-uk-tells-germany-cameron/.

McElroy, Damien, and Ahmad Vahdat. "Iranian cyber warfare commander shot dead in suspected assassination," *Telegraph*, October 2, 2013. http://www.telegraph.co.uk/news/worldnews/middleeast/iran/10350285/Iranian-cyber-warfare-commander-shot-dead-in-suspected-assassination.html.

McNamara, Robert S. "The military role of nuclear weapons: Perceptions and misperceptions," *Foreign Affairs*, 62, No. 1 (Fall 1983): 59–80.

Mearsheimer, John. *Conventional Deterrence*. Ithaca, NY: Cornell University Press, 1983.

Mearsheimer, John J. "A strategic misstep: The maritime strategy and deterrence in Europe," *International Security*, 11, No. 2 (Fall 1986): 3–57.

Mehta, Aaron. "Mattis: No such thing as a 'tactical' nuclear weapon, but new cruise missile needed," *Defense News*, February 6, 2018. https://www.defensenews.com/space/2018/02/06/mattis-no-such-thing-as-a-tactical-nuclear-weapon-but-new-cruise-missile-needed/.

Menn, Joseph. "Exclusive: U.S. tried Stuxnet-style campaign against North Korea but failed—sources," *Reuters*, May 29, 2015. https://www.reuters.com/article/us-usa-northkorea-stuxnet/exclusive-u-s-tried-stuxnet-style-campaign-against-north-korea-but-failed-sources-idUSKBN0OE2DM20150529.

Meyers, John Speed. "Mainland strikes and U.S. military strategy towards China: Historical cases, interviews, and a scenario-based survey of American national security elites," *Pardee RAND Graduate School*, August 2019.

Microsoft Digital Security Unit. "Special report: Ukraine, an overview of Russia's cyberattack activity in Ukraine," *Microsoft*, April 27, 2022. https://query.prod.cms.rt.microsoft.com/cms/api/am/binary/RE4Vwwd.

Milken Institute School of Public Health of the George Washington University. "Ascertainment of the estimated excess mortality from Hurricane Maria in Puerto Rico," August 27, 2018. https://publichealth.gwu.edu/sites/g/files/zaxdzs4586/files/2023-06/acertainment-of-the-estimated-excess-mortality-from-hurricane-maria-in-puerto-rico.pdf.

Miller, James, and Richard Fontaine. "A new era in US-Russian strategic stability: How changing geopolitics and emerging technologies are reshaping pathways to crisis and conflict," *Center for a New America Security*, September 19, 2017. https://www.cnas.org/publications/reports/a-new-era-in-u-s-russian-strategic-stability.

Minutes of Verification Panel Meeting, Washington, August 9, 1973, 3:40–4:31 P.M.; from Todd Bennett, ed., *Foreign Relations of the United States, 1969–1976, Volume XXXV, National Security Policy, 1973–1976*, 105. Washington, DC: GPO, 2014.

Montgomery, Bernard. "A look through a window at WWIII," *Journal of the Royal United Services Institute*, 99, No. 596 (November 1954), 507–23.

Moore, Harold G. (Lieutenant General Ret.) and Joseph L. Galloway. *We were Soldiers once... and Young* (New York: HarperCollins, 1992), 400.

Morgan, Forrest E. *Deterrence and First-Strike Stability in Space, A Preliminary Assessment.* Santa Monica, CA: RAND, 2010.

Morgan, Forrest E., Karl P. Mueller, Evan S. Medeiros, Kevin L. Pollpeter, and Roger Cliff. *Dangerous Thresholds: Managing Escalation in the 21st Century*. Santa Monica, CA: RAND, 2008.

Mukherjee, Rohan. "Climbing the escalation ladder: India and the Balakot crisis," *War on the Rocks*, October 2, 2019. https://warontherocks.com/2019/10/climbing-the-escalation-ladder-india-and-the-balakot-crisis/.

Myers, Steven Lee. "China bolsters its nuclear options with new missile silos in a desert," *New York Times*, July 2, 2021. https://www.nytimes.com/2021/07/02/world/asia/china-missile-silos.html.

Nakashima, Ellen. "China hacked Japan's sensitive defense networks, officials say," *Washington Post*, August 8, 2023. https://www.washingtonpost.com/national-security/2023/08/07/china-japan-hack-pentagon/.

Nakashima, Ellen. "U.S. Cyber Command operation disrupted Internet access of Russian troll factory on day of 2018 midterms," *Washington Post*, February 27, 2019. https://www.washingtonpost.com/world/national-security/us-cyber-command-operation-disrupted-internet-access-of-russian-troll-factory-on-day-of-2018-midterms/2019/02/26/1827fc9e-36d6-11e9-af5b-b51b7ff322e9_story.html.

Nakashima, Ellen. "Indictment of PLA hackers is part of broad U.S. strategy to curb Chinese cyberspying," *Washington Post*, May 22, 2014. http://www.washingtonpost.com/world/national-security/indictment-of-pla-hackers-is-part-of-broad-us-strategy-to-curb-chinese-cyberspying/2014/05/22/a66cf26a-e1b4-11e3-9743-bb9b59cde7b9_story.html.

Nakashima, Ellen, and Joby Warrick. "For NSA chief, terrorist threat drives passion to 'collect it all.'" *Washington Post*, July 14, 2018. https://www.washingtonpost.com/world/national-security/for-nsa-chief-terrorist-threat-drives-passion-to-collect-it-all/2013/07/14/3d26ef80-ea49-11e2-a301-ea5a8116d211_story.html.

Nakashima, Ellen, and Joseph Marks. "Russia, U.S. and other countries reach new agreement against cyber hacking, even as attacks continue." *Washington Post*, June 12, 2021. https://www.washingtonpost.com/national-security/russia-us-un-cyber-norms/2021/06/12/9b608cd4-866b-11eb-bfdf-4d36dab83a6d_story.html.

Nakashima, Ellen, and Matt Zapotosky. "U.S. charges Iran-linked hackers with targeting banks, N.Y. dam." *Washington Post*, March 24, 2016. https://www.washingtonpost.com/world/national-security/justice-department-to-unseal-indictment-against

-hackers-linked-to-iranian-goverment/2016/03/24/9b3797d2-f17b-11e5-a61f-e9c95c06edca_story.html.
Narang, Vipin. "Posturing for peace? Pakistan's nuclear postures and South Asian stability," *International Security*, 34, No. 3 (Winter 2010), 38–78.
Newman, Lily Hay. "Russian hackers haven't stopped probing the US power grid," *Wired*, November 28, 2018. https://www.wired.com/story/russian-hackers-us-power-grid-attacks/.
Nicholson, John W. "Opinion: the US must respond forcefully to Russia and the Taliban. Here's how," *Washington Post*, July 13, 2020. https://www.washingtonpost.com/opinions/the-us-must-respond-forcefully-to-russia-and-the-taliban-heres-how/2020/07/13/df13ed6c-c529-11ea-b037-f9711f89ee46_story.html.
Nitze, Paul H. "Atoms, strategy, and policy," *Foreign Affairs*, 34, No. 2 (January 1956), 187–98.
Nitze, Paul H. "Assuring strategic stability in an era of détente," *Foreign Affairs*, 54, No. 1 (January 1976), 207–32.
Nolan, Cathal. *The Allure of War*. Oxford, UK: Oxford University Press, 2019.
Ochmanek, David, and Michael Sulmeyer. *Challenges in U.S. National Security Policy: A Festschrift Honoring Edward L. (Ted) Warner*. Santa Monica, CA: RAND, 2014.
Oliker, Olga. "U.S. and Russian nuclear strategies: Lowering thresholds, intentionally and otherwise," in *America's Nuclear Crossroads*, edited by Caroline Dorminey and Eric Gomez, 37–46. Washington, DC: CATO Institute, 2019.
Oliker, Olga, and Andrey Baklitskiy. "The nuclear posture review and Russian 'de-escalation:' A dangerous solution to a nonexistent problem," *War on the Rocks*, February 20, 2018. https://warontherocks.com/2018/02/nuclear-posture-review-russian-de-escalation-dangerous-solutionnonexistent-problem/.
O'Neil, Kevin. "Building the bomb," in *Atomic Audit*, edited by Stephen Schwartz, 32–103. Washington, DC: Brookings, 1998.
Osgood, Robert. *Limited War: The Challenge to American Security*. Chicago, IL: University of Chicago Press, 1957.
Pape, Robert. *Bombing to Win*. Ithaca, NY: Cornell University Press, 1996.
Parthemore, Christine and Catharine Dill. "Paint the B-52s brightly: Reducing confusion between conventional and nuclear weapons is essential," September 18, 2024. https://warontherocks.com/2024/09/paint-the-b-52s-brightly-reducing-confusion-between-conventional-and-nuclear-weapons-is-essential/.
Paul, T.V. *Complex Deterrence*. Chicago, IL: University of Chicago Press, 2009.
The Paris Call for Trust and Security in Cyberspace, December 11, 2018. https://www.diplomatie.gouv.fr/IMG/pdf/paris_call_text_-_en_cle06f918.pdf.
Pawlikowski, Ellen, Doug Loverro, and Tom Cristler. "Space disruptive challenges, new opportunities, and new strategies," *Strategic Studies Quarterly*, 7, No. 1 (Spring 2012), 27–54.

Pear, Robert. "Arming Afghan guerrillas: A huge effort led by U.S." *New York Times*, April 18, 1988. https://www.nytimes.com/1988/04/18/world/arming-afghan-guerrillas-a-huge-effort-led-by-us.html.

Perkovich, George, and Pranay Vaddi. "Proportionate deterrence: A model nuclear posture review," *Carnegie Endowment*, 2020. https://carnegieendowment.org/files/Perkovich_Vaddi_NPR_full1.pdf.

Perlroth, Nicole. "Online security experts link more breaches to Russian government," *New York Times*, October 28, 2014. https://www.nytimes.com/2014/10/29/technology/russian-government-linked-to-more-cybersecurity-breaches.html.

Pettyjohn, Stacie. "Evolution not revolution: Drone warfare in Russia's 2022 invasion of Ukraine," *Center for New American Studies*, February 2024. https://s3.us-east-1.amazonaws.com/files.cnas.org/documents/CNAS-Report-Defense-Ukraine-Drones-Final.pdf.

Pettyjohn, Stacie, Becca Wasser, and Chris Dougherty. "Dangerous straits: Wargaming a future conflict over Taiwan," *Center for a New American Security*, June 2020. https://www.cnas.org/publications/reports/dangerous-straits-wargaming-a-future-conflict-over-taiwans.

Pickrell, Ryan. "A Russian satellite caught shadowing a US spy satellite earlier this year launched a mysterious space weapon, US Space Command says," *Business Insider*, July 23, 2020. https://www.businessinsider.com/russia-conducts-space-based-anti-satellite-weapons-test-2020-7.

Pillsbury, Michael. "The sixteen fears: China's strategic psychology," *Survival*, 54, No. 5 (October–November 2012), 149–82.

Porter, Jon. "White House now says 100 companies hit by SolarWinds hack, but more may be impacted," *The Verge*, February 18, 2021. https://www.theverge.com/2021/2/18/22288961/solarwinds-hack-100-companies-9-federal-agencies.

Posen, Barry. *Inadvertent Escalation: Conventional War and Nuclear Risks*. Ithaca, NY: Cornell University Press, 1991.

Powell, Robert. *Nuclear Deterrence Theory*. Cambridge, MA: Harvard, 1990.

Prados, John. *The Blood Road: The Ho Chi Minh Trail and the Vietnam War*. New York: John Wiley, 1999.

President's Foreign Intelligence Advisory Board report. "The Soviet 'war scare.'" February 15, 1990. https://nsarchive2.gwu.edu/nukevault/ebb533-The-Able-Archer-War-Scare-Declassified-PFIAB-Report-Released/2012-0238-MR.pdf.

Press, Daryl. *Calculating Credibility: How Leaders Assess Military Threats*. Ithaca, NY: Cornell, 2005.

Quester, George H. "War termination and nuclear targeting strategy," in *Strategic Nuclear Targeting*, edited by Desmond Ball and Jeffrey Richeson, 285–305. Ithaca, NY: Cornell University Press, 1986.

Quinlan, Michael. *Thinking about Nuclear Weapons*. Oxford, UK: Oxford University Press, 2009.

Qureshi, Tahir. "India warns Russia against use of nuclear weapons in Ukraine: Indian Defence Minister Rajnath Singh on Wednesday warned his Russian counterpart Sergei Shoigu that nuclear weapons should not be used by any side in the Ukraine war." *India.com*, October 26, 2022. https://www.india.com/news/india/india-warns-russia-against-use-of-nuclear-weapons-in-ukraine-5707075/.

Radio Free Europe. "Retired General James L. Jones: West 'too cautious about giving Ukraine weapons that could strike into Russia.'" November 26, 2023. https://www.rferl.org/a/ukraine-russia-general-jones-interview-long-range-weapons/32700251.html.

Rauchhaus, Robert. "Evaluating the nuclear peace hypothesis: A quantitative approach," *Journal of Conflict Resolution*, 53, No. 2 (April 2009), 258–277.

Reiter, Dan. "Exploding the powder keg myth: Preemptive wars almost never happen," *International Security*, 20, No. 2 (Fall 1995), 5–34.

Reuters. "Russia's Medvedev warns of nuclear response if Ukraine hits missile launch sites," January 11, 2024. https://www.reuters.com/world/europe/russias-medvedev-warns-nuclear-response-if-ukraine-hits-missile-launch-sites-2024-01-11/.

Reuters. "Putin says Russia will not attack NATO, but F-16s will be shot down in Ukraine," March 28, 2024. https://www.reuters.com/world/europe/putin-tells-pilots-f16s-can-carry-nuclear-weapons-they-wont-change-things-2024-03-27/.

Reuters. "Biden warns cyber attacks could lead to a real shooting war," *Reuters*, July 27, 2021. https://www.reuters.com/world/biden-warns-cyber-attacks-could-lead-a-real-shooting-war-2021-07-27/.

Reuters. "Russia strikes Ukraine with cruise missiles from two seas," March 20, 2022. https://www.reuters.com/world/europe/russia-strikes-ukraine-with-cruise-missiles-black-sea-caspian-sea-2022-03-20/.

Riqiang, Wu. "Certainty of uncertainty: Nuclear strategy with Chinese characteristics. *Journal of Strategic Studies*, 36, No. 4, 579–614.

Riqiang, Wu. "Sino-U.S. inadvertent nuclear escalation," Renmin University (2016), 6, 10, 13–17, 30, 33–35 (available from the author upon request).

Ritchie, Glenn. "Why low-earth orbit satellites are the new space race," *Washington Post*, August 15, 2019. https://www.washingtonpost.com/business/why-low-earth-orbit-satellites-are-the-new-space-race/2019/08/15/6b224bd2-bf72-11e9-a8b0-7ed8a0d5dc5d_story.html.

Roberts, Cynthia. "Revelations about Russia's nuclear deterrence policy," *War on the Rocks*, June 19, 2020. https://warontherocks.com/2020/06/revelations-about-russias-nuclear-deterrence-policy/.

Robles, Frances, Kenan Davis, Sheri Fink, and Sarah Almukhtar. "Official toll in Puerto Rico: 64. Actual deaths may be 1,052," *New York Times*, December 9, 2017. https://www.nytimes.com/interactive/2017/12/08/us/puerto-rico-hurricane-maria-death-toll.html.

Rogin, Josh. "The most shocking intel leak reveals new Chinese military advances," *Washington Post*, April 13, 2023. https://www.washingtonpost.com/opinions/2023/04/13/china-hypersonic-missile-intelligence-leak/.

Romano, Aja. "Jordan Peele's simulated Obama PSA is a double-edged warning against fake news: This deepfaked warning against deepfakes almost makes its point too well," *Vox*, April 18, 2018. https://www.vox.com/2018/4/18/17252410/jordan-peele-obama-deepfake-buzzfeed.

Roonemaa, Holger, and Michael Weiss. "Exclusive: Western intelligence fears new Russian sat-nav's espionage capabilities," *New Lines Magazine*, July 12, 2021. https://newlinesmag.com/reportage/western-intelligence-fears-new-russian-sat-nav-espionage-capabilities/.

Ross, Jay. "Time to terminate escalate-to-de-escalate—It's escalation control," *War on the Rocks*, April 24, 2018. https://warontherocks.com/2018/04/time-to-terminate-escalate-to-de-escalateits-escalation-control/.

Rovner, Joshua. "A long war in the east: Doctrine, diplomacy, and the prospects for a protracted Sino-American conflict," *Diplomacy and Statecraft*, 29, No. 1 (2018), 129–42.

Rubin, Uzi. "The rocket campaign against Israel during the 2006 Lebanon war," The Begin-Sadat Center for Strategic Studies, Bar-Ilan University, June 2007. https://besacenter.org/wp-content/uploads/2007/06/MSPS71.pdf.

Ruhl, Christian, John Gans, and Michael C. Horowitz. "Policy roundtable: The future of trans-Atlantic nuclear deterrence," *Texas National Security Review*, August 23, 2021. https://tnsr.org/roundtable/policy-roundtable-the-future-of-trans-atlantic-nuclear-deterrence/.

Sagan, Scott D., and Allen S. Weiner. "The U.S. says it can answer cyberattacks with nuclear weapons. That's lunacy." *Washington Post*, July 10, 2021. https://www.washingtonpost.com/outlook/2021/07/09/cyberattack-ransomware-nuclear-war/.

Samaha, Nour. "Nasrallah: Hezbollah to respond to Israeli attacks," *Al Jazeera*, January 30, 2015. https://www.aljazeera.com/news/2015/1/30/nasrallah-hezbollah-to-respond-to-israeli-attacks.

Sanders, Linley. "How does America feel about NATO? Support for alliance falls across key Western nations," *Yougov.com*, April 4, 2019. https://today.yougov.com/topics/politics/articles-reports/2019/04/04/how-does-america-feel-about-nato.

Sanger, David. "After Russian cyberattack, looking for answers and debating retaliation." *New York Times*, February 23, 2021. https://www.nytimes.com/2021/02/23/us/politics/solarwinds-hack-senate-intelligence-russia.html.

Sanger, David. "Behind Austin's call for a 'weakened' Russia, hints of a shift." *New York Times*, April 25, 2022. https://www.nytimes.com/2022/04/25/us/politics/ukraine-russia-us-dynamic.html.

Sanger, David. "Russia's missile test fuels U.S. fears of an isolated Putin." *New York Times*, April 20, 2022. https://www.nytimes.com/2022/04/20/us/politics/russia-putin-missile-test.html.

Sanger, David, Helene Cooper, and Anton Troianovski. "Girding for new battle, Russia warns U.S. on advanced weapons for Ukraine." *New York Times*, April 15, 2022. https://www.nytimes.com/2022/04/15/world/europe/ukraine-russia-us-weapons-warning.html.

Sanger, David, Julian E. Barnes, and Nicole Perlroth. "Preparing for retaliation against Russia, U.S. confronts hacking by China." *New York Times*, March 7, 2021. https://www.nytimes.com/2021/03/07/us/politics/microsoft-solarwinds-hack-russia-china.html.

Sanger, David, and Mark Mazzetti. "U.S. had cyberattack plan if Iran nuclear dispute led to conflict," *New York Times*, February 16, 2016. https://www.nytimes.com/2016/02/17/world/middleeast/us-had-cyberattack-planned-if-iran-nuclear-negotiations-failed.html.

Sanger, David, and Nicole Perlroth. "U.S. escalates online attacks on Russia's power grid," *New York Times*, June 15, 2019. https://www.nytimes.com/2019/06/15/us/politics/trump-cyber-russia-grid.html.

Sanger, David, and William Broad. "U.S. revives secret program to sabotage Iranian missiles and rockets," *New York Times*, February 13, 2019. https://www.nytimes.com/2019/02/13/us/politics/iran-missile-launch-failures.html.

Sanger, David, and William Broad. "Trump inherits a secret cyberwar against North Korean missiles," *New York Times*, March 4, 2017. https://www.nytimes.com/2017/03/04/world/asia/north-korea-missile-program-sabotage.html.

Sanger, David, and William J. Broad. "Putin's threats highlight the dangers of a new, riskier nuclear era: After generations of stability in nuclear arms control, a warning to Russia from President Biden shows how old norms are eroding," *New York Times*, June 1, 2022. https://www.nytimes.com/2022/06/01/us/politics/nuclear-arms-treaties.html.

Sang-Hun, Choe. "North Korea tried to jam GPS signals across border, South Korea says," *New York Times*, April 1, 2016. https://www.nytimes.com/2016/04/02/world/asia/north-korea-jams-gps-signals.html.

Santora, Marc. "How Ukraine's power grid survived so many Russian bombings." *New York Times*, April 11, 2023. https://www.nytimes.com/2023/04/11/world/europe/ukraine-war-infrastructure.html.

Santora, Marc, and Matthew Mpoke Bigg. "Russian missiles deliver new woe to Kyiv, knocking out tap water," *New York Times*, October 31, 2022. https://www.nytimes.com/2022/10/31/world/europe/russia-ukraine-kyiv-water.html.

Scharre, Paul, *Army of None: Autonomous Weapons and the Future of War.* New York: W.W. Norton, 2018.

Schelling, Thomas. *Arms and Influence.* New Haven, CT: Yale University Press, 1966.

Schelling, Thomas. *The Strategy of Conflict.* Cambridge, MA: Harvard University Press, 1960.

Schelling, Thomas. "The threat that leaves something to chance," *RAND*, 1959. https://www.rand.org/pubs/historical_documents/HDA1631-1.html.

Schlosser, Eric. *Command and Control.* London, UK: Penguin, 2013.

Schlosser, Eric. "What if Russia uses nuclear weapons in Ukraine?" *The Atlantic*, June 20, 2022.

Schmitt, Eric, Zolan Kanno-Youngs, and Julian E. Barnes. "Zelensky's weapons wish list goes mostly unfulfilled on trip to Washington," *New York Times*, December 22, 2022. https://www.nytimes.com/2022/12/22/us/politics/ukraine-zelensky-biden-weapons.html.

Schmitt, Michael (general editor), *Tallinn Manual 2.0 on the International Law Applicable to Cyber Operations*. Cambridge, UK: Cambridge University Press, 2017.

Schmuki, Yann. "The law of neutrality and the sharing of cyber-enabled data during international armed conflict," in *The 15th International Conference on Cyber Conflict*, 25–38. Tallinn, EE: CCDCOE, 2023.

Schneider, Jacquelyn. "Cyber and crisis escalation: Insights from wargaming," 2017. https://paxsims.files.wordpress.com/2017/01/paper-cyber-and-crisis-escalation-insights-from-wargaming-schneider.pdf.

Schneider, William, Jr. "China sees its nuclear arsenal as more than a deterrent; Beijing is adding warheads, missiles and subs at an alarming rate. The goal is global dominance," *Wall Street Journal*, September 7, 2021. https://www.wsj.com/articles/china-nuclear-arsenal-deterrent-navy-new-start-proliferation-national-security-11630524535.

Schneier, Bruce. "Class breaks," *Schneier on Security*, January 3, 2017. https://www.schneier.com/blog/archives/2017/01/class_breaks.html.

Sechser, Todd S., Neil Narang, and Caitlin Talmadge. "Emerging technologies and strategic stability in peacetime, crisis, and war," *Journal of Strategic Studies*, 42, No. 6 (2019), 727–35.

Segal, Adam, Samantha Hoffman, Fergus Hanson, and Tom Uren. "Hacking for ca$h: Is China still stealing Western IP?" *Australian Strategic Policy Institute*, September 24, 2018. http://apo.org.au/node/194141.

Sevastopulo, Demetri and Kathrin Hille, "US warns China on aggressive acts by fishing boats and coast guard; navy chief says Washington will use military rules of engagement to curb provocative behavior," *Financial Times*, April 28, 2019.

Shafer, Jack. "Opinion | The White House treats the public like morons. Again," *Politico*, May 5, 2022. https://www.politico.com/news/magazine/2022/05/05/white-house-morons-public-russia-generals-ukraine-00030476.

Shagina, Marina. "How disastrous would disconnection from SWIFT be for Russia?" *Carnegie Moscow*, May 28, 2021. https://carnegiemoscow.org/commentary/84634.

Shepardson David. "Canadian who helped Yahoo email hackers gets five years in prison," *Reuters*, May 29, 2018. https://www.reuters.com/article/us-yahoo-cyber/canadian-who-helped-yahoo-email-hackers-gets-five-years-in-prison-idUSKCN1IU2OE.

Shubik, Martin. "The dollar auction game: A paradox in cooperative behavior and escalation," *The Journal of Conflict Resolution*, 15, No. 1 (March 1971), 109–11.

Shurkin, Michael. "Plus ça change: A French approach to naval warfare in the 21st century," *War on the Rocks*, October 13, 2023. https://warontherocks.com/2023/10/plus-ca-change-a-french-approach-to-naval-warfare-in-the-21st-century/.

Skylar Mastro, Oriana. "How China is bending the rules in the South China Sea," *Lowy Institute*, February 17, 2021. https://www.lowyinstitute.org/the-interpreter/how-china-bending-rules-south-china-sea.

Smeets, Max. "There are too many red lines in cyberspace," *Lawfare*, March 20, 2019. https://www.lawfareblog.com/there-are-too-many-red-lines-cyberspace.

Smoke, Richard. *War: Controlling Escalation*. Cambridge, MA: Harvard, 1977.

Snyder, Glenn. *Deterrence and Defense: Toward a Theory of National Security*. Princeton, NJ: Princeton University Press, 1961.

Snyder, Glenn, and Paul Diesing. *Conflict among Nations: Bargaining, Decision Making and System Structure in International Crises*. Princeton, NJ: Princeton University Press, 1977.

Sonne, Paul. "U.S. military arms its submarines with new 'low-yield' nuclear warheads," *Washington Post*, February 4, 2020. https://www.washingtonpost.com/national-security/us-military-arms-its-submarines-with-new-low-yield-nuclear-warheads/2020/02/04/b43e0244-4766-11ea-8949-a9ca94a90b4c_story.html.Sorenson, Theodore. *Kennedy*. New York: Harper & Row, 1965.

Specia, Megan, and Ben Hubbard. "Britain says it will give Ukraine tanks, breaching a Western taboo: Western countries have balked at giving Ukraine tanks and other powerful weapons. As increased spring fighting looms, that seems to be changing," *New York Times*, January 14, 2023. https://www.nytimes.com/2023/01/14/world/middleeast/britain-ukraine-tanks-leopards.html.

Srubas, Paul. "Russians suspected of hacking Wisconsin Dems," *USA Today*, January 24, 2017. www.usatoday.com/story/news/politics/2017/01/24/russians-suspected-hacking-wisconsin-dems/97023222/.

Starkey, Sarah. "Putin reminds everyone that Ukraine joining NATO could lead to nuclear war," *Bulletin of the Atomic Scientists*, February 11, 2022. https://thebulletin.org/2022/02/putin-says-ukraine-membership-in-nato-would-make-nuclear-war-more-likely/.

Stavridis, James. "What the West should do if Putin uses a nuclear weapon," *Time*, October 26, 2022. https://time.com/6225138/putin-nuclear-weapons-what-the-west-should-do/.

Stein, Janice Gross. "Escalation management in Ukraine: 'Learning by doing' in response to the 'threat that leaves something to chance.'" *Texas National Security Review*, 6, No. 3 (Summer 2023), 23–50.

Stibbe, Matthew. "Germany's 'last card,': Wilhelm II and the decision in favour of unrestricted submarine warfare in January 1917," in *The Kaiser: New Research on Wilhelm II's Role in Imperial Germany*, edited by Annika Mombauer and Wilhelm Deist. Cambridge, UK: 2003.

Stillion, John, and Bryan Clark. "What it takes to win: Succeeding in 21st century battle network competition," *Center for Strategic and Budgetary Analysis*, July 10, 2015. https://csbaonline.org/research/publications/what-it-takes-to-win-succeeding-in-21st-century-battle-network-competitions.

Sugden, Bruce. "A primer on analyzing nuclear competitions," *Texas National Security Review*, 2, No. 3 (July 16, 2019), 104–26.

Sugden, Bruce. "Nuclear operations and counter-homeland conventional warfare: Navigating between nuclear restraint and escalation risk," *Texas National Security Review*, 4, No. 4 (Fall 2021), 59–89.

Suhas, Prashant Hosur and Christopher K. Colley, "It's still the Indian Ocean: Parsing Sino-Indian naval competition where it counts," May 7, 2024. https://warontherocks.com/2024/05/its-still-the-indian-ocean-parsing-sino-indian-naval-competition-where-it-counts.

Sutton, H. I. "Positions of two NATO ships were falsified near Russian Black Sea naval base," *USNI News*, June 21, 2021. https://news.usni.org/2021/06/21/positions-of-two-nato-ships-were-falsified-near-russian-black-sea-naval-base.

Suzanne, Smalley. "Nakasone says Cyber Command did nine 'hunt forward' ops last year, including in Ukraine," *Cyberscroop*, May 4, 2022. https://www.cyberscoop.com/nakasone-persistent-engagement-hunt-forward-nine-teams-ukraine/.

Swaine, Michael and Andrew Bacevich. "A restraint approach to U.S.–China relations," *Quincy Institute*, April 2023. https://quincyinst.org/report/u-s-relations-with-china-a-strategy-based-on-restraint/.

Talmadge, Caitlin. "Emerging technology and intra-war escalation risks: Evidence from the Cold War, implications for today," *Journal of Strategic Studies*, 42, No. 6 (2019), 864–87.

Talmadge, Caitlin. "Would China go nuclear? Assessing the risk of Chinese nuclear escalation in a conventional war with the United States," *International Security*, 41, No. 4 (Spring 2017), 50–92.

Tankersley, Jim, and Edward Wong. "The C.I.A. director meets with his Russian counterpart to warn against the use of nuclear weapons in Ukraine," *New York Times*, November 14, 2022. https://www.nytimes.com/2022/11/14/world/europe/cia-burns-ukraine-russia-nuclear.html.

Tannenwald, Nina. *The Nuclear Taboo*. Cambridge, UK: Cambridge University Press, 2007.

Team B (Report). "Intelligence community experiment in competitive analysis," December 1976. https://www.cia.gov/library/readingroom/docs/LOC-HAK-545-28-1-5.pdf.

Thornton, Read. "Limited strategic war and tactical nuclear war," in *Limited Strategic War*, edited by Klaus Knorr and Thornton Read, 67–116. New York: Praeger, 1972.

Tierney, Dominic. "The future of Sino-U.S. proxy war." *Texas National Security Review*, 4, No. 2 (Spring 2021), 49–73.

Times of Israel. "TV: Israel believes Iran struck ship in response to cyberattack on train system," August 1, 2021. https://www.timesofisrael.com/tv-israel-believes-iran-struck-ship-in-response-to-cyberattack-on-train-system/.

Troianovski, Anton, and David E. Sanger. "Russia issues subtle threats more far-reaching than a Ukraine invasion," *New York Times*, January 16, 2022. https://www.nytimes.com/2022/01/16/world/europe/russia-ukraine-invasion.html.

Trucker, Patrick. "The NSA is studying satellite hacking," *Defense One*, September 20, 2019. https://www.defenseone.com/technology/2019/09/nsa-studying-satellite-hacking/160009/.

Unal, Beyza, and Patricia Lewis. "Cybersecurity of nuclear weapons systems: Threats, vulnerabilities and consequences," *Chatham House*, January 2018. https://www.chathamhouse.org/publication/cybersecurity-nuclear-weapons-systems-threats-vulnerabilities-and-consequences.

Union of Concerned Scientists. "US ballistic missile defense timeline: 1945-today," March 29, 2019. https://www.ucsusa.org/resources/us-missile-defense-timeline

United Nations. *Agreement between India and China 1996*. https://peacemaker.un.org/sites/peacemaker.un.org/files/CN%20IN_961129_Agreement%20between%20China%20and%20India.pdf.

US Department of Defense. *Annual Report to Congress: Military and Security Developments Involving the People's Republic of China 2017*. https://dod.defense.gov/Portals/1/Documents/pubs/2017_China_Military_Power_Report.PDF.

US Department of Defense. "News briefing on the 2018 Nuclear Posture Review," February 2, 2018. https://www.defense.gov/News/Transcripts/Transcript-View/Article/1431945/.

US Department of Defense. *Military and Security Developments Involving the People's Republic of China 2021*, November 3, 2021. https://media.defense.gov/2021/Nov/03/2002885874/-1/-1/0/2021-CMPR-FINAL.PDF.

US Department of Defense. *The Summary DoD Cyber Strategy*. https://media.defense.gov/2023/Sep/12/2003299076/-1/-1/1/2023_DOD_Cyber_Strategy_Summary.PDF.

US Department of Defense. *Annual Report to Congress: Military and Security Developments Involving the People's Republic of China 2023*. https://media.defense.gov/2023/Oct/19/2003323409/-1/-1/1/2023-MILITARY-AND-SECURITY-DEVELOPMENTS-INVOLVING-THE-PEOPLES-REPUBLIC-OF-CHINA.PDF.

US Department of Justice. "United States v. Viktor Borisovich Netyksho et al," Case 1:18-cr-00215-ABJ Document 1 Filed 07/13/18. https://www.justice.gov/file/1080281/download.

US Federal Bureau of Investigation. "Update on Sony investigation," December 17, 2014. http://www.fbi.gov/news/pressrel/press-releases/update-on-sony-investigation.

US Office of the Director of National Intelligence. "Annual threat assessment of the US intelligence community," April 9, 2021. https://www.dni.gov/files/ODNI/documents/assessments/ATA-2021-Unclassified-Report.pdf.

US Office of the Director of National Intelligence. "Assessing Russian activities and intentions in recent US elections," January 6, 2017. https://www.dni.gov/files/documents/ICA_2017_01.pdf.

US Office of the Special Trade Representative. *Findings of the Investigation into China's Acts, Policies, and Practices Related to Technology Transfer, Intellectual Property, and Innovation under Section 301 of the Trade Act of 1974.* March 22, 2018. https://ustr.gov/sites/default/files/Section%20301%20FINAL.PDF.

US President Biden on our nation's cybersecurity. March 21, 2022. https://www.whitehouse.gov/briefing-room/statements-releases/2022/03/21/statement-by-president-biden-on-our-nations-cybersecurity.

US President Biden remarks before the Democratic Senatorial Campaign Committee Reception. October 6, 2022. https://www.whitehouse.gov/briefing-room/speeches-remarks/2022/10/06/remarks-by-president-biden-at-democratic-senatorial-campaign-committee-reception/.

Valeriano, Brandon. "Managing escalation under layered cyber deterrence," *Lawfare*, April 1, 2020. https://www.lawfareblog.com/managing-escalation-under-layered-cyber-deterrence.

Valeriano, Brandon G., and Jensen, Benjamin. "De-escalation pathways and disruptive technology: Cyber operations as off-ramps to war," in *Cyber Peace: Charting a Path Towards a Sustainable, Stable, and Secure Cyberspace*, edited by Scott Shackelford, Frederick Douzet, and Chris Ankersen, 64–93. Cambridge, UK: Cambridge University Press, 2022.

Ven Bruusgaard, Kristin. "How Russia decides to go nuclear: Deciphering the way Moscow handles its ultimate weapon," *Foreign Affairs*, February 6, 2023. https://www.foreignaffairs.com/ukraine/how-russia-decides-go-nuclear.

Ven Bruusgaard, Kristin. "Russian nuclear strategy and conventional inferiority," *Journal of Strategic Studies* 44, No. 1 (2021), 3–35.

Vigliarolo, Brandon. "77% of security leaders fear we're in perpetual cyberwar from now on," *The Register*, August 27, 2022. https://www.theregister.com/2022/08/27/in-brief-security/.

Vindman, Yevgeny. "Is the SolarWinds cyberattack an act of war? It is, if the United States says it is," *Lawfare*, January 26, 2021. https://www.lawfareblog.com/solarwinds-cyberattack-act-war-it-if-united-states-says-it.

Ward, Alex. "11 US troops were injured in Iran's attack. It shows how close we came to war," *Vox*, January 17, 2020. https://www.vox.com/2020/1/17/21070371/11-troops-injured-trump-iran-war.

Warden, John K. "Limited nuclear war: The 21st century challenge for the United States," *Livermore Papers on Global Security*, No. 4, Lawrence Livermore National Laboratory Center for Global Security Research, July 2018.

Warrick, Joby, and Ellen Nakashima. "Officials: Israel linked to a disruptive cyberattack on Iranian port facility," *Washington Post*, May 18, 2020. https://www.washingtonpost.com/national-security/officials-israel-linked-to-a-disruptive

-cyberattack-on-iranian-port-facility/2020/05/18/9d1da866-9942-11ea-89fd
-28fb313d1886_story.html.
Washington Post. "Read Putin's national address on a partial military mobilization," September 21, 2022. https://www.washingtonpost.com/world/2022/09/21/putin
-speech-russia-ukraine-war-mobilization/.
Watts, Barry. "Nuclear-conventional firebreaks and the nuclear taboo," *Center for Strategic and Budgetary Alternatives*, 2013. https://csbaonline.org/uploads/documents
/Nuclear-Conventional-Firebreaks-Report1.pdf.
Weedon, Brian, and Victoria Samson. "Global counterspace capabilities: An open-source assessment," *Secure World Foundation*, April 2020. https://swfound.org
/media/206970/swf_counterspace2020_electronic_final.pdf.
Wertheim, Steven. "Can America really envision World War III?" *New York Times*, December 2, 2022. https://www.nytimes.com/2022/12/02/opinion/america
-world-war-iii.html.
White House Office of the Press Secretary. "Remarks by President Obama and President Xi of the People's Republic of China in joint press conference," September 25, 2015. https://obamawhitehouse.archives.gov/the-press-office/2015
/09/25/remarks-president-obama-and-president-xi-peoples-republic-china
-joint.
Wilkening, Dean. "Hypersonic weapons and strategic stability," *Survival*, 26, No. 4 (October–November 2010), 129–48.
Winkler, David Frank. *The Cold War at Sea: High-Seas Confrontation between the United States and the Soviet Union*. Annapolis, MD: Naval Institute Press, 2000.
Wohlstetter, Albert. "The delicate balance of terror," *Foreign Affairs*, 37, No. 2 (January 1959), 211–34.
Wong, Edward. "Zelensky says Western allies must allow Ukrainian strikes deep into Russia," September 24, 2024. https://www.nytimes.com/2024/09/24/us
/politics/zelensky-ukraine-russia-strikes.html.
Wong, Yuna Huh, John M. Yurchak, Robert W. Button, Aaron Frank, Burgess Laird, Osonde A. Osoba, Randall Steeb, Benjamin N. Harris, and Sebastian Joon Bae. *Deterrence in the Age of Thinking Machines*. Santa Monica, CA: RAND, 2020. https://www.rand.org/pubs/research_reports/RR2797.html.
Woolf, Amy. "Nonstrategic nuclear weapons," *Congressional Research Service*, September 6, 2019. https://fas.org/sgp/crs/nuke/RL32572.pdf.
Woolf, Amy. "Russia's nuclear weapons: Doctrine, forces, and modernization," *Congressional Research Service*, April 21, 2022. https://sgp.fas.org/crs/nuke/R45861
.pdf.
Wright, Nicholas. "China and escalation in the 'gray zone-entangled space age,'" in *Outer Space; Earthly Escalation? Chinese Perspectives on Space Operations and Escalation*, edited by Nicholas Wright, August 2018. https://nsiteam.com/social/wp-content
/uploads/2018/08/SMA-White-Paper_Chinese-Persepectives-on-Space_-Aug
-2018.pdf, 5–14.

Xiao, Eva. "China's WeChat monitors foreign users to refine censorship at home," *Wall Street Journal*, May 7, 2020. https://www.wsj.com/articles/chinas-wechat-monitors-foreign-users-to-refine-censorship-at-home-11588852802.

Zhai, Qiang. *China and the Vietnam Wars, 1950–1975* (Chapel Hill: University of North Carolina Press, 2000).

INDEX

Pages in *italics* refer to figures and pages followed by "n" refer to notes.

Acton, James, 102n17, 115, 124, 133n32
Albon, Courtney, 82n41
Ali, Indris, 79n2
Alperovitch, Dmitri, 59n66
Anderson, Ross, 136n79
Anderson, Scott R., 49
Ankersen, Chris, 60n74
Anti-Ballistic Missile (ABM) treaty, 10n12
Arbatov, Alexei, 118, 131n18
arms races *vs.* arms negotiations, 2
Army Tactical Missile System (ATACMs), 140, 165
Aron, Raymond, 33n54
Ashford, Emma, 9n10
automated identification system (AIS), 43
Avey, Paul C., 34n65
Azizi, Hamidreza, 32n46

Bahney, Benjamin W., 79n12
Baker, Peter, 79n1
Baklitskiy, Andrey, 117, 133n43
Baratov, Karim, 54n20
Barnes, Julian E., 9n2, 57n48, 58n55, 60n75, 60n77, 60n79, 176n22, 179n49
Bateman, Aaron, 178n41
Bateman, Jon, 59n67
Beaufre, Andre, 9n3
Beebe, George, 44, 57n47
Berger, Eric, 82n39

Berger, Miriam, 33n49
Biden, Joe, 26, 35, 45, 57n51, 165
Bigg, Matthew Mpoke, 102n26
Birnbaum, Michael, 60n78, 102n25
Blackwill, Robert D., 168, 181n62
Blair, Dennis, 123, 135n63
Blank, Stephen, 57n50
Blume, Susanna, 85, 101n5
border gateway protocol (BGP), 42
Borghard, Erica D., 57n53
Bracken, Paul, 107, 131n10, 131n11
Brands, Hal, 57n52
Broad, William, 55n31, 180n56
Brodie, Bernard, 140
Buchanan, Ben, 54n16
Bundy, McGeorge, 27
Burgess, Matt, 55n26, 56n41, 59n68
Burns, William J., 29n15

Cameron, David, 17
Carson, Austin, 32n43, 103n37, 178n43
Cave, Damien, 34n63
Cevallos, Astrid Stuth, 101n3
Charap, Samuel, 26, 34n60
Charney, Scott, 54n11
Chinese ASAT test, 69
Chow, Brian, 80n26
Christensen, Thomas J., 116, 133n35
Churchill, Winston, 28n11
Cimbala, Stephen J., 150n13
Clement, Peter, 61n88
Clem, Ralph, 55n24

Cliff, Roger, 9n6
Coalson, Robert, 82n40
Colby, Elbridge, 175n6
Colchester, Nico, 32n45
Cold War, 1
Colonial Pipeline ransomware attack, 48
Command and Control (Schlosser), 48
conflict escalation, 8; conventional–nuclear threshold, 184; lethal and nonlethal conflict, 184; tactical and strategic nuclear weapons, 184
conventional attack, 174
conventional-nuclear threshold, 184
conventional strategic warfare, 94
Convention on Cybercrime of the Council of Europe, 39
Cooper, Eric, 178n35
Cooper, Helene, 60n75, 60n77, 60n79, 179n49, 192n3
Cooper, Zack, 26, 34n59, 79n13
Corkery, Michael, 60n73
Cossa, Ralph, 155, 175n8
Costello, John, 177n27
counternuclear campaign, 106, 107, 112; escalatory consequences, 114–20; inadvertent attacks, 120–24
Cristler, Tom, 81n31
Crowley, Michael, 79n1
Cunningham, Fiona, 116, 133n36–n40
cyberattacks: DDOS attacks, 42, 43; homeland facility, 95; kinetic attack, 24; normalization of, 5; nuclear systems, 124–29; penetration mechanisms, 45; Russian cyberattack, 47; on satellites, 69; signal escalation into kinetic attacks, 48; US electric grid, 15; Western infrastructure, 52
cyberespionage, 37–38
cyberspace: complicate escalation, 50–51; escalation beyond, 44–46; escalation dynamics, 43–44; ironclad guarantees, 69; LOAC norms, 38;
offenses and defenses, 109; substantial and continued improvements, 2
cyberwar: clarity, 23; cyberespionage, 37–38; economic sanctions, 46–47; effects of, 35; formal norms-making, 38–41; GPS jamming, 43; normalization, 41–43; peacetime activity, 36; perils of ambiguity, 36–37; spoofing, 43

Dadouch, Sarah, 79n3
Davenport, Brandon, 80n15
dazzling, 69
Debre, Isabel, 103n28
de facto threshold, 187
defender's options: ambiguity, 73; bodyguard satellites, 72; peacetime norms, 72; resilience, 72; terrestrial backup, 72–73
Demchak, Chris, 55n29
Democratic National Committee, 24, 40
deterrence, 186
Deveraux, Brennan, 134n46
DeYoung, Karen, 179n47
Diesing, Paul, 30n23
Dill, Catharine, 135n57
Dixon, Robyn, 33n49
Dougherty, Chris, 103n34, 174n1
Douhet, Giulio, 102n15
Douzet, Frederick, 60n74
downlink jamming, 68
dreadnought-class battleship, 147

Economist, 17, 66, 79n11, 81n27, 81n28, 101n9, 101n12, 155, 174n4, 177n28, 181n63
Eddy, Melissa, 58n59
Edmonds, Jeffrey, 28n7
electronic jamming, 68
Engstrom, Jeffrey, 79n7
Erwin, Sandra, 81n30

escalation: beyond cyberspace, 44–46; complicate management, 6; decisions, 3; fears of Armageddon, 17–20; information assistance, 49–50; initiating, 12–15; matching, 16–17; overview, 11; spiral, *154*; thresholds, *4, 153*; warfighting outcomes, 12

Fahim, Kareem, 79n3
fairness and legitimacy, 187
Faulconbridge, Guy, 176n23
Fearon, James D., 177n29
Ferdinando, Lisa, 176n18
Fernholz, Tim, 176n25
Fifield, Anna, 181n68
Finazzo, Tristan, 62n91
Fink, Anya, 28n7
first-strike conventional instability, 83–85
Fischerkeller, Michael P., 33n57
Fitzpatrick, Mark, 141, 150n10
Fitzsimmons, Michael, 9n7, 155, 175n10
Fix, Liana, 26, 34n61
Flaherty, Mary Pat, 80n20
Flanagan, Stephen, 28n4
Fluornoy, Michele, 84, 101n4
Fravel, Taylor, 116, 133n36–n40
Fredrick, Bryan, 60n71
Freedman, Lawrence, 30n28, 151n22
Friedberg, Aaron, 132n27

Gambrell, Jon, 103n28
Ganguly, Simit, 31n38
Ganske, Rich, 80n15
Garafola, Cristina L., 101n3
Garanich, Gleb, 102n20
Gates, Robert, 52
gauging escalation, 183
geosynchronous earth orbit (GEO), 67
Gershgorn, Dave, 102n14
Gibbons-Neff, Thomas, 103n38
Gibbons, Rebecca Davis, 32n47

Glaser, Bonnie S., 26, 34n59
Glosserman, Brad, 175n8
Godwin, Paul H.B., 103n36
Goldenberg, Ilan, 180n57
Goldstein, Avery, 123, 135n64
Goldstein, Matthew, 151n28
Gomez, Eric, 103n32
Gompert, David, 9n8, 82n45, 101n3
Gorman, Siobhan, 57n48
Gravity (movie), 70
Gray, Colin, 178n39
Greenberg, Andy, 56n37, 57n45
Green, Brendan, 10n12, 107, 131n9
Grigsby, Alex, 53n9
Guest, Edward, 22, 32n44
Gunness, Kristen, 62n91
Guyer, Jonathan, 61n88

Haenle, Paul, 181n61
Hagerty, Devin, 31n38
Haifa cyberattack, 59n63
Halberstam, David, 34n62
Harknett, Richard J., 33n57
Harris, Mark, 56n43
Harrison, Todd, 56n39, 71, 74, 79n13
Harris, Shane, 60n78, 61n80
Heath, Timothy, 62n91
Heras, Nicholas A., 180n57
Herken, Greg, 62n89
Hern, Alex, 53n6
Hersman, Rebecca, 33n58
highly elliptical orbit (HEO), 67
High Mobility Artillery Rocket System (HIMARS), 140, 165
Hille, Kathrin, 178n36
Hogeveen, Bart, 53n8
homeland threshold, 93–97
Hooker, Richard D., 52, 61n86
Hopfield, J.J., 101n13
Horowitz, Michael, 63, 79n4
Hubbard, Ben, 178n42
Hunzeker, Michael A., 102n27

Ignatius, David, 61n81, 61n85
Ilyushina, Mary, 179n44
India's ASAT test, 69
instability paradox, 19
Iranian DDOS attacks, 43
Irshad, Muhammad, 134n54
Israel's campaign, 166

Jensen, Benjamin, 29n17, 60n74
Jervis, Robert, 31n29, 135n58, 151n27
Johnson, Dave, 29n12, 118, 134n52
Johnson, James S., 85, 101n6, 151n24
Johnson, Kaitlyn, 79n13
Johnson, Mark, 54n10

Kahn, Herman, 24, 33n50, 162
Kania, Elsa B., 177n27
Kanno-Youngs, Zolan, 9n2
Karazy, Sergiy, 102n20
Kardon, Isaac, 181n60
Kehler, Robert, 125
Kendall-Taylor, Andrea, 53, 61n88
Kessler effect, 70
Kimmage, Michael, 26, 34n61
kinetic attack, 48
Kissinger, Henry, 25, 138, 169
Knorr, Klaus, 9n4
Kofman, Michael, 28n7, 53, 61n88
Kostyuk, Nadiya, 58n62
Kozłowski, Andrzej, 59n67
Kramer, Andrew, 57n51
Krebs, Brian, 58n56
Kreps, Sarah, 58n61
Kroenig, Matthew, 112, 123, 132n24
Krutskikh, Andrei, 50

Lambeth, Benjamin S., 102n18
Lamothe, Dan, 60n78, 61n80
launch-under-attack (LUA), 84
Lavrov, Sergey, 60n70
laws of armed combat (LOAC), 8, 37–39, 47, 95, 120, 168, 188

Leavitt, Lydia, 80n18
Leong, Clarence, 176n24
lethal/nonlethal threshold, 77–78
Lewis, Jeffrey, 134n55
Liang, Qiao, 9n9
Libicki, Martin, 33n51, 61n82, 136n73, 174n2
Lieber, Keir, 32n47, 101n10, 132n23, 133n34, 176n20
Lifshitz, Itamar, 180n59
Lindsay, Jon, 53n3
Lin, Herbert, 82n44
local–global threshold: countries panic into escalation, 90–92; fight to a superpower, 97–98; first-strike conventional instability, 83–85; homeland threshold, 93–97; large versions of small wars, 98–100; missile defense assets, 100; *post hoc* justification, 99; precision warfare, 85–90
Logan, David C., 135n67
Logevall, Fredick, 29n19
Lonergan, Erica, 53n2
Lonergan, Shawn, 53n2
Long, Austin, 107, 131n9
Lovegrove, Stephen, 159
Loverro, Doug, 81n31
low earth orbit (LEO), 67

MacArthur, Douglas, 192n4
Majumdar, David, 80n17
Manzo, Vincent, 175n7
Markey, Michael, 79n12
Markoff, John, 55n33
Marks, Joseph, 54n13
Massa, Mark, 123
Mastro, Oriana Skylar, 177n34
Mattis, James, 144, 150n21
Matuschak, Jennie, 180n57
Mauroni, Al, 150n11
Mazzetti, Mark, 56n36, 60n79, 179n49

INDEX

McDermott, Roger N., 150n13
McDonald, Andrew, 30n22
McElroy, Damien, 59n63
McNamara, Robert, 29n12, 144, 149n4
Mearsheimer, John, 65, 79n10, 132n26
Medeiros, Evan S., 9n6
Medvedev, Dmitry, 29n13
Menn, Joseph, 55n30
Meyers, John Speed, 31n33
Miller, Alice L., 103n36
miscalculations, 15
Mitchell, Billy, 102n15
Montgomery, Bernard, 31n40
Morgan, Forrest, 5, 9n6
Mueller, Karl P., 9n6
Mukherjee, Rohan, 31n39
mutual assured destruction (MAD), 10n12
Myers, Steven Lee, 130n4

Nakashima, Ellen, 54n13, 54n19, 55n32, 55n34, 56n44, 61n83
Narang, Neil, 177n30
National Command Authority, 143
Neuberger, Anne, 58n57
Newman, Lily Hay, 55n27
Nicholson, John W., 17, 30n26
Nitro Zeus, 42
Nitze, Paul, 137n86, 181n66
no-first-use (NFU) policy, 129
Nolan, Cathal, 178n37
nonkinetic attack, 48
nonkinetic warfare, 185
nonlethal attacks, 76–77
nonlethal space war, 64–67
norms and thresholds, 188–90
North Atlantic Treaty Organization (NATO), 2, 12–13, 24, 66, 89, 165–166
nuclear Armageddon, 7, 11
nuclear command-and-control (NC3), 75
Nuclear Posture Review (NPR), 74

nuclear systems: China's land-based missiles, 108; China's mobile missiles, 110; counternuclear campaign, 106, 107; counternuclear operations strategy, 111–14; cyberattacks on, 124–29; cyberspace operations, 107; electronic warfare tricks, 109; nuclear weapons, 110–111; peacetime search program, 110; technology and political geography, 105; ten-ton conventional bomb, 105
nuclear threats, 191–92

Obama, Barrack, 2, 40, 84, 170
Ochmanek, David, 136n71
Oliker, Olga, 117, 133n43, 150n19

Pape, Robert, 28n6
Parrish, Molly, 85, 101n5
Parthemore, Christine, 135n57
Pawlikowski, Ellen, 81n31
Pearl Harbor, 66, 91
Pearl, Jonathan, 79n12
People's Liberation Army (PLA), 64
Perkovich, George, 135n56
Perlroth, Nicole, 54n10, 56n35, 58n55, 58n59, 151n28
Peskov, Dmitry, 23
Pettyjohn, Stacie, 174n1
Pickrell, Ryan, 81n29
Pollpeter, Kevin L., 9n6
Poplin, Cody, 54n14
porcupine defense, 94
Porter, Jon, 58n54
Posen, Barry, 123
Powell, Robert, 19, 31n35
Prados, John, 102n16
Precision navigation and timing (PNT), 68
precision warfare, 85–90
Presidential-level agreements, 172

Press, Daryl, 101n10, 133n34, 176n20
Putin, Vladimir V., 14, 47, 50, 52, 53, 55n28, 60n77, 61n85, 66, 164, 165, 192n2

Quester, George H., 33n53
Quinlan, Michael, 151n25

RAND assessment, 53
Rauchhaus, Robert, 31n37
Rauhala, Emily, 102n25
Read, Thornton, 9n4
Rein, Lisa, 80n20
Reiter, Dan, 28n5
Riqiang, Wu, 131n7
Ritchie, Glenn, 80n14
Roberts, Thomas G., 79n13
Robles, Frances, 58n60
Rogozin, Dmitry, 110
Ross, Jay, 29n12
Rubin, Uzi, 102n19
rules of escalation, 8
Russian ASAT test, 69
Russian escalation behavior, 163–66
Russo-Ukrainian war, 48, 52, 163

Sagan, Scott D., 57n49
Samenow, Jason, 80n20
Samson, Victoria, 80n21
Sanders, Linley, 133n42
Sanger, David, 52, 55n31, 56n35, 56n36, 58n55, 58n57, 60n73, 60n79, 61n87, 151n28, 179n49, 180n56, 192n3
Sang-Hun, Choe, 56n40
Santora, Marc, 102n26
Santoro, David, 175n8
satellites: communications satellites, 67; cyberattacks, 69; dazzling, 69; downlink jamming, 68; electronic jamming, 68; GEO satellites, 67; LEO satellites, 68; satellite jamming, 68; surveillance satellites, 68; uplink jamming, 68
Schellingesque focal point, 185
Schelling, Thomas, 17, 19, 25, 27, 31n34, 34n64, 145, 146, 149n6, 151n23, 151n29, 159
Schlosser, Eric, 48, 60n72, 179n53
Schmitt, Eric, 9n2, 60n77, 79n1
Schmitt, Michael, 53n7
Schmuki, Yann, 60n79
Schneider, Jacquelyn, 57n53, 58n61
Schneider, William, Jr., 130n5
Schneier, Bruce, 131n15
Schwartz, Stephen, 150n14
Sechser, Todd S., 177n30
Segal, Adam, 54n15
Selva, Paul, 158
Seri-Levy, Erez, 180n59
Sevastopulo, Demetri, 178n36
Shackelford, Scott, 60n74
Shanahan, Patrick, 192n1
Shapiro, Jeremy, 26, 34n60
Shavitt, Yuval, 55n29
Sher, Nathaniel, 181n61
shipboard sensors, 92
Shubik, Martin, 9n11
Silver-Greenberg, Jessica, 60n73
Smeets, Max, 41, 55n25
Smoke, Richard, 5, 9n5
Snyder, Glenn, 30n23, 131n16
Sonne, Paul, 60n78, 176n21
Sorenson, Theodore, 31n31
South China Sea (SCS), 160–61
space warfare, 67–71, 75
special operations to destroy critical infrastructure targets (SODCIT), 93
Specia, Megan, 178n42
Starkey, Sarah, 151n31
Stein, Janice Gross, 149n7
Stern, David L., 33n49, 102n25
Stewart, Phil, 79n2
Strategic Support Force, 159
Sugden, Bruce, 103n29, 134n48

INDEX

Sulmeyer, Michael, 136n71
Sutton, H.I., 56n42

tactical–strategic nuclear threshold: cruise missile, 143; cumulative effect, 145; deliberate signal, 146–48; dreadnought-class battleship, 147; exemplary nuclear, 144–46; official DoD definition, 142; self-defeating, 148; strategic level, 143; Warsaw Pact armies, 138; weapon's warhead, 141
Talmadge, Caitlin, 79n8, 116, 159, 176n26, 177n30
Tankersley, Jim, 179n52
Terrorist Information Awareness program, 42
Thomas, Kaleigh, 180n57
thresholds, 187; accidental escalation, 26; declarations, 166–71; definition and purpose of, 20–26; escalation dominance, 162–63; inadvertent escalation, 26–27; and lattices, 6; lethal/nonlethal, 77–78; mismatched and missing rungs, 153–60; negotiations, 171–74; Russian escalation behavior, 163–66; separate measure and countermeasure, 160–62
Tierney, Dominic, 104n39
Trenchard, Hugh, 102n15
Troianovski, Anton, 61n87, 192n3
Trucker, Patrick, 80n19
Trump, Donald, 40, 63

Ukraine refrain, 165
universality, 22
uplink jamming, 68
US ASAT test, 69
US CyberCommand (CYBERCOM), 42, 47, 51

US freedom-of-navigation assertion (FONA), 6
US Office of Personnel Management (OPM), 37
US policymakers, 30n27

Vaddi, Pranay, 135n56
Vahdat, Ahmad, 59n63
Valeriano, Brendon, 28n10, 60n74
Ven Bruusgaard, Kristin, 62n90
Vigliarolo, Brandon, 55n22
Vindman, Yevgeny, 53n4
von der Burchard, Hans, 30n22
Vorontsov, Konstantin, 81n32

Ward, Alex, 82n42
Warden, John K., 134n47
Warrick, Joby, 55n32, 56n44
Warsaw Pact, 51, 86, 123, 138
Wasser, Becca, 174n1
weapons of mass destruction (WMDs), 155
Weedon, Brian, 80n21
Weiner, Allen S., 57n49
Wilkening, Dean, 102n21
Winkler, David Frank, 55n23
Wohlstetter, Albert, 101n2, 102n23
Wong, Edward, 179n52, 180n55
Woolf, Amy, 134n44, 150n16
World Trade Center attack, 63
Wright, Nicholas, 56n39, 157

Xiangsui, Wang, 9n9
Xiao, Eva, 79n9
Xi-Obama agreement, 38, 40, 171

Zelikow, Philip, 168, 181n62
Zhai, Qiang, 175n14
Zhenjiang Naval Base, 154
Zhukov, Yuri M., 58n62

ABOUT THE AUTHOR

Martin C. Libicki (PhD, UC Berkeley 1978) holds the Keyser Chair of Cybersecurity Studies at the US Naval Academy. In addition to teaching, he carries out research in cyberwar and the general impact of information technology on domestic and national security. He is the author of a 2021 textbook on cyberwar, *Cyberspace in Peace and War* (2nd edition), as well as *Conquest in Cyberspace: National Security and Information Warfare* and various related RAND monographs. Prior employment includes twelve years at the National Defense University, three years on the Navy Staff (logistics), and three years for the US Government Accountability Office.